Twelve Years Away from Constantinople, 1896 - 1908 (My Memoirs)

Yervant Odian

Translated with an introduction and annotations
by

Nanor Kebranian

Gomidas Institute
London

This publication was made possible by a generous grant from the Dolores Zohrab Liebmann Fund

Acknowledgements
I am deeply grateful to the Dolores Zohrab Liebmann Fund for their generous financial support, without which this translation would not have been possible. As always, I cannot thank Ara Sarafian of the Gomidas Institute enough for his thoughtful reading and insights in the process of completing this work.
—Nanor Kebranian
Vienna, March 2025

© 2025 Nanor Kebranian. All Rights Reserved.

ISBN 978-1-909382-81-7

Gomidas Institute
42 Blythe Rd.
London, W14 0HA
England
Email: *info@gomidas.org*

CONTENTS

Introduction   vii

Preface   3

Chapter 1

An attempt on Arpiar Arpiarian's life. – "Take Arpiarian down!" – "Stop Reading *Hayrenik*!" – *Hayrenik*'s dominance. – Izmirilian's election. – The role of Mihran Askanaz. – Arpiarian's character. – A. Vramian. – The Babiali demonstration. – Threatening letters from the Tashnags. – The H. Shahnazar-Yousoufian incident. – The article in *Hayrenik*. – The murder of Dikran Karageozian. – The uprising in Zeitoun. – Arpiar flees Constantinople. – L. Pashalian departs. – The *Hayrenik* cohort dispersed. – Shahnazar incarcerated. – *Hayrenik* dissolves. – Vahé Arzouyan and his friends. – The incident involving Charlié. – The services rendered by Albert Rouet. – The women of the Henchag party.   5

Chapter 2

The Bank demonstration. – The mob. – On board the *Sidon*. – The *sopaci*s try to storm the steamer. – Scenes of massacre. – The nightmarish night. – Robbing corpses. – Bloody Thursday. – The foreign interpreters' visit. – The sick passenger. – I move from the *Sidon* to the *Gironde*. – At Moda. – The Tashnags who stormed the Bank board the steamer. – Hrach and Armen Garo. – Interaction with the Tashnags is prohibited. – In Izmir. – Song and wine. – The *Gironde* reaches Piraeus. – My short-lived heroism.   31

Chapter 3

In Athens. – Prime Minister Deligiannis. – The Athenians and the refugees. – The people of Divrig and Moush. – The prayer. – The Philanthropic Committee. – Threats and accusations. – Sensible people. – Krikor Meohtemetian.   57

Chapter 4

Dikran Yergat. – His lecture. – His illness. – The Belgian Antoine. – An epic plan. – Reteos Mouradian. – The paper *Miyoutiun*. – A bunch of stamp-collectors. – Nazarpeg's bad example. – The patriotic Mr. Kokinos. – The Armenian refugees. – A week in Egypt. – The Kneipp regimen. – Arpiarian's dream. – Reprobate refugees. – Departure from Athens. – The steamship *Urania*. – An alarming trip through Crete. – We reach Alexandria.   69

Chapter 5

The farm in Sharabas. – A strange way to hunt. – The fratricidal youth. – Execution by hanging. – A mother's consolation. – A kind executioner. – Arpiarian in Egypt. – The Bolsetsis of Cairo. – Arpiarian at Sharabas farm. – Making dessert. – Arpiar's ravings. – Nshan Keshishian. – A bitter illusion. – The fake hero. – The phony Haji Minas Oghlus and the genuine article. – A new life. – The novel *Mardig Agha*. – Mikayel Giurjian. 83

Chapter 6

Jangiulian in Egypt. – He is eagerly sought after. – "Masked Men." – An incident. – Imprisonment and fine. – The Delegation's decisions. – Diran Arpiarian's homesickness. – He returns to Constantinople. – The Tower of Galata and the Eastern Question. – Dikran Yergat in Egypt. – Khazhag. – Friar Goundzig. – Departure from Egypt. – The desperate Italian. – Mgrdich Portoukalian. 101

Chapter 7

Arshag Chobanian's room. – The enemy of Sahag and Mesrob. – One way of solving the Armenian Question. – Andronik Ianesco. – We leave together for Vienna. – Ianesco's dictionary. – The Vienna Mekhitarists. – Several small incidents. – Rupture. – London. – Mrs. Raffi. – Arpiar in London. – Ohanchan's linguistics. – A duel that does not take place. – The prerequisites for unity. 121

Chapter 8

The Armenians and the Dreyfus Affair. – French fervor and English sobriety. – Guidon Lusignan and his dictionary. – The Prince's medals. – A lucrative trade. – Miss Marguerite. – The various branches of the Lusignan tribe. – Prince Vitanval. – Queen Wilhelmine of Holland and the Melusinian sash. – The open-mindedness of Prince Lusignan. – The Egyptian-Armenian knight. – Rupture and trial. 143

Chapter 9

Ianesco again. – My provincial dialect. – Chobanian and his opponents. – The Pashalian event. – Souren Bartevian's speech. – Arpiar and Vahé Arzouyan. – Bartevian takes over *Nor Gyank*. – Chobanian against Arpiar. – *Azad Khosk*. – Arpiar comes to Paris. – An innovative *poghacha*. – Chobanian's three projects and the ivory mines. – The fair and its victims. – The Persian Shah's birdkeeper. 167

Chapter 10

The Parisian Society of Christian Youth. – Cheap meals, cheap baths. – A reading of the Holy Bible. – A successful start. – The Society of Temperance and its president. – Drunk on water. – The newspaper *En Avant*. – The Salvation Army. – Its officers and soldiers. – News of a battle. – A gymnastics prayer. – A public confession. 183

Epilogue

[By Yervant Odian] 239

About the Translator 275

Illustrations

Map	vi
Yervant Odian, cir. 1922	2
Hayrenik newspaper, 1894.	7
Galata (Istanbul).	10
Arpiar Arpiarian.	12
Levon Pashalian.	17
Arshag Vramian (Onnig Tertsagian).	18
Constantinople and the 1896 Armenian Massacres (map).	30
Messageries Maritimes *Sidon*.	35
Abdulhamid II	49
Armenian revolutionaries transported to Marseille.	50
Armen Garo (Karekin Bastirmajian).	53
Piraeus, Greece.	55
Athens, Greece.	59
Alexandria, Egypt.	77
Cairo, Egypt.	85
Rural Egypt.	93
Galata Bridge, Constantinople.	111
Messageries' steamer, *Saghalien*	116
Marseille, France.	119
Paris, France.	123
Zabel Yessayan.	127
London, England.	131
Minas Cheraz.	133
Mrs. Raffi (Anna Hormouz)	135
Arshagouhi Teotig.	155
Imaginary portrait of Guy of Lusignan	164
Haroutiun Alpiar.	165
Arshag Chobanian.	173
Paris.	185
Street demonstration, 1908.	251
Adana 1909.	273

Note. The photo-illustrations of cities are from the Library of Congress. The profiles of individuals are from unidentified, on-line, public domain sources. The illustration on page 50 is credited to M. J. Fabre - *L'Illustration*, n° 2801, 31 October 1896. The imaginary portrait of Guy of Lusignan on page 164 is by François-Édouard Picot (19th century).

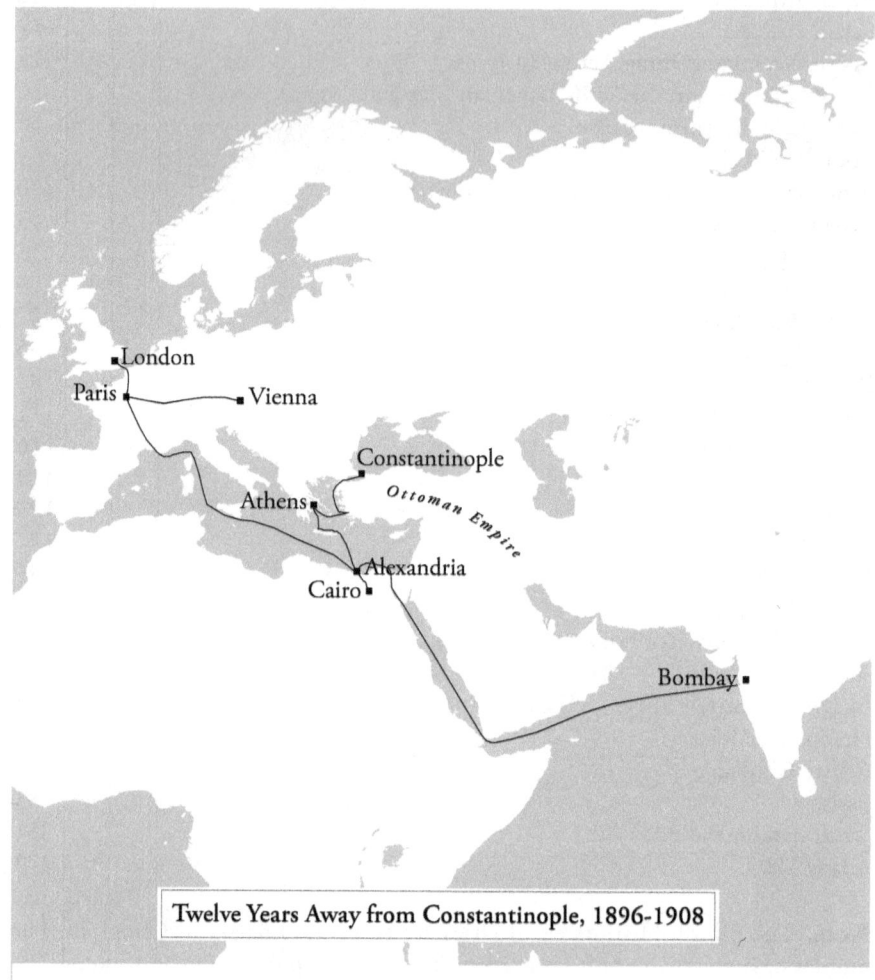

Introduction

Few works of Western Armenian literature have received as much praise or endured for as long as Yervant Odian's *Twelve Years Away from Constantinople (1896 – 1908)* [*Dasnergou Dari Bolsen Tours*]. This memoir was conceived and prepared between 1902 and 1912[*] as a series of daily instalments for the still extant newspaper, *Jamanak* (Time, Istanbul). Published almost entirely uninterrupted between August 23, 1912 and March 22, 1913, it became an overnight sensation in its time. And more than a century later, it remains one of the great classics of the Western Armenian canon.

According to the author, the series was compiled into a book due to popular demand. It was published as a standalone volume for the first time by the Haig Goshgarian Press and O. Arzouman printers in 1914. Importantly, the title of this first edition identifies it as Volume I, covering the period 1896 to 1908 and concluding with the tenth chapter. A subsequent volume never appeared, however, presumably due to the outbreak of the First World War and Odian's deportation during the Armenian Genocide.

The 1914 volume integrated another series of remembrances by Odian.[†] Published under the penname 'Vahram,' these appeared as the four instalments of "Bloodstained Memories" [Ariunod Hishadagner] in *Nor Gyank* (New Life, London) between January and September 1898.[‡] This brief text recounts the horrific episodes – depicted in Chapter 2 of the 1914 volume – surrounding the Armenian revolutionaries' siege of the Ottoman Bank in August 1896 and Odian's concomitant escape from Constantinople. Odian dedicated *Bloodstained Memories* acerbically to the authoritarian Sultan Abdülhamid II (r. 1876 – 1909), adding the trenchantly ironic epigraph, "render therefore unto Caesar the things which are Caesar's" (Matthew 22:21) below the dedication. The book was published by Mikayel Der-Sahagian (Constantinople) in 1920.

---

[*] Artsrun Avagyan, "Chzhbdatsogh Martu: Yervant Odian" [The Man Who Never Smiled: Yervant Odian], *Yervant Odian yev Levon Shant* [*Yervant Odian and Levon Shant*] (Yerevan: Yerevan State University, 2020) 19.

[†] Avagyan, "Man," 19.

[‡] Odian recounts his collaboration with *Nor Gyank*, under the direction of his closest friend Arpiar Arpiarian (1851 - 1908), in Chapters 5 and 7 of this translation.

In his preface, the author explains that he edited the original serialized version of *Twelve Years* heavily. His significant revisions, additions, and redactions unfortunately entailed the removal of extensive and highly informative sections on his life and work in Egypt and India. But as Odian states, he felt that ultimately, these changes rendered his memoir "more perfect and authentic" than its serialized version. In 1922, four years before Odian's death in 1926, the 1914 version was republished by Der-Sahagian Publishers (Constantinople). It is difficult to determine the memoir's exact month of publication, and therefore, whether the second edition appeared before or after the Kemalist army's 'Burning of Smyrna' in September of that year. That event resulted in the destruction of countless Armenian and Greek homes, businesses, and institutions and thousands of deaths. And it sent a clear message to the Armenians of Constantinople.

The 1922 edition contained ten more pages at the end of the final tenth chapter. It also included two additional sections narrating Odian's return to Constantinople following the Second Constitutional Revolution and concluding with a long epilogue relaying the counter-revolutionary tensions and terrors of 1909. While the cover and title page of this 1922 edition identify the memoir's timeframe as 1896 – 1908, the memoir's opening page indicates the closing year – printed just above the chapter heading – as 1909. To remain consistent with the twelve-year timeframe of the memoir's title, I have opted to use the less accurate period of 1896 – 1908 for the translation. *Twelve Years* was republished just once more in 1937,[*] although a compilation of excerpted segments also appeared in 1939.[†] This translation is based on the memoir's 1922 version, which was the first and last complete revised edition of the work published during the author's lifetime and with his approval and consent. Although the complete work has remained out of print since 1939 and there do not appear to be any new initiatives to republish the memoir, it is still nonetheless widely read and commented on.[‡] The fact that it was never

---

[*] Yervant Odian, *Dasnergou Dari Bolsen Tours (1896 - 1908)* (Beiut: Zartonk Print, 1937).

[†] Yervant Odian, *Dasnergou Dari Bolsen Tours (Hadvadzner)* (Sophia: Massis Print, 1939).

[‡] The National Library of Armenia hosted a 155th anniversary exhibition of Odian's works as recently as November 2024. See https://nla.am/blog/ervand-otyan-155, Accessed March 7, 2025.

reissued over the course of the past ninety years is indicative perhaps less of its relevance or circulation than of a reluctance to contend with many of Odian's exceedingly uncomfortable observations about the Armenian nationalist revolutionary parties, which came to dominate the social and political life of the post-Genocide Armenian diaspora. By contrast, his purely fictional – and thus, presumably harmless – satire of Armenian revolutionary activism, *Comrade P. Panchouni* (*Unger P. Panchouni*), has been reissued almost a dozen times since its original 1911 publication.

The very first 1912 – 1913 publication of *Twelve Years* was declared and hailed – rightly, as history would reveal – a momentous event by the editors of *Jamanak*. The work's forthcoming serialization was boldly announced on the prominent left-hand column of the August 22, 1912 issue of the newspaper's front page, where the editors described it as: "Real, historical, Armenian, international, satirical, and literary." Yervant Odian – or 'Yerod,' as he also liked to sign his works by combining the first two letters of his first and last names – was one of the most prominent Armenian public figures by this time, thanks to his involvement in almost every aspect of Armenian cultural, social, and political life, but especially through his innumerable and ubiquitous writings. The editors of *Jamanak* were, therefore, clearly overjoyed at the exclusive opportunity to publish his memoir. "Yervant Odian," they wrote, "is no stranger to the public. His writings – which appeared in every genre on the pages of numerous periodicals, from *Hayrenik* [Fatherland] to its various counterparts abroad – were devoured more eagerly and ravenously than any previous work by members of every class." Writing thirty years later, Hagop Oshagan – who is often regarded as the greatest Western Armenian writer of his generation and one its most influential literary historians – confirmed that Odian was the most beloved and sought-after writer of his time.[*] "We must thank him," Oshagan asserted, "first and foremost for the fact that every day for almost twenty years (1908 – 1926), he uplifted despondent spirits with a

---

[*] Hagop Oshagan, *Hamabadger Arevmdahay Kraganoutyan: Arvesdaked Serount VIII* [*Panorama of Western Armenian Literature: The Generation of Literary Masters*] (Antelias: Armenian Catholicosate of Cilicia, 1980) 367. See https://www.digilib.am/book/4805/Համապատկեր%20արեւմտահայ%20գրականութեան,%20ութերորդ%20հատոր, Accessed March 7, 2025.

bit of humor ...[and] newspapers were left with no choice but to purchase anything that he put his name to."*

Jamanak's announcement also provides valuable contemporaneous insights into Odian's literary reception and rise to popularity. The editors apprise their readers that:

> Odian really achieved the pinnacle of perfection after his return from abroad, and the socialist letters from Dzabulvar† gave him pride of place among Armenian satirists. If we Armenians were his only fans, one could perhaps chalk it up to nationalist self-regard. However, foreigners have recognized his talent far more than we. And today, having been translated into French, Turkish, and Greek, Odian's writings are snatched up everywhere by anyone who can get their hands on them.

As for the uniqueness of *Twelve Years*, the editors – and every subsequent astute reader over the next century – observed that it provides a veritable "panorama" not only of Odian's own life, but of what Oshagan dubs the "senior diaspora"‡ of refugee or émigré Armenians abroad. Very few writers have attempted to dramatize that world spanning several continents over the most repressive years of Sultan Abdülhamid II's reign, from the mid-1890s until 1908. This senior diaspora was home to the Ottoman-Armenian intellectual and literary elite – from writers and painters to journalists and editors – who were lucky or well-heeled enough to flee the Hamidian snare. Apart from Odian's memoir, their situation was also wryly dramatized in Zabel Yessayan's satirical novel, *Geghdz Hanjarner: Veb Deghagan Gyanke*, (Phony Geniuses: A Novel from Local Life, 1905), where the author exposed the self-involved pseudo-intellectualism of her émigré contemporaries during her years living and studying in Paris. Similar to *Twelve Years, Phony Geniuses* appeared as a series of instalments in the literary and political review *Arevelian Mamoul* (*Eastern Press*, Smyrna) in 1905.** It was published as a standalone volume

---

* Oshagan, *Panorama*, 367.
† This is a reference to Odian's novel, *Unger Panchouni*.
‡ Oshagan, *Panorama*, 428.
** Hayk Hovhannisyan, "Yerkidzagann ou Voghperkaganu Zabel Yessayani 'Geghdz Hanjarner' Vibagoum" ["The Comic and Tragic Aspects of Zabel Yessayan's Novel, *Phony Geniuses*"], *Vem Hayakidagan Hantes* 13 (19), No. 3 (75), July - September 2021: 121.

in 1909 by Piuzantian Publishers in Constantinople. Yessayan dedicated this volume to her close friend, the writer Ardashes Haroutiunian, who, she claimed "gave her the heart and moral impetus to complete the work."[*] She described her novella as "the expression of our intellectual life's peculiar psychological states at a specific point in time,"[†] striving to remain as honest as possible to the representation of these individuals and "without harboring any hatred" towards them. She explains that the work was written in a spirit of "compassion" ["*khantaghadank*"] for some of the phony geniuses it depicts, many of whom she claims she cared for deeply.[‡] These disclaimers responded to some of the discomfort the work had already provoked by ridiculing various prominent and easily recognizable émigré writers.[**]

The public's response to Yessayan's satire contrasted with the reception of Odian's much more openly factual and often bitingly critical memoir. Perhaps the difference lay in the fact that, despite being a "marvelous retelling,"[††] Odian's satires, including his panorama of Armenian émigré life, tended to offer journalistic passing glimpses rather than thought-provoking interpretations. Odian did not – and apparently seemed to be incapable of – offending the objects of his satire, be it in *Twelve Years* or in his other works. Oshagan wondered, "Was it that he was not prickly or malicious by nature? Perhaps. Was it that he did not have much of a personality? That is not impossible." Whatever the case may be, "[n]o one," wrote Oshagan, "was ever offended by Odian's attacks, especially after the Constitution's reinstatement."[‡‡] "The extraordinary thing about him was that he was both for everyone and against them."[***] And this personal impartiality, it seems, forestalled any potential hostility or antagonism. Odian evidently struck a perfect balance between pro and con, for and against, approbation and opprobrium, such that neither side prevailed or cancelled the other out. And this ultimately served to shield him from the traps of both belonging and rejection.

---

[*] Zabel Yessayan, *Geghdz Hanjarner (Veb Deghagan Gyankè)* (Constantinople: O. Arzouman, 1909) 5.
[†] Yessayan, *Phony*, 5.
[‡] Yessayan, *Phony*, 5.
[**] Hovhannisyan, "Comic," 121 - 122.
[††] Oshagan, *Panorama*, 428; Avagyan, "Man," 22 – 23.
[‡‡] Oshagan, *Panorama*, 366.
[***] Oshagan, *Panorama*, 359.

Odian may have indeed been constitutionally incapable of taking sides. However, as he indicates at various points in *Twelve Years*, his neutrality was also a principled stance, which he put into practice conscientiously. Nowhere is his commitment to remain uncommitted more evident than in his open declaration that he never registered as an official member of any Armenian revolutionary organization, despite actively collaborating with the Henchag party. By his own memoir's account, whenever Odian officially joins any organization or cause – such as his highly amusing membership in the Parisian branch of the Salvation Army –, he does so purely out of cynical self-interest, until eventually his conscience gets the better of him. That "[h]e did not speak in the name of principles" or that "he did not don the mantle of morality and sermonize"* illustrate – contrary to Oshagan's interpretations – that Odian adopted neutrality as a basic condition for ensuring his fidelity to the truth, no matter how uncomfortable or multi-faceted it might turn out to be. Hence, his insistence at various points throughout *Twelve Years* that the contemporaneous observations of his memoir present nothing but the truth, without embellishment or prejudice. As he writes in Chapter 6, "Some of my readers might be tempted to assume that I am exaggerating, that I am distorting contemporary Armenian history. But all the witnesses to these facts are fortunately still alive and well. And, if need be, they can vouch that my reminiscences are entirely devoid of any exaggeration."

Odian maintained neutrality not simply out of a personal proclivity; his stance was, rather, arguably a direct response to the rampant socio-political hostilities that plagued late 19th – early 20th century Ottoman-Armenian society. Internecine conflicts were nothing new to this community, which seemed incorrigibly unable to forge any kind of consensus. Ottoman-Armenian life was riven with longstanding socio-economic power struggles; class tensions; internal divisions within the Armenian Patriarchate of Constantinople; and violent – quite literally – clashes between Apostolic Armenians and their Catholic and Protestant counterparts. These existing frictions were exponentially exacerbated in the late 19th century by the sweeping influence of the Armenian revolutionary movement and its two dominant and highly antagonistic parties: the Armenian Revolutionary Federation [*Hay Heghapokhagan Tashnagtsoutioun*] – known as the Tashnagtsoutioun or Tashnag party for

---

* Oshagan, *Panorama*, 366.

short – and the Social Democratic Henchagian Party – known as Henchag for short. *Twelve Years* provides a grim portrait of how these often ideologically blind parties not only deepened existing divisions within Ottoman-Armenian society, but also cost Armenian lives both through intra-party attacks and by granting the Ottoman state with further pretexts to commit atrocities in the Armenian provinces. Odian's memoir achieves the extraordinary on that front through its relentless and cutting exposure of both parties' violent and self-defeating dysfunctionalities – remarkably, without subsequently being made the target of their retribution. This unflinching portrayal of Armenian revolutionary activism is arguably the work's greatest strength and a singular contribution to Armenian socio-political history. It provides a salient and sobering - and also, at times, out and out funny - counterpoint to the revolutionary parties' own self-righteous official histories and, as importantly, to the Armenian diaspora's silences on the still unfolding socio-cultural damages inflicted by nationalist-revolutionary ideology. If Armenian thought and culture proved to be incapable of working through the aftermath of the Armenian Genocide or to devote itself to the development of social values and moral virtues – such as consensus, sociality, solidarity, and honesty – by discarding nationalistic narcissism, the fault lay not in reading the wrong books or failing to mourn. It stemmed, rather, from an inability – quite understandable under the authoritarian circumstances – to shake off the narrowly defined and xenophobic nationalist identitarianism that became more or less official policy among Armenian diasporic cultural, social, and political institutions thanks to the stranglehold of their still card-carrying nationalist-revolutionary leadership.

Importantly, *Twelve Years* lays bare how entrenched the revolutionary movement was even in the mainstream Armenian political and cultural life of the 19th century. At various times, it exerted enormous influence on public opinion and hence also on communal politics and policies, while remaining mostly wary of the imperial authorities' watchful eyes. That said, Odian also provides an often-surprising glimpse into the audacity of revolutionary activists, not least in their public acts of resistance, be it through peaceful marches and demonstrations or through more violent tactics. Indeed, Odian's escape from Constantinople and his twelve years away were partly the result of just such bold activism as planned and implemented by the Tashnag party: the seizure of the Ottoman Bank and other acts of terror throughout the imperial capital.

On August 24, 1896, a seventeen-year-old Tashnag recruit, Papgen Suni, led twenty-six of his revolutionary comrades to ambush and occupy the Bank, where the group presented a list of twelve demands. As with many acts of violent Armenian protest pre- and post-Genocide, their intention was to compel the intervention of European Powers, which were already primed to exploit any opportunity to interfere in Ottoman domestic politics. They hoped and expected the Powers to exert their influence in ensuring the implementation of reforms in the Armenian provinces under direct European supervision. The first three of the revolutionaries' demands required the appointment of a European official to carry out such reforms in the capacity of High Commissioner of Armenia, notably by appointing the members of regional government and local law enforcement. The revolutionaries also demanded the implementation of a European-style judicial system and various civil and religious liberties; major overhauls in taxation and the distribution of wealth; and protections and amnesties for convicted or perceived enemies of the state, including Armenian emigres and political prisoners. The group gave the authorities forty-eight hours to meet their demands. Otherwise, they threatened to blow up the bank and everyone, including themselves, in it.

Meanwhile, four of the revolutionaries had died in the initial seizure and five had been wounded by the fallout from their own grenades. Twelve hours into the occupation, the European Powers represented by the Russian Embassy's dragoman, Maximov, agreed to take steps to meet the revolutionaries' demands. The revolutionaries accepted this offer and were given safe passage out of the bank and into the secure locations of European-owned maritime vessels. Seventeen of the revolutionaries were subsequently smuggled out of Constantinople on the same ship, *La Gironde*, that would transport Odian to safe harbor in Greece. *Twelve Years* provides a rare depiction of both his and the revolutionaries' voyage on that steamer. Meanwhile, contrary to European promises, reforms did not follow. In fact, the entire demonstration had been allowed to unfold in order to justify the authorities' heavy-handed reaction. The government had secret foreknowledge of the Bank's planned seizure. It had permitted the occupation to proceed precisely so as to stage a brutal and crushing response.

The Bank's seizure became the second bloody Armenian demonstration in two years, following the intended peaceful demonstration – now known as the 1895 'Bab-ı Ali Demonstration' – planned by the Henchag party. These Henchag-led protesters also demanded the end of mass violence in the Armenian provinces and the implementation of reforms that would ensure civil and political liberties as well as equal rights governed by the rule of law. But a violent police crackdown on the demonstrators led to mass incarcerations, beatings, and murders on the streets of Constantinople. These scores of deaths, injuries, and injustices anticipated the even bloodier massacres that took place in response to the Ottoman Bank protest.* Odian was a first-hand witness to the ensuing carnage, which his memoir depicts in chilling and halting detail. Violent mobs armed with truncheons and blades sought out any Armenian – man, woman, or child – to exact their vengeance. And, according to one count, more than 6,000 people were viciously cut down. Despite eliciting the European Powers' outrage, these deaths sadly did not lead to any meaningful reforms. On the contrary, the demonstration merely intensified the Ottoman State's more or less stated policy of suppression towards its Armenian subjects.†

The bloodless Second Constitutional Revolution of 1908 was expected to put an end to such violent outbreaks. Spearheaded by the multi-ethnic Committee of Union and Progress (*İttihad ve Terakki Cemiyeti*) and assisted in part by the Armenian revolutionary parties, the 'Young Turks' – as the leaders of the CUP have come to be known – forced Sultan Abdülhamid II to reinstate parliamentary rule according to the abrogated Ottoman Constitution of 1876. Odian was in Egypt at the time and therefore missed the euphoric celebrations of this momentous event. He returned to Constantinople in 1909 after a twelve-year hiatus. He was therefore in the capital when euphoria quickly turned into horror. In the spring of 1909, purportedly reactionary Muslim mobs massacred the Armenians and other Christians of Cilicia. Known as the 'Adana Massacres' and often identified as the prelude to the genocidal events of 1915, these atrocities resulted in tens of thousands of deaths and untold devastation perpetrated over just a few weeks. The new government's reluctance and/or failure to appropriately prevent, quell, or punish the crimes sent a clear – and familiar – signal to Armenians.

---

* Louise Nalbandian, *The Armenian Revolutionary Movement: The Development of Armenian Political Parties through the Nineteenth Century* (Berkeley: University of California Press, 1963) 122 – 126.
† Nalbandian, *Revolutionary*, 176 - 178.

Two violent massacres thus bracket the beginning and end of *Twelve Years*. Importantly, Odian depicted the first of these with typically irrepressible honesty, without shying away from the gory details. On the other hand, the memoir mentions the Cilicia massacres only as a passing reference, presumably because Odian had not personally witnessed the events. What the author does provide is a unique account of the darkness and dread that enveloped the lives and minds of Armenians as they witnessed the unabashed resurgence of authoritarian reactionary elements – and their terrorizing mobs – throughout Constantinople. This situation threatened to become a full circle moment for Odian, a repetition of the past violence with which his memoir begins. However, the author concludes the work ostensibly by emphasizing the ultimate triumph of the Constitutionalists over their reactionary foes.

Odian was perhaps at least partly sincere in this evident optimism. Yet, the ambivalence of the work's concluding sentence – "And our lives resumed in the shadow [*hovaniyin dag*] of our restored Constitution…" – suggests otherwise. I have chosen to underscore that meaningful ambivalence – emphasized by the phrase's concluding ellipses – by translating "*hovani*" – meaning both "protection" and "shadow" – as "shadow" rather than "protection." Tellingly, it is this act of translation that foregrounds Odian's depiction of the Constitutional regime's ambivalence: an institution of anticipated or presumed protection that ultimately turned into a space of all-encompassing darkness. Although it appeared several years after the CUP-orchestrated Armenian Genocide during WWI, the 1922 version of the memoir makes no mention of the Genocide. The book's suggestive concluding ellipses serve as a retrospectively meaningful silence to evoke the disillusionment and distrust that by then had come to define the Armenians' perception of ever-genocidal modern Turkish politics.

If Odian left his experience of the Genocide out of *Twelve Years*, he chronicled it in his more widely read memoir, *Accursed Years: 1914 – 1919 (My Memoir)* [*Anidzyal Dariner: 1914 – 1919 (Antsnagan Hishadagner)*].* These remembrances were also published as a series of instalments in *Jamanak* between January 26 and September 12, 1919 alongside news

---

* This memoir's translation was published by the Gomidas Institute. See Yervant Odian, *Accursed Years: My Exile and Return from Der Zor, 1914 - 1919*, trans. Ara Stepan Melkonian (London: Gomidas Institute, 2009).

reports chronicling the genocidal fate of Ottoman-Armenian victims and the indictments, arrests, and prosecutions of their perpetrators. Odian's Genocide memoir is an exceedingly rare artefact. The Genocide left few surviving writers to chronicle their experiences during those events. After all, one of the CUP's first genocidal plans was to ensure their immediate extermination. That plan was put into effect on April 24, 1915 (or April 11, 1915 according to the Julian calendar also in use at that time) with the mass arrest of hundreds of Armenian cultural, social, and political leaders. These individuals were then deported to internment camps in Ayaş and Çankırı, and almost all of them were eventually murdered. Odian was able to elude these arrests and go into hiding for several weeks, where he remained in relative safety. He decided to come out of hiding at the end of May, when he learned that several prominent Armenians had been allowed to return from exile. Odian was arrested on September 8th, several months after his emergence from hiding, but not told on what grounds. After six days in prison, he was supposedly exiled to Konya circa September 14. However, his exile took him further through Tarsus, Osmaniye, Aleppo and Hama, and eventually Deir ez-Zor, and beyond.* Importantly, his relatively sheltered experiences did not reflect the extreme violence and deprivation he witnessed regarding the fate of his compatriots, especially those from the eastern provinces of the Ottoman Empire. It was not until 1918 that he was heard from again. He announced his survival and return to Constantinople with a now famous declaration – "Greetings to You All" ["*Voghchouyn Tsez*"] – published on the front page of *Jamanak*'s November 8, 1918 issue. Although only a few paragraphs long, this emotional call to fellow survivors constitutes one of the most touching, evocative, and unforgettable texts of the Armenian Genocide. I have therefore translated it in full below:

> Greetings, fellow Armenians! – pardon me, greetings to you, remnants of the Armenian people –, I have returned from afar, from very great distances.
>
> I have returned from Deir ez-Zor, whose bridge was crossed by "three-hundred thousand" Armenians, of whom only "one thousand five hundred" women and orphans survived.
>
> I have returned from Osmaniye, where "sixty-thousand Armenians" received a downpour of lashes as they were forced to march through the mountains.

---

* Avagyan, "Man," 22 – 23.

I have returned from that deadly road linking Buzantiye to Tarsus, where Armenian infants were abandoned by their mothers, left to die beneath the fir trees, and consumed like carrion by the dogs and coyotes.

I have returned from those accursed deserts that lead from Aleppo to Deir ez-Zor, where, for three years, tens of thousands of Armenians who were forced to live in camps perished from dysentery, typhus, and various other fevers.

I have returned from the camps of Sabil, where starving parents auctioned their own children, and ten-year-old girls were sold for only sixty paras to the Arabs and Jews.

I have returned from Syria, where, faced with the threat of extermination, more than one-hundred-thousand Armenians denied their God.

I have returned from Hama and Homs, Meskene, Hammam, Mayadin, Al Busra, Sultaniye, and Konya, where thirty to forty-thousand Armenian orphans held in Turkish houses were screeching, "mother, mother," from caged windows.

I have returned from those hellscapes of atrocity, where men like Zohrab, Agnouni, Khazhag, Zartarian, Siamanto, Taniel Varouzhan, Diran Kelegian, Sevag, Daghavarian – in short, the mind of an entire nation was crushed by hands deserving to be dubbed the heirs of Tamerlane and Genghis Khan.

Greetings to you, the wreck and remains of the Armenian nation!

Odian's Genocide memoir, *Accursed Years*, presents one of the most unusual accounts of the Armenian deportation routes and internment camps. Other such rarities include Teotig's serialized memoir, *My Years of Exile and Incarceration* [*Pandi yev Aksori Dariner*] published in the 1916 – 1920 edition of his journal, *Everyone's Almanac* [*Amenouyn Daretsouytsu*, Constantinople]; Mikayel Shamdanjian's slim 1919 volume, *The Atrocity's Toll on the Armenian Mind: Reflections and Impressions of a Deportee* [*Hay Mdkin Hargu Yeghernin: Aksoragani Mdadzoumner yev Zkatsoghoutyounner*];* and Aram Andonian's renowned 1919 book, *In Those Black Days... (Impressions)* [*Ayn Sev Oreroun... (Badgerner)*].

---

* An English translation of this work is available. See Mikayel Shamtanchian, *The Fatal Night: An Eyewitness Account of the Extermination of Armenian Intellectuals in 1915*, Ed. and Trans. Ishkhan Jinbashian (Studio City: H. and K. Manjikian Publications, 2007).

Odian was fundamentally altered by the psychological and physical traumas of deportation and internment. Yet in his typically irrepressible manner, he sublimated his pain through writing. As the editors of *Vosdan* (*Metropolis*, Constantinople) observed, "Yervant Odian is the most prolific survivor on this side of the Armistice, in spite of the indignities he suffered at the hands of the infidels in Deir ez-Zor. Every day, now more than ever, he channels his vast, innovative talents into granting us all in our insufferable tedium the precious gift of humor through his 'postcards,' literary instalments, and Iknad-esque reflections."[*] The years 1918 – 1922 became one of the most productive periods of Odian's life, when he published countless articles and commentaries in the Armenian press; founded his own satirical magazines; penned a plethora of fiction, including remarkably voluminous satires, historical novels, and plays;[†] and, of course, produced his aforementioned memoirs, as well as the much lesser known but extraordinarily interesting serialized instalments of his childhood memories, *Literary Memoirs (1894 – 1914)* (*Kragan Hishadagner: 1894 – 1914*). These were initially published in his short-lived satirical magazine, *Iknad Agha* (Constantinople). They were then taken up by *Vosdan* and published between May 1, 1920 and January 16, 1922. Despite their enthusiastic reception, it seems that Odian's *Literary Memoirs* never appeared as a standalone volume or in an anthology.

Although sadly very brief, this mini-autobiography relays Odian's extraordinarily cosmopolitan Euro-Ottoman upbringing, including his experiences living with his legendary uncle, the Constitutionalist Armenian and Ottoman functionary, Krikor Odian (1834 - 1887), in Paris. His education was likewise exceedingly unusual. His uncle insisted on home-schooling, which was in part dutifully if not always patiently undertaken by his aunts. Given his prominent uncle's own cultural standing and literary social circles, the young Yervant was constantly surrounded by writers and publishers. This early exposure to print culture eventually influenced him to join their ranks. Finally, it was thanks once again to his uncle that Odian also developed fluency in French, a skill that he later applied to the translation of numerous French-language works.

It was perhaps this untethered, free-floating upbringing and education that shaped Odian's independent spirit and kept him out of the fray of

---

[*] Editorial, *Vosdan* No. 11 - 13 (17 - 19), 1 May 1920 (Constantinople): 466.
[†] Avagyan, "Man," 24.

political allegiances. On that basis, Oshagan perhaps hastily dubbed him a consummate *'bohème.'*[*] But this suggests that Odian's psychological and literary perambulations were always made by choice. It would perhaps be more accurate to identify Odian as a consummate *diasporan*. Not coincidentally, he was the first to use the foreign term 'diaspora' – and not its Armenian equivalent *'spiurk'* – to refer to the post-Genocide Armenian condition in the title of his novel *The Armenian Diaspora: On Contemporary Life in Dispersion* [*Hay Diasporan: Zhamanagagits Asdantagan Gyanku*, 1924 – 1925]. Odian fully lived and witnessed the dispersion of Armenians over the course of his entire life spanning at least ten countries on three continents. And it was in the "junior diaspora," as it were, that he ultimately ended his days. In 1922, anticipating the Kemalist forces' incursion into Constantinople, Odian once again took to his heels and fled to Romania. Thereafter he moved to Lebanon, eventually settling in Egypt, where he died in 1926.

This modest introduction cannot do justice to Odian's many talents and insurmountable body of work. But suffice it to end with the eulogy of Vahan Tekeyan (1878 – 1945), one of the giants of Western Armenian poetry, for his colleague and friend: "Those little brooks that he brought forth out of sand and rock created the immense river of Odian's corpus, which will course forevermore through the landscape of our literature."[†] May that river flow forth with this translation.

---

[*] Oshagan, *Panorama*, 359.
[†] Vahan Tekeyan, "Tampanagan Vahan Tekeyani" ["Vahan Tekeyan's Eulogy"], *Arev* [Sun] (Cairo), 5 October 1926: 1.

Twelve Years Away from Constantinople, 1896 - 1908
(My Memoirs)

Yervant Odian, cir. 1922

Preface

This memoir of my twelve years abroad was published as a series of instalments in *Jamanak* ten years ago. It received a very warm reception from my charitable readers, many of whom voiced their wish – both verbally and in writing – that it be published as a book. At last, I can now grant them their wish.

When I undertook the publication of this second edition, I realized that it required extensive revisions. I have, therefore, made significant additions, excisions, and corrections, since this memoir was initially prepared somewhat hastily to meet the newspaper's erstwhile needs.

These important revisions have rendered my memoir far more accurate and authentic than its serialized version.

Whenever possible, this edition also includes the photographs[*] of various individuals mentioned throughout the work.

Yervant Odian

---

[*] This translation's 1922 edition does not include any images. Those images were published in the original 1914 edition. To the extent possible, this volume includes copies of the very same images, substituting alternative better-quality photographs of the same individuals whenever possible. It includes only the images of those individuals who are actually mentioned in the work. It also includes the photographs of several prominent women whose images do not appear in the 1914 edition. (Tr.)

Chapter 1

An attempt on Arpiar Arpiarian's life. – "Take Arpiarian down!" – "Stop Reading *Hayrenik*!" – *Hayrenik*'s dominance. – Izmirilian's election. – The role of Mihran Askanaz. – Arpiarian's character. – A. Vramian. – The Babiali demonstration. – Threatening letters from the Tashnags. – The H. Shahnazar-Yousoufian incident. – The article in *Hayrenik*. – The murder of Dikran Karageozian. – The uprising in Zeitoun. – Arpiar flees Constantinople. – L. Pashalian departs. – The *Hayrenik* cohort dispersed. – Shahnazar incarcerated. – *Hayrenik* dissolves. – Vahé Arzouyan and his friends. – The incident involving Charlié. – The services rendered by Albert Rouet. – The women of the Henchag party.

On the afternoon of Monday, December 25, 1895, Arpiar Arpiarian – who lived in Pangalti with his brother, Dikran Arpiarian, on a property belonging to the Church of Sourp Hagop (St. Jacob) – was on his way home when he was stabbed by a Tashnag individual just outside the park in Taksim.

Despite sustaining severe injuries, Arpiar made it home and knocked on the street-side door. But when they opened the door, he already lay sprawled on the ground, blood-soaked and unconscious.

Doctor Zohrab, who lived nearby, was summoned immediately and administered first aid.

This assassination attempt did not come as a surprise, either to him or to us. The Tashnags had been plotting something against *Hayrenik* [newspaper], and more specifically, against Arpiarian for some months.

There had been orders to "take Arpiarian down!" And now those orders were being implemented conscientiously, for lack of a better term. The Tashnags had been spreading rumors that Arpiar was an informant; that he was one of Nazim Pasha's cronies; that they dined together every evening, and so on. They even planned a successful but short-lived boycott against *Hayrenik*, but it only lasted a few days.

This propaganda had been underway for two months, leading up to the assassination attempt. And Arpiarian had responded with his article of October 8, "Stop Reading *Hayrenik*," where he wrote:

> For the past four or five days, several individuals have been going through all the neighborhoods in Constantinople telling people to "stop reading *Hayrenik*." Why, one wonders? Their response is to slander my person, hurling accusations that are as

reprehensible as the idiocy of my accusers and the naivete of their followers. The truth is that I am in the habit of ignoring nasty gossip. Neither enmity nor friendship will divert me – not even by a hair's breadth – from the path I have chosen in public life. But, if this one time, I now feel compelled to make a statement, the reason is that a group of antagonistic rivals is intent on bringing me down in their efforts to undermine *Hayrenik*. But they can rest assured that their machinations over the past five years will prove to be futile both now and hereafter.

Arpiar then went on to elaborate on the circumstances that had provoked this hostility against him – that is, within the permissible constraints of censorship at that time –, and he concluded: "I have one response to the slanderous charges spread by this petty contingent of malicious agitators: They are absolutely false. Let me also add that not one of them has the gumption to come out and accuse me in public. They are a bunch of liars scheming in the dark."

What was the motive behind their savage persecution of Arpiarian?

There could have been multiple reasons.

First and foremost, Arpiarian had attained to the exceptionally powerful status of a revolutionary leader. He edited the unprecedentedly popular periodical, *Hayrenik*. He was a member of the Henchag party's central committee in Constantinople. He worked as a correspondent for both *Meshak* and *Hentchag* – two extraordinarily influential periodicals in revolutionary circles.

Hayrenik was especially prominent in Constantinople. It had taken charge of national politics over the entire previous year. It was *Hayrenik* that endorsed Izmirlian's election.

That election took place on Wednesday, December 7, 1894 – exactly one year before the assassination attempt – at the church of the Mother See and during a period of tremendous hope and anticipation. Abdulhamid had placed a moratorium on meetings of the National Council. Eventually, he issued a sultanic decree permitting elections for the offices of the Patriarchate and the Administration. Bishop Hmayag gathered all the representatives and opened the session. The first vote was held for the Office of the Chancery, and Kapriyel Effendi Noradoungian was elected as the First Chairman. This was followed immediately by a vote to appoint the Patriarch. And, with 67 ballots cast by 76 voters, the preacher of Scutari, Madteos Izmirlian was elected as the Patriarch. Bishop

Partoghimeyos had only received three votes; Ghevont Alishan, two; Hmayag Timaksian, two; Bishop Bedros, the Prelate of Sivas, one; with one abstention.

Hayrenik newspaper, 1894.

This election constituted a phenomenal protest against Abdulhamid, who despised the patriotic and incorruptible Patriarch-elect. It took a full twenty days for him to issue the decree ratifying this election. However, ultimately, the Sultan was obliged to ratify the election and, on Monday, December 26, Izmirlian took his oath.

The next day, *Hayrenik* described that magnificent ceremony in the evocative lines penned by L. Pashalian and me. L. Pashalian insisted that we somehow include Hentchag's name in that precis, and he devised the following sentence: "Outside, the church bells (in Scutari's Church of the Holy Cross) rang jubilantly, their rousing chimes* propelling all the excitement of this joyous news into the heavens above."

That "*hunchaganoutyoun*" – which the Armenian censor did not fail to notice – almost landed us in hot water. Fortunately for us, Mihran Askanaz, who was approached for further clarification of that term, quelled their suspicions.

Many years later, Arpiar Arpiarian relayed those events in one of his "graveyards:"†

After His Holiness Izmirlian's election was ratified, this Patriarch of the Renaissance was led to the Mother See in an

---

* The suggestively used Armenian term is "*Hunchaganoutyoun*," meaning "resonance." (Tr.)

† Arpiarian wrote a series of essays and remembrances on late 19th century Ottoman-Armenian society, politics, culture, and literature under the general title of "Hoghvrdik," meaning "cemetery" or "graveyard." (Tr.)

unprecedented ceremonious procession, at the sight of which, Armenian hearts fluttered with visions of an Armenian king's consecration. That day, the Armenian people came dangerously close to blurting out the words, "Holy King Madteos," as their forebears must have done once upon a time when they had witnessed the coronation of Pakradouni Ashod. A shared faith in a better tomorrow enveloped the congregation. "And the Cathedral rang out with rousing chimes,"[*] wrote Pashalian the next day in *Hayrenik*. His account presented a perfect rendition of the Armenian people's emotional upheavals during the year 1894, one that, like an illuminated manuscript will be preserved in history for all time. Not one of us had the heart to excise those two audacious words. Their excision would have been tantamount to vandalizing a pair of masterfully depicted eyes in an elegant portrait. The censors, meanwhile, failed to see that depiction for what it was. Sometimes, censorship took an "off-hand" approach. When Pashalian met with an artist we both knew several days later, he was alerted that *Hayrenik* had just eluded a major threat – a threat that would have probably culminated in the paper's closure and its editors' exile. "You should light a candle for Askanaz. You'd both be done for, if it weren't for him," stated the source. This is what had transpired: After the Ministry of the Police translated *Hayrenik*'s report, it sent it off to the Ministry of the Interior requesting further review of the two "provocative" words, "rousing chimes,"[†] marked in red. An influential member of the Ministry of the Interior – a noble Turk – received the text and decided to expedite matters. So, he pocketed that issue of *Hayrenik* and that very same night, he invited the aforementioned artist to his residence in Kadikeuy. He showed him the words marked in red and requested their precise translation, while also impressing upon him that "those poor wretches are in for some serious trouble." The Armenian was lost for words. As soon as he saw the term, "*hunchag*," he panicked. Later, he told Pashalian, "I was about to cross myself, but I was sitting across from a Muslim." He suggested that they call on Askanaz Effendi, who lived nearby. "He is a formidable Armenologist. He can provide the

---

[*] "*Hunchaganoutyamp.*" (Tr.)
[†] "*Havadardzardz hunchaganoutyoun.*" (Tr.)

most precise translation." Someone was dispatched to the renowned Armenian language instructor's home, and he arrived straightaway. Askanaz, along with everyone else, had grasped the hidden meaning of "*havadardzardz hunchaganoutyoun*," and "he couldn't help clearing his throat repeatedly," he told the artist afterwards. But when asked for the precise translation of those words, he had replied casually that "*hunchaganoutyoun*" merely means the same as "*sonorité*" in French. He did not let on in the slightest that "*Hunchagyanoutyoun*" might have also crossed his mind. And when he was apprised of the police report, Askanaz had replied with his inimitably naive and innocent chuckle – in what was perhaps his very first act of deceit or half-deceit –, "There is a big difference between '*Hunchagyanoutyoun*' and '*hunchaganoutyoun.*' Ali Effendi and Veli Effendi differ by only one letter, but they are not the same man, after all." During this consultation, it was also duly and dutifully explained to the employee of the Ministry of the Interior that *Hayrenik* enjoyed immense popularity. And concerns were raised that the paper's closure and its editors' exile might perhaps elicit some outrage, which could occasion some dire consequences. The Turkish Effendi had compiled all this information and relayed it to the Minister of the Interior the following day, thereby successfully stifling the whole business.

To adequately foreground the magnanimity of Askanaz during this ordeal, I must emphasize that relations between him and *Hayrenik* had been "severed." I do not recall why. That wittiest, and hence, most remorseless of editors – whose name will now rise to the lips of every Egyptian-Armenian reader – used to pick on him mercilessly. Askanaz was deeply offended. Teachers are easily riled by criticism. And suddenly, *Hayrenik*'s life depended on him, on the lips of the very same teacher who had been the target of those attacks. Fortunately, his lips were moved by his heart, and his heart was good. Askanaz did not resort to spite, which also meant that this kind man had been unjustly subjected to those unwarranted attacks.

Many tumultuous days were to follow in Constantinople. And I did not have another opportunity to meet Askanaz. But, when I arrived in Alexandria in the autumn of 1897, we suddenly came face to face on the street, and our hands reached for one another. I took this opportunity to express my profound gratitude and to

Galata (Constantinople).

convey my immense awe at his act of kindness. He seemed to be taken by surprise and stood wondering at who might have revealed his "secret." I mentioned the artist's name. He laughed. It was all true.

This kind man was all but martyred by the harassment and torment to which he was subjected. That teacher who had devoted himself wholeheartedly to Armenology, whose dedication was an inspiration to many young Armenians, did not perish in the dungeons of Constantinople, his skull bashed in by his Turkish tormentors. Instead, he wasted away out in the free world, where Armenian hands needled and pierced his bleeding heart up to the very end of his life.

That was to be expected. After all, "what was spoken was to be fulfilled." And it is said that Armenians perform no task more fully than staging an extravagant funeral.

The administration which was appointed to work with Izmirlian was vetted through a list prepared by the *Hayrenik* cohort. It consisted of: Chairman I – Sahag Ghazarosian; Chairman II – Mihran Hovagimian; Secretary I – Mgrdich Manougian; Secretary II – Avedis Tngrian; Misak Kaytanjian, Garabed Eknayan, Hovhannes Msrian, Hovhannes Boyajian, Doctor Seghposian, Smpad Kyatibian, Arsen Arsenian, Badrig Giulbengian.

As one can see, none of them was an effendi.

The Religious Council, meanwhile, consisted of: Chairman I – Krikoris Aleyatjian, Hmayag Timasian, Father Hovhannes Arsharouni, Father Kevork Yeretsian, etc.

Hayrenik's other victory was the election for Pera's Town Council. Every single candidate on its list won by a devastating majority.

As expected, the overwhelming influence and authority of *Hayrenik* and its Editor-in-Chief presented an obstacle to the Tashnag party, which found it difficult to bolster itself against an opposition of this magnitude. Yousoufian was the representative or head of the Tashnags in Constantinople at that time. And he was the one who initiated the attacks on *Hayrenik* and Arpiarian. Arpiarian had been his close friend and confidant, up to a certain point – namely, when he realized that Arpiarian and his comrades had been deceiving him.

Arpiarian lacked integrity. This was the main reason for all the hostility directed at him. He was a consummate intriguer throughout his life, a fact that he openly acknowledged. And this vice seemed to be instinctive to his nature. He schemed for the sheer pleasure of it, and not in pursuit of some agenda, reward, or conquest. He simply relished the act of manipulating his hapless victims. It was a veritable psychological compulsion.

He concealed his Henchag affiliation from Yousoufian for quite some time. He pretended that he supported the Tashnags, joining their efforts to improve the Henchag party's standing. When he was finally exposed, the Tashnags were furious at both him and *Hayrenik*.

Up to that point, the Tashnags were avid supporters of *Hayrenik*. In fact, Onnig Tertsagian (better known now as A. Vramian) was a regular contributor, as evinced by the appearance of his signature, "O.K.T.," on some of *Hayrenik*'s best-written pieces in its early years.

Apart from this literary collaboration, Tertsagian was a close friend of Arpiarian, and he often visited the newsroom for their regular tête-à-têtes. Back then, he was a lovely, lively young man with a smooth, beardless face. And he always supported the most radical ideas. He worked for the Russian Postal Service in Galata, and that enabled him to assist both parties – Tashnag and Henchag alike – in disseminating their correspondences.

The Tashnag party began to attack Arpiarian after the June 1895 Babiali [Sublime Porte] demonstration. Everyone knew that the demonstration was organized exclusively by the Henchag party – in principle, to pressure the government into hastening its implementation of reforms in Armenia, but which, in fact, became nothing more than a pretext for the massacres. The consequences of that demonstration included people sheltering in churches, closing their shops, and so on, on the advice of the Henchag leaders, who had orchestrated everything.

Arpiar Arpiarian.

The center of Henchag activity during that tumultuous period was Pera's Church of the Holy Trinity, where more than one thousand people took refuge. Among them were Aliksan Arzouyan (Vahé), Sarkis Siungiujian (Sarkis Svin), Kegham Barsamian, Antreas Mgrian (Parebashd), in short, the entire Henchag planning committee.

A number of Tashnags had joined forces with the Henchags.

Doctor N. Daghavarian, who was deemed a zealous Tashnag at the time, went around reassuring everyone in the church that the British navy would be entering the Dardanelles any moment now. Many were so anxious for this turn of events that they even *heard the booming cannons*.

It was when successful diplomatic interventions had ostensibly restored peace – and enabled people to leave the churches and reopen their shops – that the Tashnag committee began its intimidation campaign. It sent Armenian newspapers threatening letters and demanded that they stop their presses as an act of protest.

This type of protest would not only be meaningless and futile; but coming at such a critical moment, it would also endanger the newspaper directors and editors, whom the government would surely dub as revolutionaries and agitators.

Letters containing the proverbial red stamp were sent to *Hayrenik*, *Arevelk*, and *Jeride-i Sharkiye*. *Arevelk* and *Jeride-i Sharkiye* panicked, and

Zareh Yousoufian, Piuzant Kechian, and Dikran Jivelegian rushed over to ask us how we planned to respond, so that they could follow our lead. It goes without saying that everyone opposed such an ill-conceived protest and gleaned the disastrous personal consequences. And yet, the red stamp – which back then exerted almost supernatural powers on everyone concerned – had fallen into their hands.

Hovhannes Shahnazar and Arpiar Arpiarian categorically declared that they would not succumb to those threats, and that they would continue to print *Hayrenik*. They advised the others to follow their example.

Arpiar already surmised that the Tashnags had him in mind with this plan to stop the Armenian presses. And if the Tashnag party ever decided to act on its threats, he would be the sole target of an assassination attempt. He made this point to reassure the two newspaper directors, because, it must be said, they were terribly anxious about the red stamp on their letters.

Having realized that its threats were futile and deducing correctly that *Hayrenik* was responsible for this, the Tashnag party sent another round of threatening letters. This time, they were addressed not to *Hayrenik*'s directors, but rather to Shahnazar, Arpiarian, Levon Pashalian, and me personally.

This prompted Shahnazar to confront Yousoufian for an explanation. And he asked me to join him.

We went to Tepebashi, where Yousoufian was renting a room in a Greek man's house located opposite the Toma dairy warehouse.

The discussion got very heated. Yousoufian insisted that the presses must be stopped, even if that put the directors and editors at risk of being incarcerated or exiled. Shahnazar objected that *Hayrenik* would be of better use to the revolution by continuing to publish, not by stopping its press, which would have absolutely no influence on the government. As I already noted, the discussion got very heated, often flaring into an out and out argument, and I had to step in repeatedly to defuse the situation.

Ultimately, a resolution proved to be impossible. Incensed, Shahnazar stood up, and we left.

I cannot remember the exact words that were exchanged. However, I can attest to the fact that Shahnazar never once threatened to turn Yousoufian in, contrary to what one Armenian-American newspaper claimed many years later to discredit Shahnazar.

"I'll have you taken out of Constantinople," Shahnazar said at one point.

But this warning – which came in response to Yousoufian's "we'll kill you," – did not mean that Shahnazar intended to inform on Yousoufian. It was simply tit for tat, with Shahnazar driving home the point that if the Tashnag party resorted to extremes, then the Henchag party – which had a much stronger network in Constantinople at the time – would retaliate.

And Yousoufian got Shahnazar's drift.

After that, the next time I saw Yousoufian was at the Mother See of Koumkapou during the election of Patriarch Arsharouni. He had just returned from the Caucasus and was on his way to Europe, where he was due to receive minor ear surgery. Our greetings were amicable, but I did not have an opportunity to ask him whether he had prior knowledge of the Armenian-American newspaper's story.

I believe that perverting the truth to smear someone's reputation – something which, alas, our revolutionary press often resorts to – is one of the most reprehensible acts of sabotage.

Arpiar's assault on the streets of Taksim took place after that meeting.

Our house – which was located next to the Dame de Sion school on the road to Pangalti – was just a few minutes away from Arpiarian's residence.

I was still having dinner, when Arpiarian's nephew, Pilig – a skinny, pale ten-year old boy –, rushed in with the awful news.

I sprinted over to their house. There were two rooms on the ground floor, one that abutted the courtyard on the right, and another that faced it. I noticed Dikran Arpiarian in the room on the right, wearing a cardigan and sitting cross-legged on the sofa. He was swaying pensively back and forth in front of a grill. Judging by his appearance, he could have been mistaken for the attack victim.

Arpiar was lying motionless on the sofa in the opposite room. Doctor Makhokhian, who had arrived after Dr. Zohrab, was still there, giving orders to the landlady, Mrs. Pembe Sanjakian, who doted over Arpiar, her tenant, with unwavering devotion throughout this entire ordeal.

The doctor, who was a great admirer and friend of Arpiar – as well as one of *Hayrenik*'s contributors – appeared very anxious.

"Is his life in danger?" I asked when he left the room.

"He has an extremely critical wound just below his chest," he replied. "If he develops a fever, it will prove to be catastrophic."

"Does he realize the gravity of his situation?"

"I told him, because he forced me to tell him the truth…"

Then I approached Arpiar, and we embraced.

He had grown even paler than usual, but his eyes twinkled as mischievously as ever.

"You must find Shahnazar and bring him here as soon as possible," he told me… "There is a good chance that I am going to die; I have some things to discuss with him."

"But you don't look like you're about to die," I said laughing.

"Makhokhian can't be sure yet," he replied, "and I want to put my affairs in order. Go, quickly, and find him… Tell him discreetly that I've been attacked and bring him here."

Fifteen minutes later, I was at Tokatlian's, where I was sure I would find Shahnazar.

And indeed, there he was reading a newspaper at one of the tables. I gave a little chuckle as I approached him.

"How do you like Arpiar's move?" I said.

"What?" he asked.

"He got a Tashnag to try and kill him just to get everyone talking…"

Shahnazar paid me no mind, assuming that I was just kidding.

"It's true," I continued, "three stabs, one of them pretty deep. Come on, let's go over to his place, he wants to see you… He wants to draw up his will."

Shahnazar could now tell that something was amiss.

"Did they get him?" he exclaimed.

"Yes," I replied softly, "but it's just a flesh wound."

We quickly climbed into a cab and went back to Arpiar's place. He was perfectly composed as he recited his "will" to Shahnazar. As wills go, it was no more than a set of instructions for the Henchag party.

We spent the night there. The fever, which the doctors had feared, did not develop. And, by the following day, the patient's condition had markedly improved.

It wasn't until the next morning that Levon Pashalian, who lived in Scutari, learned what had happened and came running as fast as he could to his beloved's bedside.

Hayrenik reported the assassination attempt in its Wednesday, December 27 issue. The article cited here was penned by Shahnazar and prompted the newspaper's indefinite closure:

Attempted Murder

On Monday evening, around two o'clock, Arpiar Effendi Arpiarian left *Hayrenik*'s newsroom and was on his way home to Pangalti. As he approached the Military Barracks in Taksim, the man who had been following him put one hand on Arpiar Effendi's shoulder and, with the other, thrust a knife into his chest. Arpiar Effendi was stabbed three times as he tried to fend off his assailant with his umbrella.

As soon as the soldiers across the road noticed the scuffle, they rushed to the scene. Arpiarian told them, "Everything is fine," and went straight home. In the meantime, his assailant ran toward Taksim and disappeared.

Two thrusts were aimed at his heart, but they missed and slashed his upper arm. The third, however, went into the lower right part of his chest. His many friends will be relieved to learn that his life is no longer in danger. We are hopeful that his wounds will heal over the next few days.

The motives for this attempted murder remain a mystery to us. It is true that recently, we received death threats demanding that we cease publishing official reports. However, since Arpiar Effendi is merely an editor at *Hayrenik* – an editor who is, moreover, entirely ignorant of Ottoman-Turkish –; and, since *Hayrenik* can only publish those reports with the owner's and director's permission twenty-four hours after going to print in the Turkish press and once they have been translated for the Armenian papers; one can only assume that this time, those same anonymous people who felt that *Hayrenik*'s very existence obstructed their aims – and, who, therefore, went around every home and *han* instructing unsuspecting young boys to slander Arpiar Effendi or telling everyone they ran into to "stop reading *Hayrenik*!" – also wished to hit several targets with one stone by arming a hapless wretch and convincing him that killing Arpiar Effendi was a crime worth committing, because it would serve the greater good.

***

On Monday evening, Dr. Makhokhian, Zohrab, and Elmasian bandaged the victim's wounds and, yesterday morning, they discovered that the patient's condition had improved measurably.

His many friends rushed to his side from near and far. And one of the first to arrive was the deacon of Pera, Fr. Nerses Kharakhanian.

***

Back then, only Hovhannes Shahanazar had the temerity to write and publish this sort of thing.

Two days later, *Hayrenik* was closed down indefinitely.

News of the attempted murder had scarcely reached Constantinople, when visitors did indeed flock to Arpiar's home, which turned into something of a pilgrimage site. Even several Tashnags paid him a visit. As I recall, Onnig Tertsagian (A. Vramian) was among them. He came to convince Arpiarian that the attempt on his life was justified.

Levon Pashalian.

Naturally, the Henchags did not take the news of their leader's attack well. They were furious and inconsolable. And they would stop at nothing in their passionate calls for revenge. Vahé Arzouyan, in particular, was set on retaliation and had picked out several notable Tashnags as prime targets.

Fortunately, several days later, Arpiarian was no longer in critical condition and was expected to make a full recovery. That was the only reason that the Henchags desisted from their plans to retaliate. Arpiar staunchly opposed vendettas and wrangled at length on this matter with Vahé and his supporters.

Meanwhile, just as I was walking into Tünel in Galata, I ran into Vahé Arzouyan who told me, out of the blue, "We're staging a protest against the bourgeoisie this evening."

"What do you mean?"

"There will be an attempt on Dikran Karageozian's life."

"Does Arpiar know?"

"No, I was on my way there now to let them know," replied Vahé. "Although I would prefer not to, seeing as I have other important business to attend to. But since you're here, why don't you go back and tell them; let them know that everything is set to move ahead with the plan. See what he says."

"But what if he objects?" "Let me know right away. I'll be waiting for you in Yanni's tavern."

I ran out of breath to Arpiar, who was out of bed and sitting up in a corner of the sofa.

I reported what Vahé told me. Arpiar was terribly upset and agitated.

"You have to run over there right now!" he shouted. "Tell him to put a stop to the whole thing... I absolutely object. Quick, go find him..."

Arshag Vramian (Onnig Tertsagian).

I went back to Yanni's tavern and, true to his word, Vahé was waiting there.

I relayed Arpiar's message. He looked at his watch and replied, "I think it's too late by now. The deed is probably done..."

"But," I insisted, "Arpiar is absolutely opposed to that assassination attempt."

"I'll go over there and find out. If it isn't too late and there's a chance we can stop it, we'll postpone the mission," said Vahé as he got to his feet.

We walked out together. He left me at Galatasaray, and I went into Tokatlian's café, which had become our unofficial headquarters at that time.

"They got Dikran Karageozian..."

That was the first thing I heard when I went in.

We were already too late...

I could not bring myself to go back and face Arpiar. And it wasn't until the following day that I learned what had happened.

Dikran Karageozian's wounds were initially thought to be light, but the poor man died a couple of days later.

The main contention with him was that, apart from not making any donations to the revolution, or to the "Sacred Work," as they used to say, he also used to advise – and even compel – other wealthy individuals not to donate to the cause.

At the time, the Zeitoun Insurgency was underway, and the Henchags were sending collections to Nazarpeg and his wife, Maro, in London, so that the funds could be distributed to the insurgents.

It was eventually revealed that Nazarpeg and his wife had appropriated all those funds and sent a mere trifling to Zeitoun.

The events in Zeitoun had roused the Armenians of Constantinople to their feet. And if only a handful of wealthy individuals felt compelled to make a donation, it goes without saying that the population at large was only too eager to contribute its meager earnings.

Epic tales of the insurgents' victories had begun to circulate. There were some claims that the Armenians had claimed a sovereign territory; that they were using their own currency printed with the image of an Armenian prince; that people arriving from Zeitoun had obtained Armenian passports…and so on and so forth.

Some people even averred that they had actually seen banknotes printed with the name of the prince of Zeitoun – Prince Babig, I believe.

Meanwhile, Nazarpeg was busy in London. He was innovating his efforts to rouse the Armenians of Constantinople – and, as it was later revealed, to exploit their naiveté. He would embellish every issue of *Henchak* with astonishing correspondences from Zeitoun reporting incredible feats such as the annihilation of entire regiments.

When Arpiar recovered fully, he decided to leave for London, because it had become impossible for him to stay here.

The Tashnag party's assassination attempt exposed Arpiar as a Henchag, whereas Nazim Pasha had been under the impression that after delivering his infamous written confession and giving his solemn oath in the Church of the Mother See, he had withdrawn from the revolution. Moreover, his presence in London had become a matter of urgency as there were mounting complaints about Nazarpeg and his wife.

Levon Mgrdichian, Mihran Damadian, Andon Rshdouni and Ardavazt or Artiur Ohanchan had already left Constantinople after the Babiali demonstration.

At the time, the latter – who had orchestrated the assassination of Maksoud Simon Bey – was also Nazarpeg's plenipotentiary. He was thought to be a ringleader in Van or Erzurum and was armed when apprehended. He was brought to Constantinople to stand trial, where he was incarcerated and then released shortly before the Babiali demonstration. He was an amiable young man and could speak Russian, English, and French fluently. He was not a fervent revolutionary, but he threw himself into that profession simply to satisfy his need for adventure. He looked like a perfect gentleman, as he never left the house without a black redingote, a pair of gloves, and an *haute forme* hat. And those who did not know him never suspected he was Armenian. A revolutionary, moreover? Never. No one would have guessed that.

Artiur Ohanchan was so charismatic that many people joined the Henchags thanks to him. One of them was my brother, Hrant Odian, who had never gotten involved in the revolution directly or indirectly, until he met Artiur. All of a sudden, he was a fervent Henchag and a member of its administration.

His departure was a great loss for us all, and things generally began to deteriorate afterwards.

Arpiar escaped Constantinople fairly easily. Ten liras were enough to bribe the officers guarding the French steamer, and they let Arpiar, as well as those seeing him off – including me – board the steamship unimpeded.

After Arpiar's departure, Levon Pashalian also left for Salonica and then from there, for Europe, with the proviso that he would not return.

That was how the *Hayrenik* cohort dissolved. Arshag Chobanian had been first to leave and settle in Paris. Vahram Svajian had taken his mother and left. Only Shahnazar and I remained from the original group, in addition to a handful of other associates such as Dikran Yergat and Friar Goundzig.

Yet, Shahnazar had made up his mind to keep the paper running; and he tried every single day to resume printing. Eventually, after a five-month hiatus – it was April '96, I believe – we received a pardon, and *Hayrenik* began to publish again.

We assumed that the absence of several central figures would impact the paper negatively, and that we would not be able to garner the success of bygone days. But, contrary to our expectations, the public embraced its beloved paper effusively, and the number of subscriptions even went up.

But we had lost our enthusiasm. These were bleak times, and the massacres in Armenia had sapped our energy and shattered our dreams.

It had been scarcely a month since *Hayrenik* resumed printing, when one morning, someone from the police station came by and told us that the minister wanted to see Shahnazar posthaste.

"He's not here. We'll send him over when he gets back," we replied.

And the man left.

When Shahnazar returned, we gave him the news, and he went at once to meet with Nazim Pasha.

"If I take too long, Adrouni should come to see about the situation," he said as he was leaving.

We did not think much of it. And Friar Goundzig – who was now a permanent staff editor – and I kept working.

Yet, several hours went by, and Shahnazar did not appear.

In the evening, Adrouni brought word that he was in prison and that the paper would no longer be published.

The immediate reason, or more precisely, excuse, for Shahnazar's incarceration had been the return of two female students whom *Hayrenik* had dispatched to Nancy. Several letters from Shahnazar had been found in their possession.

In describing the country's dire conditions, the director of *Hayrenik* had advised the students to remain in Nancy and continue their studies instead of returning to Constantinople, as they had intended to.

I do not know how, but I believe that these letters somehow found their way into the hands of Father Vahan and were conveyed to the police.

The police were already looking for an excuse to get rid of *Hayrenik*, and this served as the perfect pretext for Nazim Pasha to have the director jailed and the paper shut down.

After Arpiar and Levon Pashalian left for London to work in the headquarters of *Henchak*, our "true colors" were completely exposed to the government. And even if the incident with the letters had not occurred, they would have probably concocted another excuse to permanently shut *Hayrenik* down.

At the same time, the Henchag party in Constantinople had almost completely dissolved. Its main leaders – Arpiar, Levon Mgrdichian, Mihran Damadian, Andon Rshdouni, Artiur Ohanchan – had all left. Several months after joining, my brother Hrant Odian also had to flee. Others such as Sarkis Svin were arrested and jailed. Everyone who had not been captured – Vahé Arzouyan, Kegham Barsamian, and several other friends – was being sought by the police and had to hide out at a Greek woman's home on Abanoz Street in Pera.

Meanwhile, Vahé Arzouyan and his friends had fallen out with Yervant Chavoushian and his friends. My brother, who left Constantinople at very short notice, was unable to hand over his Henchag stamp. And now, both sides were hounding me for it on the assumption that my brother had left it with me and that I was being uncooperative.

Finally, I received a letter from Athens, in which my brother specified where he had hidden the stamp and instructed me to hand it to Vahé – which I did, in spite of Yervant Chavoushian's threats, since he wanted in no uncertain terms to take possession of that priceless object.

I do not know what happened then, but Vahé lost the stamp. So, he wrote to his friends in Athens asking them to prepare another one and send it to him.

At the time, the distribution of Henchag party correspondences was facilitated by a young Swiss man by the name of Charlié. That foreigner was a friend of Artiur Ohanchan who had made the necessary arrangements to obtain his services.

He worked as accountant and cashier at the Pera Palace Hotel, our drop-off point for all correspondences. My task was to retrieve and deliver them to Vahé. He had arranged the stamp's delivery from Greece. And Charlié was aware of the urgency of the situation as well as our desperation to finally get our hands on it.

One day, when I went as usual to pick up our correspondences, Charlié, looking shaken, told me, "Oh no, sir, there has been a terrible catastrophe..."

"What catastrophe?" I exclaimed, trembling.

"Look!" he said, showing me his desk drawers. "They've locked them up, and soon, they'll be stamping them... Unfortunately, your envelopes, as well as the stamp which arrived this morning, are among them... Dear God, what a catastrophe!..."

In his desperation, Charlié was hitting himself on the head.

"How could this happen? Tell me!" I demanded.

He eventually pulled himself together and explained, "I had removed about fifty liras from the coffer, and I wanted to store them somewhere safe. But, suddenly, this morning, the chief comptroller conducted a review, and discovered the missing amount... I had to confess everything. So, the comptroller seized the keys to the chest and drawers, locked everything up, and said that he was going to inform the hotel management, so that they could proceed accordingly... I begged and pleaded with him and eventually got a one-day extension to replace the fifty liras and settle the whole affair quietly... I had placed all my hopes on you. Tell Vahé to send me that amount without delay. Otherwise, I'll have to drop everything and run away. And that means you'll probably be discovered, because the police are liable to get involved..."

It all sounded dubious to me, but what was I to do? I returned to Vahé and reported everything.

"That guy is trying to put one over on us," he said, "because we made some financial gifts in the past and he hasn't been receiving anything for a little while... since we're completely broke."

And indeed, all the party members who had stayed behind were in dire financial straits, especially Vahé and his friends.

Still, we had to come up with a solution.

We put our hopes on Diran Kelegian to do something. And I decided to take Charlié to Kalamish, where I had been lodging at the beachside Bellevue Hotel. Diran Kelegian also lived in that village with his family.

Charlié came along, ate, drank, and had a wonderful time at the hotel, but we were unable to arrive at a resolution. Kelegian attempted in vain to wrest the truth from his lips, promising that he would pay him the required amount in good time, if he immediately handed over the correspondences and stamp.

"That's impossible. I can't. They confiscated the keys," insisted Charlié adamantly.

The next morning, he and I went down to Pera Palace.

"You need to meet with the chief comptroller. You might be able to convince him to wait another few days," he told me.

We went up to his office, and he introduced me to a young man. He was supposedly the chief comptroller but looked more like a common clerk.

After making several threats, he acquiesced to extending the deadline to that evening. He also emphasized that, if necessary, the drawers could be unlocked in the presence of police officers and embassy personnel.

I apprised Vahé and Kegham of the situation. As I mentioned, they had taken refuge in a Greek woman's house and had not come out for weeks, because the police were in hot pursuit.

We talked briefly, and then Vahé suddenly stood up, pulled out two revolvers from under the bed, and gave one to Kegham.

"Let's go pay Charlié a visit," he said.

He ordered me to follow a short distance behind, so that I would know if they were apprehended *en route*.

We took the side streets and reached Pera Palace in Tepebashi unmolested. Vahé and Kegham went in, while I paced outside, my heart in my throat as I awaited the outcome of this visit.

About twenty minutes later, Vahé and Kegham reappeared. Their expressions led me to believe that everything had gone smoothly.

When we returned to the house on Abanoz Street without incident, Vahé reported what had happened.

The two friends enter Charlié's office, where the young gentleman, whom he had introduced as the chief comptroller, is waiting for them.

Kegham shuts the door and blocks it. Vahé takes a step forward, removes the revolver from his pocket, and cutting out the small talk, demands that they immediately turn over the stamp and correspondences. He warns them that otherwise, he will have to shoot them down.

This produces immediate results. Trembling, Charlié opens the drawers and hands all party items over to Vahé, who does not bat an eyelash as he turns to leave with Kegham.

Some have speculated – even in writing, I believe – that Vahé put his comrades in the line of fire, while he shied away from risk. Being very close to Vahé and having observed his conduct on numerous occasions, I cannot corroborate these unfair charges.

He did not make demands that he was not willing to personally fulfil. And he always prioritized his friendships.

I may be reminded of other such examples involving Vahé throughout this narrative.

After thwarting Charlié's chantage and despite the difficulties that plagued him, Vahé nonetheless tried to restore the Henchag administration in Constantinople. It had fallen into utter disarray due to the absence of its many departed or incarcerated members.

He was confined to his room and could do little to ameliorate the situation. So, I had to run around recruiting anyone who would agree to being christened a Henchag.

Several unsuccessful attempts later, I remembered the sculptor and architect, Arabian, an exuberant and straight-talking young man, who had recently returned from Paris. He had a workshop in Pera, on Istiklal Avenue, not far from the Café Luxembourg.

I broached the topic with him and was so persistent that he ultimately acquiesced.

"Who would I be working with?" he asked.

It was a tough question, because everyone was gone.

"You'll find out when you become an official member of the Administration," I replied enigmatically.

I then took him to Vahé's hideout, which he visited on several more occasions to parley with Vahé. But, when it became evident to him that there was a shortage of members, organization, and active momentum, he quietly withdrew.

Vahé was most concerned about his incarcerated friends, whom we tried to help any way we could.

We decided to draft a memorandum addressed to the embassies and requested – in somewhat alarming terms – their mediation on behalf of the prisoners.

After some searching, I found our irreplaceably kind comrade, Garabed Bilezigjian (Dikran Yergat), and apprised him of our plan. He immediately drafted a memorandum in French. We made six copies, which received the Henchag stamp and were entrusted into the hands of a very young girl tasked with delivering them to the embassies.

The memorandum was composed in such elegant French, in such a moving and poignant tone that it aroused great interest among embassy staff, and several French and English newspapers published some excerpts from it.

Albert Rouet – the nephew of the chief interpreter in the French embassy – had excellent contacts and was one of our close allies. He indicated to me that the memorandum had led some embassy staffers to believe that various distinguished diplomats must surely be among the Henchag party ranks.

Despite these efforts, however, the prisoners were not released.

Albert Rouet – who recently passed away – never wavered in his profound support for the Armenian revolutionaries both then and much later.

We always appealed to him whenever we needed to smuggle someone out of Constantinople. And, somehow, he always found a way thanks to his contacts. On many occasions, he took matters into his own hands and smuggled the fugitives personally onto a steamship. Arshag Chobanian, Souren Bartevian (born Sisag Bardizbanian), Sarkis Svin, and many others were able to escape Constantinople thanks to him.

As though that weren't enough, he also hid many fugitives in his own home for extended periods of time. These included people like Diran Kelegian, Vahé Arzouyan, and, if I am not mistaken, also Sarkis Svin, among many others.

His support went above and beyond any other's. The Armenian revolutionaries had an irreplaceably steadfast friend in Albert Rouet.

Not once did he withhold his assistance, not even when we tried to secure Shahnazar's release from prison. Unfortunately, that proved to be impossible.

One French embassy staffer, Mister Quinet, had taken it upon himself to mediate with the Minister of the Police on Shahnazar's behalf. After several meetings, he concluded that his release was impossible and that the case would be taken to court. During those discussions, he also warned me, "You would do well to leave this place sooner rather than later. You have been blacklisted, and they will be coming to arrest you too any day now."

"But I'm not a revolutionary," I protested. This was absolutely indisputable. Because the fact is that I had never officially signed up as either a Henchag or a Tashnag.

"Your name was on a list of suspects submitted by the minister," persisted Mister Quinet. "I am hereby advising you to leave this place."

Of course, this was an extremely serious warning. And since I already intended to leave Constantinople, I began to make preparations urgently.

I knew that a Tashnag demonstration was going to take place in the coming days. And I was certain they would come for me this time – that is, if they even bothered to wait that long.

Everyone was talking about the Tashnag demonstration. We knew that they were planning to set off several bombs. But we had no idea how they intended to go through with it.

This was an era of extraordinary fervor and passion. After the Babiali demonstration, young Armenians felt less despair than a redoubled zeal to mobilize. They worked feverishly to prepare for another confrontation.

In Scutari, Psamatia, Balat, and other neighborhoods, Armenian girls were busy making bombs.

One day, Mrs. Kayané Madagian – the Senior Superintendent for Kindergartens in several neighborhoods – led me to Scutari to show me "these female bombmakers." They ranged from schoolteachers to little girls.

Those women and girls – both Henchag and Tashnag – had banded together in a now inconceivable demonstration of harmonious collaboration.

One of the earliest female Armenian revolutionaries – and, I believe, a student in Pera's workshop – was Miss Marie Beylerian (now Mrs. Beylerian, Director of the secondary school in Izmir). She currently enjoys great notoriety as a leading woman of letters and the founder of the first feminist Armenian journal in Egypt.

Miss Marie Beylerian, along with two of her girlfriends, had participated in the Babiali demonstration. Unfazed by the presence of officers and soldiers, she had stood up and read a revolutionary treatise for all to hear.

Like Vahé and his comrades, she somehow eluded the police after this bold display of defiance and went into hiding for several months.

It bears mentioning that Sarkis Svin was tasked with overseeing the Henchag women, which is why his comrades had sarcastically nicknamed him, "kizlar aghasi."[*]

After the Bank demonstration, Miss Beylerian somehow eluded capture and fled Constantinople. She settled in Egypt, where she remained for many years thereafter, working as a teacher in Alexandria's Boghosian and Cairo's Kalousdian schools.

Several weeks before the Constitution was restored, a Constantinople newspaper reported that the Criminal Court had sentenced Marie Beylerian to death *in absentia*.

She was finally receiving the punishment she deserved for her transgressions twelve years earlier.

Would you believe that some people still complain that Justice is not served swiftly enough in Turkey?

There was another female Henchag, who rendered extraordinary services, despite her young age. She was no more than ten or twelve years

---

[*] In Turkish meaning, "the girls' boss." (Tr.)

old, the daughter of a woman who hailed from Julfa and had relocated here from India. I mentioned her earlier as the young girl who delivered Dikran Yergat's memorandum to the embassies.

This well-known little Henchag inspired dread among our householders every time Vahé dispatched her to see me.

As soon as my mother or grandmother would catch sight of her, they would scurry and hide in terror at the back of the house; and if the maid happened to open the door, she would simply run away. No one had the courage to approach her or speak with her, such was the dread that this little revolutionary aroused.

I eventually told Vahé to stop dispatching this terrorist to our home.

Not all the women revolutionaries of Constantinople were as lucky as Marie Beylerian. And many of them accepted the Communion of prison, remaining steadfast and defiant to the very end.

It bears mentioning the Tashnag Minassian sisters, whom I met in Alexandria.

But, to keep a long story short, the point is that all of revolutionary Constantinople was hard at work in the summer of '96, and the demonstration was due to take place very shortly.

I had decided categorically to leave Constantinople as soon as there was an opportune moment. The one thing that could facilitate my departure – money – was in short supply. Back then, I knew nothing of traveling with empty pockets, something I eventually came to learn.

My cousin, Ardavan Hovveyan had just received ten liras from his employer. He worked for the Public Debt Administration. At some point, he had been incarcerated for his Henchag activities but was eventually released. To avoid being arrested again, he had moved into Shishli's French La Fe Hospital as a precaution.

He decided to give me eight of his ten liras, so that I could leave Constantinople. But there was a problem. He could only get the money by leaving the hospital and going into the administration's offices. This meant that Ardavan would have to violate his parents' agreement with the hospital's nuns, who had accepted him on the proviso that he would never leave the premises without their consent.

So, he first had to sneak out of the hospital, which was a much more complicated affair than one would expect.

On the appointed day, I visited him in his private room at the hospital. We took advantage of the nuns' momentary absence and hurried out, speeding across the rooftop, leaping down to the garden, and hiding in a barn, as we waited for the right moment to make our getaway.

But, unfortunately, the elderly gatekeeper and one of the nuns had placed a couple of chairs by the door and seemed to have no intention of leaving their seats.

These desperate times called for desperate measures. We climbed onto one of the cows, squeezed ourselves through a small window, and sprinted out of the hospital like a couple of escaped convicts.

CONSTANTINOPLE
and the 1896 Armenian Massacres

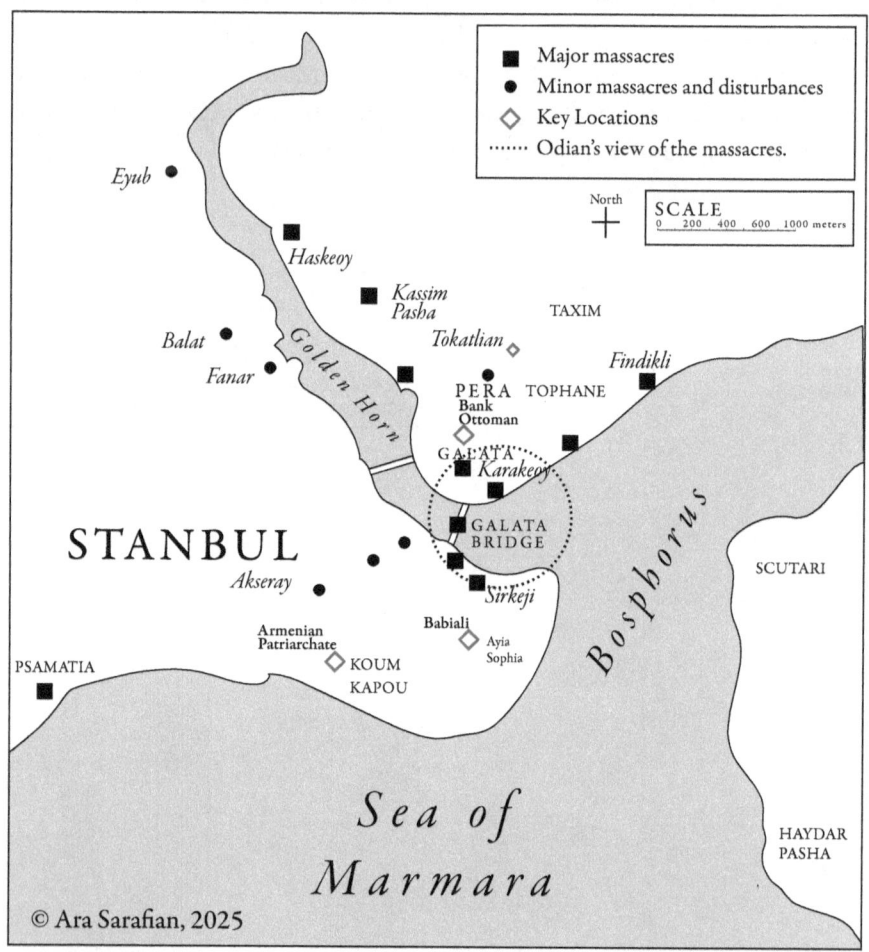

This map is based on "The Armenian Massacre in Istanbul (1896)" by Sinan Dinçer and *Twelve Years Away from Constantinople, 1896-1908* by Yervant Odian.

Chapter 2

The Bank demonstration. – The mob. – On board the *Sidon*. – The *sopaci*s try to storm the steamer. – Scenes of massacre. – The nightmarish night. – Robbing corpses. – Bloody Thursday. – The foreign interpreters' visit. – The sick passenger. – I move from the *Sidon* to the *Gironde*. – At Moda. – The Tashnags who stormed the Bank board the steamer. – Hrach and Armen Garo. – Interaction with the Tashnags is prohibited. – In Izmir. – Song and wine. – The *Gironde* reaches Piraeus. – My short-lived heroism.

The next morning, my relative retrieved his gift and gave me the eight liras.

The thirteenth of August, a Tuesday.

I decided to leave the very next day.

On Wednesday, I left home as usual, notifying everyone that I would not be returning that evening, because I was going to visit my uncle, Kevork Aslanian, in San Stefano. Word was spreading that this would be the day of the demonstration. So, before leaving home, I told my father to cancel his trip to the neighborhood around the Sublime Porte.

"Why, what's the matter?" he asked.

"I think they're going to stage a demonstration."

"Nonsense," he replied.

"Nonsense or not, it's best that you stay home today," I said.

I learned later that my father did follow my advice.

I left home and went to find Ardavan, who walked with me to Galata. We saw Dikran Yergat outside Komisyon *han*. I let him know about the demonstration and advised him to stay at home as well. And I told him that I would be leaving in the evening.

How or where the demonstration would take place, I did not know. However, I did know that they would be setting off bombs. After dining with Ardavan in a beachside tavern, we went for a walk along the piers.

How could I board a steamship? Would I even find a steamship? Back then, only the Messageries' steamers ever docked at the port. And by midday, there was none to be seen.

I went to the company's offices, where I learned that the steamer *Sidon* would be arriving from Samson that evening. The following day, it would be leaving for Marseille via Salonica and Shira.

As I was leaving their office, I ran into Mr. Sbantiarian, who worked as a teacher in Constantinople but was thought to be a revolutionary.

He approached me with a smile on his face.

"They're moving ahead with the demonstration today," he said.

"I know... but where?"

"In Psamatia... And in some other neighborhoods too, but it's going to start in Psamatia ... We have five-hundred bombs."

And he hurried away.

Several moments later, there was a terrifying blast, followed by another and another...

They sounded very close by and seemed to be coming from the direction of Galata.

The port went quiet. Everyone appeared stunned, their eyes darting around to make some sense of the situation.

This confusion persisted for approximately ten minutes. When the explosions stopped, we saw a sudden rush of people running madly through the street leading to the port.

Not a sound was heard, not a word was uttered as they began to climb into the boats. They ordered the boatmen to steer toward the open water. And a few minutes later, the sea was teeming with boats. My relative and I had no idea what was going on, so we decided to follow along and jumped into a Greek man's boat. There was an outpouring of questions on the open sea. No one had any inkling as to why they had fled and taken refuge on the boats.

But, little by little, everyone began to agree on one point.

"Something happened at the Bank..."

But, what?

Some said, "The Cretans are attacking the Bank."

Others corrected them, "Not the Cretans! The Macedonians."

Still others claimed, "No. They're government employees who haven't been paid for a while. They're protesting against the Bank."

Eventually, we learned what had really taken place.

"The Armenian revolutionaries are occupying the Bank."

Meanwhile, it was getting late. The *Sidon* had already arrived from the Black Sea and was close to port. Our elderly Greek boatman was complaining that he needed to return to shore, telling us that his family in Fener was expecting him soon. Many had already returned to the docks.

So, he turned the boat around.

Chapter 2

Looking East. Galata bridge over the Golden Horn. Galata Tower is on the horizon. Ottoman Bank is below the tower. Karakeoy is in the distance to the right of photograph.

Ardavan noticed a bearded man on another boat and said, "That man is a spy. He works for the police. I met him in prison. He must know something. Let's ask him."

And he yelled out, "Ahmed Effendi, Ahmed Effendi!..."

The bearded man turned to greet us.

"What is going on?" asked my relative.

"Nothing," the man calmly replied.

"Then what's all this commotion about...?"

"*Effendim, haraketi arz oldou gechti* (There was an earthquake, and now it's over)," he replied nonchalantly.

And then he advised us to head back.

When we finally returned to the docks, a group of people was plying an officer for more information.

"*Effendim*, some scoundrels tried to storm the Bank and were immediately apprehended..."

"How many?"

"Two or three."

"So, what was that explosion?"

"There was no explosion. Just a few gunshots..."

In an apparent objection to this supposed explanation, two more powerful blasts were heard.

The officer and the spy sped away in haste.

The crowds were dispersing, and I told Ardavan that it was probably best for him to take a cab back to Pera.

We bid each other farewell, and I meandered alone along the piers.

The passengers of the *Sidon* had disembarked. I went through the customs office and approached the steamship. But I realized that it was impossible to board, because there were two officers sitting at the foot of the ladder.

I returned to the pier hoping that the officers might step away for a moment, and I might get a chance to sneak onto the steamer.

It was getting dark, and the port was emptying out.

At one point, I realized that I would have been the only person there, were it not for a few boatmen and several Turkish porters working in the grubby cafes.

The officers did not step away from the *Sidon*.

So, I made my way towards the bridge where I planned to take a boat out onto the open water in hopes of boarding an anchored steamer.

I had scarcely walked a few paces, when I heard a commotion of terrifying screams and obscenities coming from the bridge.

The first thing I saw was an Armenian porter and a man in black – who, as I later learned, was an Armenian jeweler – sprinting frantically towards me.

An instant later, the two men were standing next to me. An angry mob of some forty or fifty people was about fifty steps away. They were racing towards them armed with truncheons and cursing violently.

Until that moment, the gravity of our situation had eluded me. I had assumed that all the shouting and crowds were nothing more than a bunch of brawling porters or boatmen. But it suddenly dawned on me that I was in mortal danger. So, I turned around and joined the Armenian porter and the old tradesmen, and we ran as fast as our legs would carry us.

We were speeding by a café, when an elderly Turk donning a bright white beard stood up, grabbed his square stool, and threw it at our feet.

The chair fell between the porter's legs, and the poor man toppled headfirst.

The mob had almost closed in on us. It reached the porter before he could get back up and run. And a barrage of clubs rained down on the poor

Messageries Maritimes *Sidon*. Odian sheltered on this ship in full view of the massacre of Armenians in 1896.

man's head. He did not make a peep. Terror had reduced him to stunned silence.

For the next several minutes, the murderous mob was preoccupied with its savage attack. So, I and the other old man had a chance to get away. And we hurled ourselves into the customs office, which was almost deserted at that time of night.

We had just stepped off the pier, when a group of *sopacis** reached the customs office in hot pursuit.

The *Sidon* was still moored at the port, and the two officers had not moved from their spot.

I ran frantically towards the steamer's ladder.

One of the officers got up and shouted, "*Yasaktir…!*"†

But I was in no mood to obey the authorities. I summoned all my strength to shove the officer aside and leapt up the steps, out of breath.

The old tradesman was behind me. Breathless and overcome by fatigue and anxiety, he fainted at the foot of the ladder.

I felt safe as soon as I was on the steamer.

A member of the crew asked me, "What do you want?"

"I want to see the Captain," I replied.

---

* Turkish meaning "men wielding clubs." (Tr.)
† Turkish meaning "That is prohibited." (Tr.)

"The Captain is up there," he said pointing to a man with a beard.

I went up and told him, "I am an Armenian editor. There's a mob trying to kill me, and I need to take refuge on your steamer."

"That's fine, that's fine," he replied. "You may stay here as long as you like."

"Thank you."

In the meantime, the steamship's crew noticed the Armenian man lying sprawled and unconscious at the foot of the steps. They immediately sent down a couple of crewmembers to retrieve him. They administered some treatments, and he came to.

After we took refuge on the *Sidon*, several French clergymen and a nun also boarded the steamer. They apprised us that a massacre was underway in Galata.

The port was completely deserted. And there was no one in sight on the bridge.

I had been on the steamship for at most half an hour, when a commissar and an officer – the same officer who had been guarding the steamer's ladder – boarded the *Sidon* and asked for the ship's interpreter so that they could parley with the Captain.

"Two men boarded this ship earlier. They do not have passports, and they are fugitives. You must turn them over to us."

"This is French territory," replied the Captain. "We cannot turn anyone over to you."

"But those men assaulted two officers when they boarded."

"That is none of our concern."

The commissar insisted. He seemed worried that the massacre would not be quite thorough enough without also apprehending these two Armenians.

The Captain lost his temper and yelled, "Get these people out of here!"

The interpreter explained to the commissar that there was no use in pressing the point, and that it was best for them to exercise restraint and leave immediately without resorting to any use of force.

Disgruntled by the outcome, the commissar and officer finally left.

The murderous mob showed up shortly thereafter. They lined up along the length of the steamer – probably at the commissar's urging – and demanded that they turn over the Armenians on board.

There were approximately eighty of them, howling and threatening to climb on board if their demands were not met.

At that point, the Captain ordered them to drape a French flag over the ladder. He posted two armed seamen at the top of the steps. And then he had his interpreter tell the mob below that if any of them dared to step onto the flag and climb on board, he would be shot on the spot.

This warning worked instantly. One by one, the *sopaci*s retreated through the customs office and disappeared.

No one approached the steamship after that. But, just as a precaution in case of an ambush, the Captain ordered his men to steer the ship one meter away from the docks.

An agent from the Messageries got on board and briefed us about the unspeakable atrocities unfolding outside.

The Captain introduced us and told him, "Here's an Armenian editor. That mob would have skinned him alive if he hadn't come up here."

"I see," replied the agent with the blonde beard. "I advise you not to go outside under any circumstances."

"I'm leaving Constantinople on this steamer," I said.

"We'll take you all the way to Marseille for free, if you are presently unable to pay," offered the agent.

"No. I have some money on me, and I would rather pay, if it's all the same," I told him. "I am not going all the way to Marseille. I am getting off at Piraeus."

"Even better, in that case."

So, I purchased a second-class ticket for Piraeus right then and there.

The old jeweler was in a terribly anxious state. The poor man was worried sick about his wife and children. And despite the ordeal he had just been through, he was seriously considering returning home to Pangalti. It was all we could do to convince him that he should wait at least until the following morning. We were hoping that everything would blow over by then.

It was now all quiet on the piers. Everything seemed to be back to normal, except for the occasional shooting in the distance.

We had all cocked our ears, listening for anything that could enlighten us about the events unfolding outside.

Four more people had arrived to take refuge on board – three women and a young man, all French. An old Russian had boarded the steamer with his daughter a little earlier. They were all equally distressed and confused. I went up to them and joined the conversation.

No one could provide an accurate report. They had all heard shooting and explosions. Then they had seen the shops closing for business. This was followed by a panicked rush of people, including them, running every which way. They were close to the port, so they had taken refuge on board.

Suddenly, I realize that all the passengers, including the French group, are dashing towards the beachside end of the bridge.

What was happening?

My heart was pounding. I stepped out of the kiosk.

A shocking scene.

Twenty men armed with pipes were beating four Armenian porters on the docks right in front of the *Sidon*.

They had already knocked the porters to the ground. We could not make out their screams. But we did hear a cacophony of collective howls accompanied by the dull thud of the mob's pipes. The beating stopped several minutes later. The murderers pounced on their dead victims and emptied out their pockets. Then, they swung their pipes over their shoulders and with a look of smug satisfaction, disappeared into a street off the port.

We saw a row of cavalrymen watching indifferently. They had been guarding the street leading to the scene of the crime.

The four savaged Armenian porters lay curled up on the ground.

We were trembling from the shock, and the women were weeping.

We saw two officers rushing towards the bodies. They kicked the porters in the head. One of them was still alive. He let out a muffled cry and lifted his free arm to protect his head.

But what ensued beggared belief.

One of the officers drew a knife from his waist and stabbed the man repeatedly in the abdomen. His blood gushed onto the docks.

The ship's crew shrieked, "Scoundrels! Brutes!" and stomped their feet in outrage.

One of them, the *Sidon*'s steward, drew a revolver from his pocket.

"That's enough! I cannot take any more of this!" he screeched.

The Captain realized what the steward was about to do, ran up to him, and held down his arms.

"What do you think you're doing? Have you lost your mind? Have you no idea what that would mean for you?"

He snatched the revolver from his hand and hid it away somewhere.

Moments later, we heard another round of commotion at the far end of the street facing us. An Armenian porter was racing like mad towards the docks with the same pipe-wielding murderers in chase.

We waved and gestured frantically for the man to climb aboard. The poor man saw and heard our exhortations, took heart, and ran even faster. Just as he reached the dock, he suddenly noticed his four compatriots' bodies…

He hesitated momentarily. We redoubled our appeals. But he could only reach the steamship by taking an extremely long detour around a partitioned stretch of the pier. Nevertheless, the man ran desperately, aware that the murderers were still far behind. The Captain posted two sailors at the top of the steps, ready and waiting to lift the man on board.

Mute and petrified, we watched what happened next.

They threw a wooden plank at the porter's feet. The man fell. The murderers closed in. They roared, cursed, and cheered at a deafening pitch. They almost had him when he got up and started to run. One of the cutthroats lobbed a heavy baton but just missed his back. Another baton followed, and this time the porter tumbled.

No words can encapsulate our anguish and fury.

The murderers had finally caught up with him and got straight to work.

It never ceases to astonish me that the man neither screamed nor cried. I can only assume that he was paralyzed with fear. The beat of thudding pipes filled our ears as the man died right before our eyes.

We were now forced to look upon the corpses of five men.

An officer had been watching the entire incident. He walked towards Tophane and returned some time later in a dray driven by a migrant laborer. They collected the bodies, placing them one by one upon the dray. Then they covered them with a dirty old sheet. The officer sat next to the drayman, and they drove towards the bridge.

We felt somewhat relieved when the bodies were removed.

The women stopped crying, and the steamer's crew stopped cursing.

It was now evening. Fortunately, we did not have to witness another round of carnage. We could, however, still hear shooting in Galata.

All the foreign-owned buildings were flying their respective British, French, Italian, and Greek flags. And we saw many men and women pacing anxiously across the rooftops of those buildings.

At that moment, the agent of the Messageries Maritimes – whom I had met earlier on board the *Sidon* – brought a memo from the French Embassy requesting that the steamship pull a few meters away from the docks and draw up its ladder. He also added that they had orders to open fire on anyone attempting to attack the ship and to turn away all Turkish passengers.

While he was on board, we took this opportunity to probe him about the unfolding situation.

"There's fighting everywhere," he said. "The Armenian revolutionaries are occupying the Ottoman Bank. They're using grenades to resist the surrounding forces. People are being killed in the streets. The embassies are overflowing with refugees. And everyone is terrified."

"Do the Embassies intend to do something?" we asked.

"Oh, they do have some decisive plans in place. The guard ships have received orders to take their positions at the port in Karakeoy. They are arriving in a few hours. But, at the moment, the Embassies are mainly concerned about getting the revolutionaries out of the Bank."

I forgot to mention that the Messageries' steamer, the *Gironde*, had arrived at almost exactly the same time as the *Sidon*. It was docking at the port, a little further up from us and closer to the bridge.

After the agent left, the *Gironde* and the *Sidon* pulled away from shore and drew up their ladders.

We had now severed our link with the outside world.

It was time to eat. And a bell sounded instructing us to proceed to dinner.

I intend to make my account perfectly candid. And so, I confess, that although I had just witnessed the most revolting scenes, I had a ferocious appetite. I think that the emotional turmoil of the previous six hours must have sharpened my wrenching hunger.

The conversation over dinner inevitably turned to the day's events. The old Russian and his daughter were the only other passengers at the dinner table. The rest were members of the *Sidon*'s crew. We all unanimously decried the violence. We also discussed the weakness of the European governments' response. They seemed perfectly willing to sacrifice their humanitarian responsibilities to pursue their own gains.

"Diplomacy is revolting," said one of the guests, as he emptied his glass.

Another diner said, "It shames me to be called a European."

"Is this what the French Revolution was for?" added the steamship's doctor.

"I am sure that the Embassies will soon put an end to this situation."

The waiter burst in on these naive remarks, and cried, "They're killing more people at the port."

We stood up midway through our meals and rushed up the stairs.

It was the same vicious pipe-wielding mob. They had fallen upon three Armenian porters. A relentless barrage of truncheons rained down from all sides.

And then we saw the murderers bend down over the bodies and start to pick their pockets.

This time, they were also joined by three officers.

The killers then foisted their bloody pipes onto their shoulders and left, while the three officers went to a nearby café and ordered a round of coffee and nargileh.

We returned to our meals.

After coffee, we found ourselves back on the bridge. It was now covered in total darkness but for the freshly lit gas lamps. The three bodies remained where they were, and the officers drew on their nargilehs.

Three drays arrived from the direction of Tophane. When the first dray approached the bodies, one of the officers signaled for it to stop, pointed at the three Armenian porters, and shouted, "Pick those up and toss them in."

"I don't have any room," yelled the drayman. "Why don't the others take them?"

The second approaching drayman heard this exchange and shouted, "I already have eight in my dray. There's no more room. The horse is exhausted. And I've already made this trip three times."

Seeing that it was useless to argue with the drayman, the officers bent down and threw two bodies into the first dray.

The drayman protested and jumped down, grabbed one of the bodies by the feet, and pulled it to the ground.

"Leave them here. I'll pick them up on my next round."

"No," barked the officer. "You have to remove them right now."

The third drayman tried to settle things amicably and yelled, "Why don't you give one to me? I can take it."

An officer then grabbed one of the bodies by the feet and dragged it all the way to the third dray.

Now, the other draymen felt obliged to take a body each, and the drays trundled off toward the bridge.

This was just one of the inconceivably evil acts they devised under cover of darkness. What shocked us most about this process was their conspicuous apathy.

All through the night, a succession of drays arrived, each one stacked with a pile of corpses. By midnight, I had counted thirteen. They were all coming from the direction of Tophane and then proceeding towards the bridge.

After midnight, I climbed into my cabin and tried to get some sleep. But my stricken imagination made it impossible to shut my eyes. All I could see were nightmarish visions of that day's horrific scenes. And I could still hear shooting on the shore. I got dressed and returned to the bridge.

It was a clear star-studded night. Steamers dotted the sea with their brightly twinkling red, yellow, and green lights. Steamboats hurried every which way. The sea was unusually effervescent. And the drays continued to roll onto the docks carrying their grim cargo. I did not wish to count how many.

I sank into a deckchair, turned my face towards the sea, and sat there smoking for hours. Out in the distance, near the Saray Burnu, I noticed some men on a barge lit by two small lamps. Every now and then, they would throw something into the water. I could sense that something evil was afoot on that barge. And I sharpened my attention. Little by little, I could see more clearly. Seven or eight people kept moving back and forth across the barge, occasionally throwing a large bundle overboard. I could hear the splash as they hit the water.

These were the bodies of murdered Armenians…

This process took more than two hours to complete. It took time to discard each body properly. They seemed to be attaching rocks or pieces of metal to weigh them down.

Before this barge had finished offloading its cargo, another one, also illuminated by two lamps, arrived.

Horrified, I retreated below deck and shut myself inside my cabin.

At dawn, after a sleepless night, I climbed up to the bridge of the *Sidon*. Just about everyone from the night before was also there.

Facing the *Sidon*, on one of the side-streets leading to the port, around forty people were immersed in conversation, their eyes darting at the windows of two old stone-built *hans*. The wooden shutters were closed. One of those *hans* was only accessible through the second floor, which connected to the street by a wooden staircase. Several men climbed up and tried knocking the door down. But it seemed to be too thick and firmly secured from the inside. So, they gave up and climbed back down.

A few moments later, they brought a portable wooden ladder. They leant it against the wall, and two men climbed up to one of the windows, which as I just mentioned, had been shuttered. A metal object was used to dislodge the shutters, which came off easily. One man climbed back down, while the other poked his head carefully through the window and remained in that position. Eventually, he withdrew his head, looked down at the mob below, and yelled, "Nothing to worry about here. You can come on up."

And he climbed in through the window.

Several of those Turkish men felt emboldened by this invitation, wielded their pipes, and climbed up.

The intruders opened the door to the *han*.

The *Sidon*'s crew brought several binoculars to get a clearer view, although we could already see everything perfectly well.

A moment later, three men appeared at the window and threw a half-dead Armenian porter down to the pavement. Their comrades cheered and fell upon their prey, finishing the job quickly and easily.

"Move aside," barked one of the men from the window. And the body of another Armenian fell to the ground.

We passengers were not beset, as we had been earlier, by the same heart-pounding anguish and fury.

We had grown numb to these scenes.

A crewmember, the manager, who could sketch well, took out his notebook and composed an outline of the events unfolding before our eyes.

And then, one by one, four more people were thrown out of the window and killed under a barrage of pipes.

I must not forget to add that there were three officers on the scene, but they only took part as spectators. None of them participated in the killings.

The men standing outside eventually got angry with their comrades inside. And they had a right to be.

The pockets of the discarded Armenians were void of any valuables.

Their comrades inside had already cleaned those bodies out before dropping them out of the window.

Furious, the men in the street began to climb up the steps, as the others tried to shut the door in their faces. But they did not have enough time, and a vicious fight broke out between them in the doorway.

The commotion grew out of control, and one of the officers summoned several soldiers from the Tophane garrison to put an end to the fighting and disperse the mob.

Then the officers entered the *han*. A few moments later, they brought out a migrant woman holding a small child. The woman was crying and screaming uncontrollably as the officers tried to escort her out. Eventually, they had to pull on her arms for her to come down. The woman surveyed the bodies lying on the ground. As she stood next to each one, her sobs turned into heart-wrenching screams.

One of the men must have been her husband.

The officers tried to lead her to the port.

But the woman placed her son on her husband's body and ran away. An officer took the boy, caught up with the woman, and returned him to her embrace. But the mother turned around, threw her son onto the body, and this time, began to run even faster. The officer was forced to pick up the boy and give chase to the woman, who was already a long way off. The boy wrapped his little arms around the officer's head and knocked his fez off. The officer bent down, picked up his fez, and began to run, holding the boy with one hand and his fez with the other. Meanwhile, the woman sprinted away as she wailed, her sobs broken only by her intermittent pleas. "Mother! Christ!..."

The pathos and anguish of those moments were too awful to bear.

Our hearts sank as we watched this tragic scene from the *Sidon*.

We had already spent many hours watching the most horrifying events unfold before our eyes. And we had almost grown accustomed to those images. But the heartbreaking sobs of that migrant woman reverberated loudly in our ears.

Chapter 2

The sun was now up, and the shooting had resumed.

The *Sidon* was scheduled to depart later that day, which meant that first, it had to secure enough provisions. The manager and Captain went ashore with a couple of crewmembers brandishing their revolvers. Our eyes wandered over the world beyond the steamer's bridge. And we waited anxiously for them to return and bring us some news.

To the uninformed eye, the city may have appeared positively festive. Foreign flags were flying on the rooftops. The sea was dotted with countless boats and steamers speeding through the water. The ships guarding the Embassies had arrived towards morning and taken their positions along the length of Tophane. Men and women were watching from the rooftops. Cavalrymen were patrolling the shore.

Were it not for the corpses lying before us, we may have thought a royal visit was underway at the Sultan's court. Everything was so reminiscent of that Thursday, October 15, when the German kaiser arrived in Constantinople.

The manager returned to the steamer with a Greek butcher in tow. He brought us some horrific news.

Every last one of the Armenian porters working at the customs office in Constantinople – three hundred souls in total – were slaughtered overnight.

All the Armenian homes in Haskeoy were raided, and all the men put to the sword.

All the Armenian shops and warehouses were looted, and the shopkeepers killed.

"They even made off with the doors and windows," chortled the manager.

"Have things at least settled down now?" we asked.

"Settled down?" he replied. "I saw them kill more than ten people on my way over here."

A commotion broke out on the docks and interrupted our conversation. Some officers and a group of Turkish men had arrived at the scene of the four Armenian porters' murders. They quickly removed their bodies and hid them away in one of the side-streets. Then they brought a barrow full of fine sand – the kind they scattered when Abdulhamid came to Constantinople – and covered the bloodstained ground.

Once they were done, four of them – who had been among the murderous pickpockets – moved to the head of the group, walked up the *han*'s steps, threw the window shutters open, sat down, and had a rest.

At first, we could not make heads or tails of this strange performance. But what happened next shed some light on the situation. A couple of dragomans employed by the embassies arrived from the direction of Tophane carrying briefcases. They seemed to be conducting an investigation and were accompanied by a smartly dressed Turk, who appeared to be a senior police official. The interpreters stopped briefly on the corner of the street and observed the fake Armenians smoking their cigarettes out of their windows. And then they moved on.

After breakfast, the shooting intensified. We could hear gunshots in every direction.

The port was full of cavalry and infantrymen who had taken positions all along the shore and were aiming their rifles at the buildings across the way.

We used binoculars to survey the scene around our steamer.

A group of soldiers were firing relentlessly on a house near the Karakeoy bridge. Then they forced their way in through the door and threw six people out of the windows.

We have no idea whether they were dead or alive.

Despite the great distance between us, we could nonetheless hear the stifled cries of desperate men pleading for their lives just before they were killed.

It was unimaginable.

Evening fell slowly, and the moment of our scheduled departure approached. An Armenian man by the name of Kevork Effendi Torkomian was the first passenger to board the steamer. He worked for the Public Debt Administration and was leaving for Salonica. He had walked down along the Bosphorus and was entirely ignorant of the present situation.

Then we noticed a cortege of women and servants, who were carrying a visibly ill young Turkish man up to the steamer. This entourage consisted of fifteen people, half of whom were first-class ticketholders. He was a notable agha from Salonica, who had come to Constantinople for treatment and was now returning to his city. Consumption had left its cruel mark on his thin, sallow, cadaverous face.

They carried an armchair on board and placed it on the steamer's deck. They rested him in the armchair and, notwithstanding the sun's heat, they covered his knees with a blanket. A lovely young woman stood beside the ailing man and wiped his forehead with a handkerchief every now and then.

The steamship's doctor approached the patient and demanded, "Which one of you is this man's attendant?"

"Is there a problem, sir?" asked a Jewish man, the interpreter for the Turkish agha's entourage.

"This man will surely die during our passage. He cannot be allowed to board the steamer," shouted the doctor.

"What do you mean?" replied the incensed Jew. "Your own agency sold us these tickets. Your superintendent in Salonica is our Effendi's friend and provided him with a special dispensation to receive especially good care on board."

"I do not accept it," yelled the doctor. "This man is dying and must be removed immediately."

The Jew appealed to the Captain who had been observing this exchange.

"I will not get involved. The doctor has made his decision," replied the Captain, echoing the same harsh tone. "If he believes that this man must be removed, then he must be removed. Understand?"

Their severity was quite obviously provoked by a hostility that had only recently taken root. Two days earlier, that patient would have received a compassionate welcome. But, at this point, we all wanted that wretched man to be taken away.

The Jew translated the shipmates' replies, making sure to soften their words.

But the doctor was unsatisfied. He called over the *Sidon*'s interpreter and had him tell the patient directly that since he would probably die on this trip, he was not allowed to board.

The consumptive man's pale cheeks suddenly blushed. Irate but impotent, he attempted unsuccessfully to get to his feet and cried, "Come on! Let's get out of here! I cannot abide another instant in this place!"

I reflect now on my spiteful schadenfreude during this exchange.

They carried the man, armchair and all, back down. And the women in the retinue – including his wife and mother – began to weep.

They set the armchair down on the pier and consoled the patient. He was so agitated that he was struggling to breathe through his dry hacking cough.

At that moment, the crew noticed that the customs employees had snuck on board and alerted the Captain, who ordered them to be dragged away by their arms and thrown off board.

"Not one Turk will step foot here," he shouted furiously.

Several moments later, a group of Muslim Albanian passengers boarded the steamer. They were headed for Salonica.

There was an argument as to whether they could remain.

"No, send them away!" decided the Captain.

After gently protesting his decision, the Albanians had no choice but to disembark.

The moment of our departure was fast approaching. We were all relieved that we would soon be leaving this city behind. Smoke rose from the steamer's chimney, and the *Sidon* blew its first whistle.

All of a sudden, the Messageries Maritimes' corporate agent jumped aboard with an order from the French Embassy in hand. It commanded the *Sidon* to postpone its departure while the massacres were underway, because its services might be required at a later time for the evacuation of all French citizens. The agent announced that the *Gironde* had been ordered to leave, and that only the *Sidon* would be remaining in Constantinople, until the crisis had abated.

Many European families had taken refuge on board the *Gironde* the previous day and would presently be transported to the *Sidon* by steamboat.

The agent left after communicating these developments.

As announced, the Messageries' steamboat did transport several French families to our steamer and then returned to make a second round.

I was so revolted by all that I had witnessed over the past few days that, although I felt secure on the steamer, I still wanted to leave this city far behind me as quickly as possible. So, when I realized that the *Sidon* would be remaining in Constantinople for several more days, I appealed to the Captain and requested that they transfer me to the *Gironde* by steamboat. The Captain accepted my request, but the sea was teeming with surveillance police watching for any stowaways trying to escape on a foreign steamer.

When the steamboat returned, they carefully smuggled me in and hid me among the stokers, where I crouched behind a pile of coal.

That is how I snuck onto the *Gironde*.

As soon as I stepped onto the steamer, they started releasing the ropes. At that moment, the docks resembled a battlefield. Soldiers had opened fire on the buildings across the way. Their relentless assault had shattered all the windows. Soldiers had also taken up positions on numerous rooftops. No one remained on the bridge. And both of its entrances were being guarded by cavalrymen.

Sultan Abdulhamid II. The so-called "Red Sultan."

I felt inexpressible delight at the sight of the *Gironde*'s moving windlass. We were finally leaving….

We moved slowly away from the docks, and the steamer turned its prow towards the Marmara.

But then the *Gironde* changed direction and began moving towards the peninsula of Moda in Kadikeuy. At first, we thought that the currents were pushing the ship in that direction. All the passengers rushed anxiously to the bridge. We asked one of the crewmembers for an explanation. He replied, "There is nothing to worry about. We just have to make a quick stop here and pick up a few more passengers."

The *Gironde* did indeed pause in the peninsula of Moda across from Kalamish.

These developments darkened our already gloomy imaginings. All the passengers and most of the crewmen were assembled at the gunwale, surveying their surroundings attentively.

A steamboat flying the French flag approached us. We recognized it a moment later by its distinctive white color. It was the French Embassy's steamboat.

It finally reached the *Gironde*.

Armenian revolutionaries extracted from Ottoman Bank and transported to Marseille. Odian had the occasion to converse with them during his journey to Piraeus (Greece).

Only two people were visible in its cabin. And we were surprised by the sight of several revolvers on the seats.

When the steamboat latched onto the *Gironde*'s landing, seventeen men slowly emerged from a hideout. Several were dressed as porters; some were in rags; and a couple of them looked distinguished in their black suits and hats.

They were followed by the chief interpreters of the French and Russian embassies, Mr. Rouet and Mr. Maximov.

A French passenger who had been watching from the upper deck next to me could not suppress his excitement and exclaimed, "Ah, now that is a beautiful sight! Armenian revolutionaries hiding beneath our flag! I do have a homeland, after all! My country has not let us down! Ah, what a beautiful sight! I am a truly happy man!"

That poor man was mistaken.

They were not boarding refugees, but rather some of the Tashnags who had stormed the Ottoman Bank.

The Armenians were instantly surrounded by a large circle of passengers.

Fifteen men were huddling together. The two leaders – Hrachya and Armen Garo – were standing a few paces away.

Chapter 2

Hrach or Hrachya was wearing a black redingote and a straw hat. A small bag hung from his shoulder, and he had the mild, contented bearing of a typical tourist. He was a slim, attractive young man, with a hooked nose and sparkling eyes.

The Hrach of sixteen years ago would be unrecognizable to anyone who knows him as today's portly, ruddy-cheeked, energetic Mr. Hrach working in *Azadamard*'s newsroom. He had gained so much weight by 1908, that I could not recognize him when we met again in Alexandria, after he had served time in Bodrum prison.

Garo was dressed in grey. He was a young man of average height, chubby, healthy, and robust. Topped by his leonine head, his bearing expressed a sense of power and stability that inspired both awe and affection.

I always thought that Armen Garo would remain an incorrigible revolutionary. But I have noticed many changes in him recently. With his designs for the railway system and his candidacy for parliament, the former deputy from Garin, Karekin Pastrmajian, currently bears no resemblance whatsoever to the hero of the Bank incident, Armen Garo. And perhaps he prefers it that way.

I must confess, however, that I had greater affection for the man I knew sixteen years ago. He had not drawn up his plans for the railway system yet, but in those earlier days, I suspect that his thoughts were preoccupied by aerial machines that could soar like eagles.

The other Tashnags in the group had a downtrodden, browbeaten look about them, as though they were overwhelmed by their own audacious acts. The previous day's events had left lingering effects, and they were still not quite themselves.

As soon as Mr. Maximov and Mr. Rouet boarded the steamer, they asked to see the Captain.

The two interpreters and the Captain had a brief, hushed conversation. And then Mr. Maximov raised his voice to address the Captain. "We confiscated their guns, but you should definitely search their pockets in case they're hiding something. Do be careful. These are bandits, after all (*Ce sont des brigands*)."

Hrachya and Armen Garo reacted badly to his last comment. They marched up to him and furiously objected to this insult.

Meanwhile, the Captain had already given orders to carry out Maximov's instructions, and the crew began searching the revolutionaries' pockets. They kept their cool and let them do as they were bid. Some of them even joked, "See, not so much as a razor blade in our pockets. And they've already taken our guns."

However, it is true that when Armen Garo gave the order – "Do not let them search you" –, they were fully prepared to resist. But it was all over by that point.

Hrachya and Garo were so incensed by this insulting treatment that they demanded to disembark. They told the dragomans that they would much rather risk ending up in Turkish custody than staying on board.

Garo was shouting, "You were on your knees just yesterday, pleading with us. And now you're confiscating our guns and insulting us!"

Maximov ignored these comments, although he was clearly agitated.

Mr. Rouet, the French Embassy's interpreter, finally settled the dispute. The crewmen did not search the two leaders' pockets.

The interpreters left, and the *Gironde* went on its way.

After lunch, I went up to see the heroes of the day. Hrachya and Garo were nowhere to be found. They were given a third-class cabin, and the steamer provided their meals. The others remained on the upper deck. The Captain had given instructions to move them to the steamer's prow, away from prying eyes. They were even barred from entering our quarters.

They were having dinner when I went to see them. They were laughing and looked happy now as they tucked into their meals.

One of them recognized me and called me over to join them.

We had scarcely spoken, when a crewmember asked me to leave.

The dragomans must have decided to keep them under special guard until we were out of Turkish waters.

I retired to my cabin and was about to go to sleep, when the steamer made another unexpected stop.

This time, the engine had broken down. The repairs took four hours, delaying our arrival in Chanakkale to noon the following day.

The steamer was surrounded by hundreds of boats full of curious spectators. They had already gotten wind of the incidents in Constantinople. And they wanted to climb aboard to get the full story. But the Captain strictly forbade anyone from stepping foot on the ship.

There were fears that Turkish vigilantes might take matters into their own hands and attack the Armenian revolutionaries.

This prohibition was also enforced in Izmir, where we arrived the next morning. The only people allowed on board were the American and British Consuls. And they were eager to meet the Armenian revolutionaries and speak with Armen Garo.

Once we left Izmir, they lifted all the restrictions. The revolutionaries could now move around the steamer freely, and we were all allowed to interact with them.

Armen Garo (Karekin Bastirmajian), revolutionary and future statesman.

Armen Garo and I spoke for several hours. His honest, lively disposition had an enchanting effect on me. It might be worth mentioning one of his anecdotes here.

When Garo decides to join the revolutionary movement, he writes to Nazarpeg and tells him that he is prepared to sacrifice his life and his possessions in the struggle for liberation. And he asks Nazarpeg how he may be of assistance.

"We don't need any people. Send us your money," replies Maro's husband.

On that, Garo decides to approach the Tashnags instead. And they embrace him with open arms.

Meeting with Hrachya proved to be almost impossible. He was somewhat taciturn and kept withdrawing into his cabin, where he was always busy writing something. I think he might have been drafting a report of the Bank incident for *Droschak*.

It was evening when I finally had a chance to meet the other Tashnags unimpeded.

We gathered at the ship's prow. It was a beautiful, starry night. And the *Gironde* was passing through Chios and Psara.

The fatherland of Kanaris...

The hills of Psara glowed with flickering red lights.

The Tashnags were in high spirits, drinking wine and belting out their merry songs.

As I gazed upon the lights of Chios, my memory was struck by all that I had witnessed four days earlier.

In April 1822, Kaptan Pasha arrived in Chios with forty-five ships and 7,000 men. He subjected the city to a long night of relentless bombardment. And he ordered the massacre of its entire population. The unarmed people of Chios were no different from us as they were slaughtered like sheep. The massacre continued for three days straight. Twenty-three thousand people perished, and 40,000 more were abducted and sold as slaves in Egypt.

And yet, although Chios was massacred, the island of Psara – its little sister – resisted and Kanaris – a hero of the Greek revolution and a native of Psara – inflicted disproportionate losses on the Turkish navy.

Meanwhile, the Tashnags were singing:

"The evil, vicious oppressor of Armenians

Hid in fear beneath his golden throne.

The halls of deaf Europe boomed.

The Armenians shuddered; the Henchags blushed."

Back then, the Tashnags used to sing Henchag songs. It was mutual. Those were the good old days.

But I could not suppress the inexplicable feeling that this song was somehow inappropriate under the circumstances, too boastful to be sung in these waters. And I retreated to my cabin.

The next morning, a Monday, the *Gironde* entered Greek waters.

It was a bright, cheerful morning. A brisk wind was blowing across the sea. We were approaching Attica, near the promontory of Sounion, where we could see the temple of Athena. And before us were the Aegean, Salamis; and on land, way off in the distance, glowing in the sunlight, the Parthenon.

The steamer made a dignified entrance into the port of Piraeus.

News of the occupied Bank had already reached Athens. And, as was their wont, the Greek newspapers had reported everything at length and with great hyperbole.

Chapter 2

Piraeus, Greece.

They knew that the people who had stormed the Bank were on board the *Gironde*.

The entire Armenian population of Athens and Piraeus – some of whom were revolutionary fugitives – surrounded the *Gironde* with their boats. But they were not given permission to board the ship.

I was standing by the Tashnags, who were standing along the bridge.

The spectators watching from the boats recognized Armen Garo instantly. He had visited Athens for several weeks shortly before the demonstration. We heard an eruption of cheers and applause below us.

Suddenly, a couple of people also recognized me. And before I knew it, word had spread that Odian was one of the heroes who had stormed the Bank.

Once all the official procedures had been carried out, they lowered the yellow quarantine flag and dropped the ladders. The Armenians rushed up to the steamer, threw themselves at us, and smothered us with their embraces.

I tried in vain to explain that I was not one of the heroes who stormed the Bank and that I do not deserve these displays of affection.

But my protestations fell on deaf ears. I was exasperated. And for the next half hour, I had to resign myself to my fate and pretend to be one of the heroes who had stormed the Bank.

The Tashnags were going all the way to Marseille. Some arrangements had supposedly been made – of which I know nothing – to send them from there to South America.

Since the steamer was going to dock in the port of Piraeus for several more hours, the Armenians surrounded the heroes of the day and besieged them with interminable questions.

An Italian passenger and I left the ship together. He knew Athens well and was kind enough to direct me.

That man had been a correspondent for an Italian newspaper. He had visited Athens for a period of several months before taking the *Gironde* to Constantinople. He had arrived on the very day of the Bank demonstration. And without setting foot in Constantinople, he was forced to return to Greece.

We boarded a ship for Athens together. It was only half an hour from Piraeus.

He helped me rent a room in a hotel on Omonia Square. And then he insisted that I go along with him to visit the Greek newspaper offices. We visited the newsrooms of *Estia, Acropolis, SKRIP*, and *Keri*. They all welcomed me warmly and then probed me for everything I knew or had witnessed. Naturally, I had a great deal to tell. And the next day, all four newspapers were full of my stories.

When I returned to my hotel, I was met by an acquaintance – I think the only person I knew in Greece at the time – who had been waiting for me.

He was a Henchag activist, a painter by profession called Antreassian Mgrian who was better known as Parebashd.

Parebashd had been involved in the Babiali demonstration and was a wanted man. He had fled to Athens, where he had been living for the past several months.

We had a long conversation, and then I retired to my room.

Chapter 3

In Athens. – Prime Minister Deligiannis. – The Athenians and the refugees. – The people of Divrig and Moush. – The prayer. – The Philanthropic Committee. – Threats and accusations. – Sensible people. – Krikor Meohtemetian.

Over the next several days, I inevitably met all the Armenians there.

The first piece of advice they gave me was this: "You have to change your name."

"Why?"

"That's the local custom," they replied smiling enigmatically.

I eventually learned that they had adopted this tactic to elude the spies.

A wealthy merchant from Yerznga by the name of Der Sdepanian – who had been condemned to death for allegedly making financial donations to the revolutionaries and who had fled to Athens, where they called him Garabed Garabedian – christened me as Vahram Vahramian. And during all the months I spent in Greece, I was known by that name. Many even believed that was my real name.

The first person I got to know in Athens was Zareh Kochian, who was also condemned to death *in absentia*. They called him Ardzrouni, and we became fast friends.

There was also Reverend Nshan Keshishian, an incredible young man from Kalousd Abkhanian's group of guerrilla fighters. There was also Simon Manigian, a notable figure from Armudan and a Henchag representative, who resided in Piraeus and was christened "Ambassador of the Armenian People." Parebashd, meanwhile, was designated as the Consul of Athenian-Armenians.

A week after I arrived in Athens, the refugees began to flood in. Each steamer from Constantinople brought hundreds of refugees to the shores of Piraeus. Those who had the means left for Egypt, and those who were too poor, were forced to stay.

One month later, the number of those hungry, deprived men had reached one thousand.

A solution was urgently needed to provide them with food and shelter.

We formed a committee without delay and appointed Serovpe Giurjian as President. He was an erudite man, a graduate from an American university, who had come to Athens through a twist of fate. He had lived there for many years, despite barely scraping by.

I was chosen to be Chairman of the Committee, and our members included Garabed Garabedian, Parebashd, Zareh Kochian, Simon Manigian, Reverend Keshishian, Maksoud Khanjian, Krikor Kalfayan, and Mr. Reteos. Mr. Reteos wore many hats for the monthly *Miyoutiun*. He was owner, director, typesetter, editor, distributor, and manager at the same time. Our members also included several local Armenians.

Our first initiative was to find a way to shelter the almost 1,000 homeless refugees of both sexes.

The Committee decided that it was best to appeal to Prime Minister Deligiannis and assigned that task to me.

An Armenian deacon – a filthy, ignorant, uncouth drunkard – lived in Athens at that time. I do not recall his name or place of origin.

To give a more formal air to our visit, I took that reverend with me to meet the elderly Prime Minister at the Office of Foreign Affairs.

I did not entertain much hope that Mr. Deligiannis would welcome our visit. And in case of just such an eventuality, I had also put my appeal in writing.

We asked around and found the Prime Minister's office. A guard was posted at his door.

"We would like to meet with the Prime Minister," I said sheepishly.

"You may enter," replied the guard and opened the door.

Before we knew it, we were face to face with Mr. Deligiannis. He was poring over some documents on his desk.

Keeping my words brief, I introduced myself and the deacon. But before I had a chance to finish my sentence, the elderly Prime Minister had risen to his feet and, in a show of utmost respect and humility, he was kissing the deacon's hand.

I explained the reason for our visit.

He listened attentively and asked us to elaborate on the number of refugees and their current situation. Then, he said, "I am very glad that you came to me for help. And I want to do all I can for those poor souls immediately…"

He summoned an aide and instructed him to have fifty military tents pitched in the field of Phaleron – located between Piraeus and Athens – posthaste.

Athens, Odian's first point of refuge on his 12 year exile.

"The tents are completely new and unused," he said, "so I submit them to your care. Do your best to use them well."

We expressed our deepest gratitude and parted from the elderly diplomat.

Mr. Deligiannis treated the Armenians with the same extraordinary humanity and generosity on several other occasions.

A few years ago, when this noble elder was brought down by the blade of a pathetic fool, I published a couple of articles about that Prime Minister's benevolence towards the Armenians in Alexandria's *Azad Pem*. Those pieces were reprinted in several Greek newspapers. And Minas Cheraz printed some excerpts in his paper, *L'Arménie*. Our debt of gratitude to him was thus partly repaid.

To be entirely honest, I must admit that Deligiannis was not an exception. The entire Greek government and population showed tremendous hospitality towards the Armenians.

Every time an Armenian and a Greek got into a fight, the policeman on the scene would arrest the Greek man and let the Armenian go, even if the Armenian was at fault.

"They are our guests. And we cannot blame them for their actions," was the policeman's response. Of course, he was complying with orders from the highest authorities.

But this tolerance did not last very long, because there were some Armenians who resorted to theft and murder.

The fifty enormous tents sheltered every one of those homeless refugees.

The Committee eventually created a process to identify the neediest men and to help them find work.

This was an extremely arduous process. They all claimed to be starving and tried to get on that list. But, as we later learned, many of those people had been hiding hundreds of liras under their girdles.

Once we had completed that process, we still faced the problem of finding enough money to feed hundreds of people.

Our first task was to organize a fundraiser. It produced remarkably good results, thanks to the collaboration of the Greek newspapers and their heartfelt appeals to the people.

We staged a Greek production in the Variété Theatre. And the Greek Sarah Bernhardt, Mrs. Paraskevopoulo, and her troupe gave a free performance of *Frou-Frou*.

But our scarce resources soon dried up.

We gave the refugees a daily food allowance of 60 lepta or approximately 3 kurush per person. But after taking stock, we realized that there were still 500 people on our list of the desperately needy.

New refugees were arriving on a regular basis, with groups of thirty to forty people at a time. And they all needed food and shelter.

I can recall one group from Divrig. There were about fifty of them. They had come to Piraeus in October, several months after the Bank demonstration.

Those men from Divrig were shoveling coal on an British steamer docked at the port, when the pogrom had broken out. They were forced to stay on board and to leave all their money and belongings behind in a *han*.

The Captain had agreed to hide them, provided that they work for him. They had left Constantinople for Batum, the steamer's destination, but the Russian government had not let them disembark. The steamer had picked up its cargo and returned to Constantinople. Then it had gone back to the Black Sea, this time to pick up a shipment of flour in Odessa. It had left Odessa for Piraeus, where they were finally able to jump ship after a passage of six weeks. They had been made to work continuously for forty days, hauling heavy cargo without any pay, but for some dry bread as their remuneration.

Chapter 3

"I saved your lives. How dare you ask me for pay?" was the Captain's reply, when they had worked up the courage to demand wages.

During those forty days, they were never allowed to bathe. Flour had hardened like cement on their coaldust-blackened bodies. And they looked like they had come back from the dead as menacing phantoms.

Water, water to bathe in. That was still in desperately short supply for the people sheltering in the open expanse of Phaleron's meadow. There were no springs nearby. People had to carry jugs of potable water all the way from Phaleron. And there was no way the men from Divrig could walk all the way there. The police had forbidden them from leaving the campgrounds, because they were practically naked and would therefore cause a scandal... All they had on was what they were wearing on the ship in Constantinople, namely a pair of short underwear that went down to their knees and a coal sack on their bare upper bodies. They had cut out holes in the sacks for their heads and arms. Those poor men looked like turtles standing awkwardly upright on their hind legs.

And, just beyond their reach stretched the sea, clear and blue, as far as their eyes could see. They watched while everyone else went to wash in the bathhouses.

Every day, these miserable men pined, "Oh, will we ever get to run into the sea!"

No, they had no right to be clean. They were too dirty.

And this was a great source of suffering for them, a total disaster, the ultimate Golgotha. Their misfortunes had subdued them into complacency. They had resigned themselves to all their tribulations – the loss of their money and possessions, the six weeks at sea, tent life in Greece, dry bread for food... But being confined to this state of filth, covered in coal and flour, and unable to bathe even once in all those many long months – this they could not endure.

"We did not expect this," they lamented, shaking their heads hopelessly. And that gesture made them appear ghastlier.

In addition to the group from Divrig, I must also mention another one from Moush. It included twenty to twenty-five men, who had been thrown in jail several months before the Bank demonstration. They were confined until the end of August, but one day, they were brought out and questioned. "Where are you from?"

"Moush."

"Fine. You will now leave and return directly to your homes."

A police cortege had herded them like sheep onto an Austrian steamer. Once they were on board, the group had realized that the policemen had mistakenly put them on a ship leaving for Trieste instead of Trabzon.

The police had taken care of their travel expenses for their trip to Trabzon. But now the Captain was demanding their tickets for this journey. The men from Moush did not have a single kurush in their pockets. So, as per the steamship's regulations, the Captain threatened to tie them to the flagstaff on the bridge with ropes.

Desperate, they had replied, "All right, if that's what you need to do."

And the steamer's regulations were thus duly enforced.

Twenty-six people were tied to the flagstaff. They remained there all day. And the ropes were not loosened at nightfall. The sea had been choppy. But now the swells grew bigger. And the steamship began to toss violently as the breakers lashed the poor men.

The men began to pine for their prison and lamented the day they were released. Prison seemed positively cozy compared to this.

At midnight, there was a terrifying commotion on the bridge. Some large empty barrels had been fastened to the gunwale. But as the ship had continued to toss violently, the ropes had snapped, and the barrels had begun to roll side to side. They were tumbling every which way and barreling into the sea-drenched men, who were left tied up in the middle of the bridge. They had begun to scream desperately for help.

The crew had rushed to their aid and refastened the barrels. But it was all too little too late. The men were gravely injured. Their feet, arms, legs, and heads were crushed, broken, and lacerated. Moments earlier, the waves of frigid seawater thrashing their bodies had felt like torture. Now, they offered soothing relief as they washed over their bloodied limbs.

The Captain had come to assess the carnage. He had seen for himself their slashed bodies, their disfigured faces as they wept and pleaded. He had taken pity on them...

And they were released.

When they arrived on the shores of Piraeus, we saw their bandaged limbs and assumed that the wretched men were attacked by Turks.

"No," they replied. "This was not the Turks' doing." And they told us their sad story.

Apart from the group from Divrig, they were by far some of the most unfortunate souls sheltering in the tents. Ignored by the gods and forsaken by humanity, they epitomized the figure of the tragic outcast, the eternal object of Evil's unmitigated fury.

"How much more of this do we have to take?" they mumbled anxiously, terrorized by their memories of the past and terrified of the memories to come.

Their presence consoled the other afflicted refugees, whose egotism led them to feel some degree of solace. They would compare their respective misfortunes and feel their spirits lift.

"Praise the Lord," they would think to themselves. "At least we were spared what these men from Divrig and Moush had to suffer."

Yes, praise the Lord, since God almighty could have drowned them all in the same misfortunes.

They feared what came next. The idea of tomorrow crushed these terrified creatures. They were desperate to find anything that could somehow ward off the impending danger. They were convinced that it was after them. They wanted to subdue and disarm the invisible fist that could resurface from the dark underworld and strike them down at any moment – the seven angels of the Apocalypse, who were determined to destroy them with God's wrath. And they were overcome by the compulsion, the irrepressible compulsion to prostrate themselves and implore, plead, and howl so that they might at last be worthy of forgiveness and grace.

"Let us pray, let us pray to God to have mercy on us."

This surrender eclipsed all their other thoughts. They no longer possessed the full faculties of their minds, hearts, and senses. They had lost the wherewithal to fight, to survive. The liberation of Armenia had faded from their minds. They did not harbor any spite towards their Turkish compatriots. They had forgotten everything – their wives, their children, their fields, their possessions, their fatherland.

"They snatched our wives and daughters, they looted our belongings… May they enjoy them," they thought. "If that is what it takes to rid us of this evil, to free us from its torments."

One day, I was strolling through the tents, when I noticed that a group was huddling around a man reading something.

I recognized him. It was the "Reverend Father," a sixty-year-old porter from Sivas. He had received this nickname thanks to his constant proselytization and interminable prayers.

He was a former revolutionary, a bigwig from a village in Sivas, who was eventually apprehended. After serving several years in prison, he had managed to escape by feeding his entire fortune, piecemeal, to all the prison employees. He had returned to his village and found an empty home. His wife had died. His four male children had joined a guerrilla regiment and left. And all that remained were his daughters and daughters-in-law, who had no source of income. They were living as squatters in a dilapidated little hut and subsisted on the generosity of their fellow townsfolk. The bigwig of yesterday had left for Constantinople in the hopes of earning a meager livelihood to support his family. One day, he had received news that the Kurds had raided their village and abducted his daughters and daughters-in-law. Now, he was all alone in this world, all alone with his Holy Scriptures, which he kept tucked under his arm everywhere he went.

When I approached the group, the man from Sivas was reading a selection of verses from the Psalms.

"Like water, I flowed aimlessly," he declared, his vacant gaze taking in his rapt listeners. "Like water, I was misled. My bones crumbled. Like wax, my heart melted and dissolved into my belly."

"My strength dried up like clay. My tongue stuck to the roof of my mouth. And they buried me in death's domain."

"For, the hounds surrounded me, evil besieged me and lanced my hands and feet."

"Spare me from the sword, save me from the hound's jaws."

"Long have I waited for the Lord our God. I am weary of pleading. My throat is parched. My eyes are drained of their tears."

And the pitiful elderly "Reverend Father" began to weep... The entire group was overcome with grief. Their anguish overflowed from memories of their terrible suffering. And the dread of what lay ahead made them shudder once more.

"Let us pray, let us pray!" they cried in unison. "Reverend Father, lead us in prayer."

The man from Sivas closed his book, wiped his eyes, and said, "Yes, let us turn our eyes towards the East and pray."

We walked away from the tents and formed a line in the middle of the meadow, beneath Mt. Hymettus. The Acropolis rose exquisitely in the distance before us, its Pentelic marbles golden in the resplendent light of the setting sun behind Salamina.

As the prayers commenced, we succumbed to the profound emotions stirred by this deeply moving ritual and the touchingly solemn congregation.

The elder from Sivas stood a few steps away from our group. Arms outstretched, his upturned eyes penetrated the heavens above, as he sought in vain Him to whom he would plead. He seemed to be another Moses leading his people on the exodus into the desert. His tall silhouette would sometimes bow low, kneel, prostrate itself, and kiss the earth. And the worshippers would follow suit, pressing their terror-stricken faces into the dirt as though they had just been bludgeoned to the ground.

Night fell slowly. The sun disappeared behind the Peloponnese. The peaks of Hymettus darkened from purple to black, and the Parthenon lost its brilliant luster.

Their prayers, their prostrations, the crescendos of their pain-stricken cries continued.

"Lord have mercy, Lord have mercy…"

Night was upon us. The stars twinkled, and the congregation assumed the form of a ragged shadow. The men from Moush and Divrig looked demonic with their white bandages and cadaverous, spectral appearance.

They resembled a league of sorcerers plotting inconceivable, unimaginable catastrophes under cover of darkness.

Meanwhile, the prayers, the exclamations of "Lord have mercy," the prostrations, the exhortations, carried on as before.

They had now entered a state of rapturous transcendence and awe. Unbeknownst to them, they had been led beyond the limits of mundane awareness.

Suddenly, a cry rang out. "Oh God, lead us to your light…" And the rapt congregation repeated in unison, "Oh God, lead us to your light…"

Oh, those long-suffering, pitiful souls… After all their protracted struggles and exhaustion, all they wanted was for their prayers, their prostrations, their stricken breasts, their tears, and laments to amount to something, anything. All they asked for now was a light, a sign, a small, minor miracle in the heavens above, which might soothe their spirits and give them heart.

Too poignant to forget, the memory of that prayer has stayed with me unchanged in all these years.

***

But our resources were spent. We could not rely on the Athenians' ongoing generosity indefinitely.

And just as the Committee was working feverishly to raise enough funds for the distribution of the sixty lepta daily allowance to the neediest refugees, there was an uprising in the camp.

A good-for-nothing agitator had convinced those poor people that the Henchag party had sent 5,000 liras in aid. And that we had pocketed most of it, while doling out barely enough for them to live on.

In response, when we went to distribute the usual allowance in Phaleron – which we had collected against almost insurmountable odds –, the refugees rejected it.

"We don't want that money!" they shouted at us.

All of a sudden, we were being falsely accused and subjected to threats from left and right.

We could not talk sense into those people. So, we thought it was best to leave before things got out of hand.

But our troubles did not end there. The Committee members had gathered at their favorite spot, the café on Agioi Theodoroi Square, when several people ambushed us. They threatened to make us really pay, unless we distributed the thousands that we had supposedly received from London.

Fortunately, Parebashd had already gotten wind of that ambush. And he showed up with several other people just in the nick of time and saved us from a potentially disastrous situation.

The following day, a petition was circulated demanding our resignation in the most intimidating terms. It was signed by virtually every refugee in the camp.

We saw this as an exquisite opportunity to shrug off what had become an unbearable responsibility. We decided to resign from the Committee immediately. But because we were still being hounded by unfounded accusations, we felt the need to address the refugees directly and to set the record straight by disclosing all our sources of income before we resigned from our posts.

I was tasked with delivering this address, since, as I mentioned previously, I was the Committee's Chairman.

We proceeded to the camp. We summoned all the complainants. I climbed up a tree and armed "with evidence," I explained the actual situation at hand. Then I asked our accuser to do the same by coming forward and substantiating his claims.

No one came forward.

In the end, I announced that we were resigning from our posts.

"No!" they all yelled. "We don't want your resignation. We want you to stay. We trust you."

"But you signed a petition saying that *you* wanted us to resign!" I objected.

"That didn't mean anything. They told us to sign it, so we did," replied the complainants' leaders. "We knew they were lying."

"So, why did you sign it?"

"They told us to sign it, so we did. There's no problem, Monsieur Vahram. Why don't you prepare another one, and we'll sign that too…"

I realized at that moment what "sensible people" really meant, namely, a bunch of opportunists…

I was still young, inexperienced, driven, and somewhat idealistic, when I discovered this vice in their collective character. I failed to respond wisely. I should have simply laughed off their shortcomings. But I was consumed by rage and roared, "You sheep-brained imbeciles! How can you just change your minds overnight!... How can you sign two separate petitions making completely different claims! What if I'm the liar, and the other guy is telling the truth…!"

But they already regretted everything. They groveled, kissed our hands, and begged us not to forsake them.

So, we were compelled to remain in our posts, however onerous that proved to be.

At that point, an Egyptian-Armenian man by the name of Krikor Effendi Meohtemetian came to our rescue. A native of Tokat, he had settled in Zagazig and amassed a fortune. He was in Greece for a change of scenery.

One day, out of curiosity, he had taken a tour of the refugee camp. The experience had resounded deeply in his heart, and he had heard the call of his nation. And that man, who had spent many years abroad, away from his native soil, indifferent to the fate of his compatriots, had suddenly felt unbearable sorrow at the sight of their insufferable abjection.

After his visit, he came looking for us and asked how we were managing to feed these wretched creatures. When we divulged our sources, he pledged to donate five liras per day. By the time he returned to Egypt, I believe he had contributed 80 – 90 liras.

Simon Manigian, who distributed the daily allowance, believed that Meohtemetian was sent by providence and dubbed him "The Man of God."

Later, when I was in Egypt, the Reverend Nshan Keshishian and I went to pay "The Man of God" a special visit in Zagazig. And he welcomed us graciously.

Chapter 4

Dikran Yergat. – His lecture. – His illness. – The Belgian Antoine. – An epic plan. – Reteos Mouradian. – The paper *Miyoutiun*. – A bunch of stamp-collectors. – Nazarpeg's bad example. – The patriotic Mr. Kokinos. – The Armenian refugees. – A week in Egypt. – The Kneipp regimen. – Arpiarian's dream. – Reprobate refugees. – Departure from Athens. – The steamship *Urania*. – An alarming trip through Crete. – We reach Alexandria.

It must have been October or November when one day, I paid a visit to one of the Messageries steamships that had just arrived from Constantinople – something I did often in the hopes of meeting an old acquaintance.

As soon as I arrived, I ran into Dikran Yergat standing on the bridge. He was traveling via Marseille, on his way to Paris, where he was hoping to settle down.

They were caught in a terrible storm and the poor man, who was already rather weak to start with, was awfully distressed and barely had the strength to complete his journey.

"Why don't you come down with me, take a break here for a week? You can leave on the next steamer," I advised him.

"Maybe you can give a talk in Athens, on the Armenian cause …"

"But I don't have that sort of money," he demurred. "I have barely enough to subsist on when I get to Paris."

"Don't give it another thought. You won't have to pay for a thing here in Athens."

I figured we could support him for a week on 60 – 70 drachmas.

Dikran Yergat agreed. We retrieved his bags and left the steamship together.

He could barely stand. I took him straight to a hotel, where he had a small meal and then retired to bed.

He was somewhat more energetic the following day, and we were able to visit the newsroom together, where we mooted the idea of a lecture. It was met with much excitement.

Before too long, the newspapers were announcing the arrival of Dikran Yergat, who, they claimed with great fanfare, had come to Athens with the express purpose of giving a talk on the Armenian cause.

Dikran Yergat, however, was still very frail. In fact, he took to his bed the following day.

He needed two weeks to regain enough strength to be able to speak. The lecture was held at the so-called Hall of Parnassus and attended by numerous members of the Athenian intelligentsia.

The bedridden Dikran Yergat had composed his presentation hastily. It took him a full hour and a half to read it aloud in his exquisite French. The talented young man discussed Greco-Armenian relations through the ages. And he predicted that in the future, there would be an alliance of these two historic nations, which had so many features in common.

The presentation – a terse talk replete with historical examples – provoked a powerful reaction and was received with enthusiastic applause. The next day, long excerpts were printed in all the newspapers, and everyone showered Dikran Yergat with gratitude.

But the long-suffering man had put too much stock in his abilities. The day after the lecture, he took to his bed again, this time utterly spent. He was bedridden for an entire month.

We all took turns attending to him and trying to fulfill the irritable patient's capricious demands.

There was a small desk opposite his bed, where he asked that we display the pictures of his loved ones. Then he requested a vine cutting and instructed us to wreath it around those pictures.

After hours of searching, Zareh Kochian finally snatched a cutting and sped back with it triumphantly.

Dikran Yergat also asked us to cut open a pomegranate and display it on the desk.

But that pomegranate caused us a lot of grief. The fruit was not in season. And only the biggest fruit markets were selling them for an exorbitant 2 – 3 drachmas apiece. We asked for donations just so as to fulfill our dear patient's request for a pomegranate.

The Athenians treated this illness very kindly. The doctors – who were supervised by the Prime Minister's brother, Dr. Deligiannis, the most illustrious physician in Greece – came to see the patient every day pro bono. His visitors also included various notable figures of the local literati.

Even when he finally got back on his feet and was able to take a stroll around the city, the doctors remained unconvinced that he was fit for the exertions of travel, especially given the winter weather. And they advised him to stay for another month until he had recovered more fully.

Around that time, Simon Manigian and Parebashd informed us that a young man had arrived from Europe, and that he was determined to relay an urgent message to a leading member of the Armenian revolutionary movement.

I went to meet him and get a better sense of what he wanted. He was an energetic young man by the name of Mr. Antoine. He could not have been more than 20 – 22 years old.

I asked to hear his important communique.

"Are you a revolutionary leader?" he asked.

"No," I replied.

"Then, I can't tell you anything. I must speak with a leader about what I have in mind. That is the sole purpose of my journey, to which I have devoted my life and my fortunes."

In the evening, I relayed my conversation with Mr. Antoine to Dikran Yergat, who took great interest in this development.

"I wonder how we can get him to talk," he pondered.

"Let's tell him you're a revolutionary leader. That might work," I replied.

Dikran Yergat agreed to this idea and the following day, we told Mr. Antoine that a revolutionary leader would meet with him. He was overjoyed. We gave him an appointment for a rendezvous at a café on Syntagma Square.

Mr. Antoine gave the "revolutionary leader" a vigorous handshake. Then he quietly asked whether he could speak openly in my presence.

"Yes," said Dikran earnestly. "This gentleman is one of my lieutenants. You can trust him completely."

That loosened Mr. Antoine's tongue, and he began to talk.

First, he explained that he was Belgian, a practicing Catholic, and a student at a religious school where he had learned about the massacres being perpetrated against Christians. His noble soul was outraged. And he had decided to initiate a new Crusade posthaste to aid his co-religionists.

"There are eight of us. We were united in our decision and left Belgium together. But six of my friends only went as far as Paris and refused to accompany me any further… Regardless, I do have faith in them. And I know that as soon as I give them the signal, they will hasten here to our side. But we will need more men to complete this mission… I am meeting with you in the hope that we may forge an alliance and that you might contribute to this effort… I do not want money or weapons…"

What sort of contribution do you have in mind?

"I need twenty-three men, just like the ones who stormed the Bank – fearless, daring, and dedicated."

"Why twenty-three exactly?" probed Yergat.

"Because we already have seven and are twenty-three short of having an even thirty."

"But what can you achieve with only thirty men?"

"That should suffice to free the Christians from Abdulhamid's grip," replied Mr. Antoine decisively.

"Do you have a clear plan?"

"Of course… I'll explain it presently, and you will see how simple and effective it is. Putting that plan into effect requires thirty people and 20,000 francs. The money has been secured. I have 10,000 francs of my own funds, and my six friends will contribute another 10,000 francs… All we need are the men."

"If you can actually act on your plan, then we can assign you with not just twenty-three, but three-hundred men immediately," replied Dikran Yergat. "Now, explain to me what you intend to do."

"I thought up the whole plan, and I would like you to keep it strictly confidential," said the Belgian earnestly and enigmatically.

We give our word.

"In that case, listen carefully. Those thirty men will be armed from head to toe. I will then rent a sailboat and set off for the borderlands of Asia Minor. I will start out at Chanakkale and travel as far as Yafa, stopping at every port and city along the way."

"To do what?"

"To capture all the pashas and beys and drag them on board…"

"How can you fit that many people onto a sailboat?"

"I have a solution for that as well," replied the eager Belgian. "I will take them in groups to an island in the Greek Archipelago, where they will be guarded by the locals."

"What then?"

"Then, once we capture and transport all the pashas and beys, we will parley with Abdulhamid and demand that he accept our conditions. In addition, whenever they kill a Christian, we will even things out and kill one of our captives."

One hesitates to call Mr. Antoine completely insane. But, between his mental excitement, his fanaticism, and his derring-do personality, he had obviously lost touch with reality.

Dikran Yergat patiently explained to him that however well-intentioned, his plan was nonetheless absolutely unworkable, especially because these pashas and beys could not simply be gathered up like shells on a beach.

Disheartened, the young man protested indignantly, "I can plainly see that you are not genuine revolutionaries…"

Nevertheless, he was undeterred and went on to communicate his idea to a number of other people.

Then, some months later, while I was in Egypt, I heard that Mr. Antoine had rented a boat, set out with eight to ten armed Armenian men, and traveled all the way to Egypt.

The expedition was dispersed, and the British authorities confiscated all their weapons.

Once he had convalesced, Dikran Yergat left Athens for Paris, where he published several articles on contemporary Athenian and Greek literature in the prominent periodical, *Revue de Revue*. These were translated into Greek. And his name became so popular in Greece that the Athenian Mayoralty named that talented young Armenian an "Athenian citizen." His premature death was a devastating loss to all Armenians.

I had hardly set foot in Athens when Reteos Mouradian suggested that I become editor of the paper, *Miyoutiun*. In return, I would receive two meals a day at his expense and in a restaurant of his choosing.

Mr. Reteos was a small man with a square face. He had lived in Athens for fourteen years and made his living as a lithographer.

Before our departure, he collaborated with Turkish emigres on a Turkish-language lithographic newspaper called, *Vatan*. This caused quite a stir, ultimately leading to the Ottoman Embassy's successful efforts to incarcerate Mr. Reteos in Athens and shut the paper down.

After his release, Mouradian decided to publish an Armenian paper using smuggled types from Constantinople. Unfortunately, however, several letters such as '֓' and '֊' were lost on the way. And the poor man had to publish *Miyoutiun* without them.

Mityoutyoun was a tiny paper consisting of four narrow columns. This monthly was published for unlimited distribution, free of charge, and made possible by donations.

Reteos used to tell his subscribers, "The paper is free, but we gladly accept donations." And although *Miyoutiun* did have subscribers, they failed to send in donations. Many of them simply wanted to enhance their collection of Greek stamps.

Readers would send in enquiries such as, "Why don't you use stamps that only cost 3 or 4 lepta instead of 5?" Occasionally, he would actually receive donations in the amount of 3 francs from Bulgaria, half a dollar from America, 5 kurush from Egypt. But this was hardly enough to cover the paper's expenses, no matter how low he kept the production costs.

"What made you want to print a free paper?" I asked him.

Mr. Reteos told me that Nazarpegian was indirectly responsible for that idea.

It is widely known that, for a long time, the founder of *Henchak* printed his paper in Athens, where he had settled with his wife, Maro.

Mr. Reteos knew Nazarpeg and was also employed as *Henchak*'s forwarding agent.

"It was unbelievable. When Nazarpeg was still here, we would go to the post office together, and there would be a flood of donations… Oh, that flood got me excited, alright. I made up my mind right then and there that I was going to do the same thing – print a free revolutionary paper and pocket at least 10% of the donations."

Miyoutiun was the offspring of those fond memories, although it was ultimately a total disappointment. Regardless, being an obstinate man, Mr. Reteos continued printing it for several more years, spending his earnings as a lithographer to cover the paper's costs.

I served as the paper's Editor-in-Chief for a period of only three months. But I felt that we could do better than a monthly and suggested to Reteos that we also publish a lithographic biweekly called, *Havelvadz Miyoutyan*. It would be devoted exclusively to news on politics and the nation. This supplement, which would be much more substantial than the actual paper itself, would be sold for profit. We printed six or seven issues of that lithographic paper but stopped when it failed to meet our expectations.

Chapter 4

While he was still in Athens, Dikran Yergat indulged our request for an article, although it promoted a very different agenda from that of our paper. I should add, before I forget, that our paper had an explicit agenda: namely, "to unite all the revolutionary parties."

Dikran Yergat's article was entitled, "The Benefits of Disunity." It illustrated how the existence of several different parties was more advantageous, because it would generate harmless competition and rivalry, and thus energize the movement.

Miyoutiun's manager was a local named Kokinos. His name was printed at the bottom of the paper, but his face never appeared in print. So, I never once got a look at him.

We would receive heartrending letters from readers in the farthest corners of the provinces – the revolutionary network made it possible to deliver the paper even to the most remote regions of Turkey – asking for assistance from the "patriotic Mr. Kokinos," whom, of course, they imagined to be an all-powerful Armenian revolutionary leader.

And so, for better or worse, *Miyoutiun* kept my belly full. And it was no small achievement to keep one's belly full in Athens.

Greece is a poor country with very few professional opportunities for foreigners.

The most successful Armenian in Athens was Dr. Aghapeg, who worked as a dentist for the royal court but failed to collect his dues from King Yorgos.

The Armenian refugees' struggles to earn a living defied belief.

The Reverend Nshan Keshishian – Kalousd Arkhanian's beloved friend, who had become a guerrilla fighter out of his deep love for the revolution, sheltering in the damp mountain caves for years despite his agonizing arthritis – now sat hunched under a tall pillar selling ice cream in Athens and Piraeus.

Aram Pakrad – who was a graduate of the *Mülkiyye*, once occupied an important post in Izmir, and spoke fluent Turkish, French, English, and German – was forced to leave everything behind and flee to Greece after his last assignment for the revolutionary cause. He now worked as a tour guide, loitering outside fancy hotels to greet fresh batches of British tourists. He would put on the airs of a modern Cicero and guide them around the Athenian ruins or some such place for the paltry sum of a few drachmas.

The whole business tormented him bitterly. His knowledge of those ruins was very limited. And he was prone to mistaking the hill of Areopagus for the prison of Socrates or the temple of Theseus for the theatre of Bacchus.

And whenever a tourist would consult his copy of *Baedeker* and promptly correct what he had to say about a historical source, a column, or a well, Aram Pakrad would snap back curtly, "I beg your pardon, sir, but Baedeker must be wrong. Archaeologists have not been able to settle the argument on that specific point just yet."

Simon Manigian – the baker from Armudan, who had once been hugely successful and employed dozens of laborers – now ran a tiny coffee shop in Piraeus to eke out his keep.

Zareh Kochian – the son of a wealthy merchant family in Adapazar – lived a life of destitution in Athens.

Antreas Mgrian or Parebashd applied his talents to decorating signboards for a meager wage.

We normally took our meals in the small house that Simon Manigian had rented in Piraeus. It usually consisted of tomato salad and olives, which we devoured greedily. This house became the meeting point for every down-and-out Armenian fugitive passing through Piraeus. It often provided room and board for eight to ten exceptional guests.

While I was in Athens, more Henchags arrived from Constantinople: Setrag Ambarian, Shahriman, Souren, etc.

I had met Shahriman a couple of times in Constantinople thanks to Vahé Arzouyan. But I got to know him better in Athens where he stayed for several months.

Dr. Jelalyan and Dr. Tiurab had also come to Athens as refugees from Constantinople. They both spent their days pining for Constantinople, anxiously awaiting news of any change for the better so that they could finally return with some peace of mind.

Dr. Jelalyan, who was staying at a hotel on Omonia Square, was exasperated by the refugees. They were always accosting him about all the ailments he specialized in, pleading with him, for the love of their nation, to treat them free of charge.

Vahé Arzouyan had also left Constantinople and fled to Egypt.

At one point, Zareh Kochian and I had saved enough money to travel to Alexandria – hardly a large sum, since we used to travel in second or third class –, where we stayed for a week.

Alexandria, Egypt, an important center for Armenian merchants and exiles.

It was the first time I was setting foot in Egypt. And the only people I knew in Alexandria were fugitives from Constantinople. Vahé Arzouyan was my closest friend among them.

At the time, thousands of Armenian refugees had arrived in Alexandria. The school and grounds of the Sts. Peter-Paul Church now looked like a bazaar overflowing with them. Wooden shacks crowded the large expanse around the church. They served as makeshift cafes, restaurants, barbershops, grocery stores, tobacconists, etc. The Philanthropic Committee fed and cared for all those refugees. It was much more generously funded than our Committee in Athens.

After spending a few days in Alexandria, I spent a night in Cairo.

My intention was to see Dikran Arpiarian. He had also fled Constantinople and arrived among the refugees in Egypt.

We met at the Opera Square opposite the Azabekya Garden and embraced.

Dikran had been the luckiest member of our group. The minute he had set foot in Alexandria, he was given a generous reception. They provided him with around five to ten liras and sent him to Cairo, where there was no shortage of moral and financial support.

When I saw him, he had just arrived in Cairo but was still unemployed. That said, he was given assurances that he would be employed very shortly. And, so it was.

My brief trip to Egypt convinced me to leave Greece and settle in Egypt permanently. This was what my friends and acquaintances had already counselled me to do.

In any case, Kochian and I returned to Athens and took Vahé Arzouyan with us. He was unhappy in Alexandria, where he found it difficult to follow the vegetarian diet that he hoped would cure his gastroenteritis.

Vahé was a consummate Kneippian back then. He quoted Kneipp throughout the day as though it was the Book of Psalms. Kneipp's nutritional regimen had two requirements: "a strict vegetarian diet and vapor baths."

For the entire two days of our trip on that steamer, Vahé preached his gospel. So, by the time we arrived in Piraeus, both Zareh Kochian and I had become strict vegetarians.

From a financial standpoint, Kneipp's regimen was entirely compatible with our income. And this was probably one of the main reasons why we were so eager to adopt Vahé's doctrine.

When we reached Athens, we rented a furnished room in a house, where Vahé Arzouyan, Shahriman, Zareh Kochian, Setrag Ambarian, and I all lived together.

We were all vegetarian by this point. But, apart from Vahé, the others did not take up the compulsory vapor bath regimen. We would buy baskets of seasonal vegetables and simmer them for several hours over a portable gas stove. We even skimped on seasoning, including salt. But our meals always turned out to be very tasty – at least, that's what we liked to tell ourselves. Setrag Ambarian would occasionally pine after various meat dishes, letting out a mournful sigh as the aroma of grilled ribs would waft in from the kitchen.

One day, he was so overwhelmed by the temptation that he went straight to a nearby restaurant and ordered ten different meat dishes. He cursed Kneipp and his regimen between mouthfuls as he devoured every bite.

This treachery emboldened the rest of us to abandon Vahé, who remained a staunch vegetarian to the very end – and to be fair, it did him a world of good.

Chapter 4

***

During my time in Athens, I corresponded regularly with Arpiar, who had been living in London. He would send me lengthy missives – sometimes up to 20 – 30 sheets long –, complaining firstly, about his circumstances, and secondly, about his Henchag comrades, with whom he could not see eye to eye.

What he desperately wanted was an independent source of income so that he could withdraw from the revolution and dedicate himself to writing.

That idea had taken possession of him a long time ago. But, in all his years abroad, he had never been able to turn it into reality.

He seemed to be entirely fed up with life all those months he was in London.

To be fair, the Henchag party's dysfunctionality had risen to new heights.

The opposition to Nazarpeg was only partly successful. It is true that he and Maro were ousted from the center. But those two would not concede their losses. And with the support of their backers, they carried on working under the Henchag party's banner.

The opposition, which was led by Arpiar and some others, constituted the majority. But it was short on funds. Nazarpeg and his collaborators, on the other hand, were financially far better off.

Moreover, the paper *Henchak* was registered under Nazarpeg's name in London. And it was deemed his property by law. So, Nazarpeg continued publishing *Henchak*, which made it impossible to publish any other periodical with that name.

Meanwhile, Nazarpeg's opposition – which constituted the overwhelming majority – could not come to any consensus. And Arpiar failed to reconcile with his comrades.

They published circulars full of violent mutual indictments and distributed them as widely as possible. These poured in from London, Egypt, Bulgaria, and America. And they gave the Armenian refugees from Constantinople their first glimpse into the outrageous dysfunctionality of the Henchag party's inner workings.

At that time, Vahé Arzouyan had also formed a small group. And it too attracted both supporters and fervent opponents. Arpiar Arpiarian was among the former and championed Vahé wholeheartedly.

His support continued for several more years, until, one day, it gave way to fierce antagonism.

***

I believe it was November when a continuous twenty-four-hour downpour inundated the Phaleron meadow as well as many streets in Piraeus and Athens.

The Armenian refugees had to abandon their tents and take shelter in Athens, where the tents were relocated once the downpour had stopped.

The Committee could no longer distribute any money or subsistence to the refugees. Although their numbers had dwindled, there were still too many of them.

We were very fortunate that the British Embassy came to our aid just then.

One day, our President, Serovpé Giurjian – who had some contacts in several Embassies – informed us that the British Ambassador, Mr. Edgerton, had received a substantial sum of money from London to assist the Armenians. But that money was to be used for creating employment opportunities to support the needy.

We rushed to the Embassy to verify this information. We described the dire state of the refugees, explaining that they had nothing to eat and that we could no longer feed them. We were so persistent that they agreed to take charge of the refugees.

After that, Embassy staffers started making daily rounds with their moneybags, and we would help them hand out the small notes to all the refugees.

When the latter learned that the British Embassy in London had sent financial assistance, they staged another – and, if one can imagine, even angrier – uprising to demand more money. They went so far as to threaten the British Secretary at gunpoint one day. He grabbed his moneybag and left, never to return.

Several days after all the financial assistance had been distributed, the camp was completely deserted. Everyone had left to fend for themselves.

It had been the same story in Alexandria and Cairo. The police had to be called in to stop the fights that kept breaking out every time they distributed any money.

I think the same thing had happened in Varna as well, where another Philanthropic Organization had been hard at work. A group of bald-faced reprobates were making their way from Cairo to Varna, Athens and Alexandria living off the distributed funds. Their scheme lasted all that year, until there was nothing more left to distribute.

***

Toward the end of January '97, I left Athens and settled in Egypt.

I made the trip on board a small steamship, the *Urania*, which was owned by a company called Pantaleon. The journey from Piraeus to Alexandria lasted eight days. By contrast, the Khedive's steamships made the same journey in thirty-six hours.

That said, the *Urania* did stop at every port in Crete.

When we reached Chania, the Captain – an older Greek man who had once worked for Ounjian's steamships and whom I got to know pretty well – asked me to accompany him going down to shore. Of course, I declined that risky invitation, as it could have landed me in terribly hot water.

When we left Chania, we were caught in a horrible storm. We took shelter in Souda Bay for twenty-four hours. Then we arrived at Rethymno and finally at Candia, where we had a ten-hour layover.

The Captain insisted once again that I accompany him to shore.

I said, "No, I don't want to take any unnecessary risks."

"You have nothing to worry about," he replied. "Why don't you just put on a Captain's hat and come out with me like you're one of the crew. No one will bat an eyelash."

He was so persuasive that I eventually acquiesced, mainly because I did not want to appear like a coward.

And indeed, no one on the docks paid us any mind, despite all the Turkish laborers and officers who were standing around. And we went to the Pantaleon's offices where the Captain had some business to attend to.

Once he had wrapped everything up, he took me to a café in the main square for a game of backgammon and some nargileh.

We had scarcely begun our game, when the shooting began.

The café's patrons – almost all of them Greek – rushed outside. And, of course, so did we.

The commotion on the square was indescribable. The shooting intensified as it went on.

We were very alarmed and began asking the others, "What is it? What's going on?"

"A group of insurgents is attacking Candia. They've surrounded the city," they replied.

In an instant, the streets were full of Greeks and Turks armed with rifles and revolvers, which they were firing indiscriminately on every street and from every open window.

It was impossible to go out. We sheltered in the café, which was now completely deserted. Even the waiters had left.

The aged Captain was as shocked as I was and regretted leaving the steamship.

The commotion and confusion intensified as women and children began to scream and wail, their cries broken only by the piercing howls of people being shot.

The entire city had become a battleground, with the Greeks and Turks at each other's throats.

The shooting seemed to be dying down. So, we stepped out of the cafe. The square was completely empty. We only saw women calling to each other from their windows, their faces streaked with tears.

The Captain noticed an elderly Greek man standing in the corner of the square. He rushed over to him to find out what he knew.

We learned that the city's Greeks had taken up arms and joined the rebel forces, while the Turks had quickly sided with the army to defend the city.

The old man cautioned us that the fighting could resume without warning, even in the streets.

"The rebels have a big army. And we're surrounded. The Turks can't defeat them," he said.

As I noted above, everything had quieted down for the time being. So, we seized the opportunity and ran at full speed back to the ship.

Just then, a Turkish steamer pulled into port and offloaded an army regiment. The shooting resumed and continued unabated.

The Captain thought it would be best to leave before our scheduled departure. There was no way to communicate with his associates on shore and the crew could not make any deliveries or accept any shipments.

Two days later, we arrived in Alexandria at last.

Chapter 5

The farm in Sharabas. – A strange way to hunt. – The fratricidal youth. – Execution by hanging. – A mother's consolation. – A kind executioner. – Arpiarian in Egypt. – The *Bolsetsi*s[*] of Cairo. – Arpiarian at Sharabas farm. – Making dessert. – Arpiar's ravings. – Nshan Keshishian. – A bitter illusion. – The fake hero. – The phony Haji Minas Oghlus and the genuine article. – A new life. – The novel *Mardig Agha*. – Mikayel Giurjian.

After a month of aimless unemployment, Boghos Nubar Pasha hired me to work as bursar-bookkeeper on one of his farms. This farm was a vast cotton and rice plantation about eight hours away from Alexandria and Cairo. It was located near a small Arab village called Sharabas, which is how the farm got its name.

An Eygptian *abaadiyya*[†] is not what one thinks of as a farm – surrounded by trees and meadows, full of livestock, where milk and yogurt, butter and cheese are produced in abundance.

Those cotton plantations are no more than bare fields divided by irrigation channels. There are no trees anywhere in sight. And as for sustenance, even the eggs and milk are often delivered from a nearby city, because the *fellah*[‡] do not keep hens or herd cows.

On the other hand, the Sharabas plantation had an enviable location on the banks of the Nile. And several trees dotted the grounds of our residence.

I was offered private accommodation consisting of two large rooms and a parlor with simple furnishings.

After all the bustle of Athens, Alexandria and Cairo, being alone there honestly gave me the creeps. The nights were especially difficult. I could hear bats, mice, and cockroaches scuttering around. But even worse things disturbed my sleep. I knew that snakes were often found and killed in the cellar, which doubled as a storage room for farming equipment. Moreover, I sometimes noticed scorpions crawling along the walls, and a lizard would occasional drop down from my bedroom ceiling.

---

[*] An Armenian term meaning "Constantinople Armenian." (Tr.)
[†] Egyptian Arabic, meaning "estate." (Tr.)
[‡] Egyptian Arabic, meaning "farmer." (Tr.)

This dreadful combination meant that I kept my eyes wide open during my first several nights on the farm, only sleeping for a few hours during the day. But I soon adjusted, since I realized that none of these creatures seemed to pose any threat.

In the two years that I spent on Sharabas farm, I never heard of anyone being bitten by a snake or stung by a scorpion.

What I found absolutely unbearable were the dense swarms of flies. They were so awful that I sometimes found it impossible to read or write in the house. I had to cover my desk with a mosquito net.

There were other people apart from me living on Sharabas farm. These included Boghos Pasha's deputy, Mgrdich Effendi Antranigian, although he was often called away on business; a Swiss Nazir or supervisor with his wife; and another Swiss man, who was hired for his expertise in chemical production, but who did nothing but hunt. He was an extremely skilled sharpshooter, and he never missed his target.

On one occasion, a dolphin had wandered into the Nile. I remember how he shot it from an impressive distance.

The appearance of dolphins in that section of the Nile was unsurprising. At times of drought, the Nile would drop so precipitously that the sea would surge in and bring along its various creatures. That is how we sometimes caught saltwater fish on the shores of our river.

But usually, we hunted for our fish in the fields and fished our birds out of the water.

This bizarre fact obviously requires some clarification.

Presently, Egyptian plantations typically produce cotton, rice, or Egyptian clover. It is customary to plant rice after the cotton harvest, because cotton depletes the soil, making it less fertile, whereas rice has the opposite effect. The rice fields are watered generously. In other words, the canals along the Nile are opened, and the fields are inundated under half a meter of water, turning them into vast lakes.

It takes several days for the soil to absorb all that water. And that is when the fish, which had been swimming in the Nile, start flopping around in the fields. You can now understand how one could quite naturally collect fish from the rice fields.

As for hunting wild ducks or similarly large birds, we used to go to Lake Manzala, which was less than an hour away from the farm. It would take us twenty to thirty minutes to wade into the water, because it was barely

Chapter 5

Cairo was another Armenian center in Egypt.

one meter deep, despite being so wide that it stretched from Damietta to Port Said. We used to crouch and wait for the flocks of birds to bathe or drink with their feet dangling underwater. It took very little effort to grab several birds in one go by their feet. One did need patience, however, as it could take many hours before the birds deigned to dip in.

***

While at Sharabas, I once witnessed an execution at very close quarters. It left a profound impression on me.

The condemned was a twenty-year-old youth. His mother had incited him to murder his two stepbrothers, nine and ten years old.

That youth owned and cultivated several *feddan** of land not far from our farm. He and his stepbrothers had inherited them from their father. When he is called up for military service, his mother tells him, "You will suffer terribly in the army. You may even die. Then, your brothers will inherit all your lands. You should kill them before you leave. That way, they won't be able to seize what is rightfully yours. And if you do successfully complete your military service and return, you will be very well-off."

Her incitements eventually drive her son to murder.

---

* Arabic, referring to a unit of land measurement. (Tr.)

One night, the young man axes his two brothers to death in their sleep. The murderer is apprehended the very next day. And after a weak attempt to deny his crime, he confesses everything. As a result, his mother is also arrested.

The mother is ultimately released, but the son is condemned to death.

The execution – which is done by hanging in Egypt – was set to take place in the city of Faraskur, an hour and a half away from our farm.

It was local custom for the sentence to be carried out at dawn. So, the Swiss Nazir and I left in the middle of the night to attend the gruesome event.

There were very few sources of entertainment on the farm, and one could not be too picky. We leapt at every opportunity we had.

The scaffold had already been erected when we arrived. And a large crowd of people was waiting in the prison square.

We were given a place of honor right by the scaffold, next to the Governor and Commander of Faraskur.

The prison gates were opened at dawn, before sunrise. And a police retinue brought out the condemned man. The Chief Executioner – a formidable negro from Said – and his two assistants stood patiently at the foot of the scaffold.

The murderer looked frightful, his face a bluish green. But he advanced with steady steps, arms tied firmly behind his back.

A woman and her daughter were standing near us.

"The criminal's mother and sister," whispered the Governor. "The one who incited her son to commit the murders…"

The murderer was first led towards those two women. The daughter was sobbing, but the mother remained unmoved. Without a word, the young man turned his head away from her. But the woman placed a hand on her son's shoulder and said, as though to console him one last time, "*Hali dünya, ya veled, hali dünya*" ("That's the way of the world, my son").

I think the old witch was secretly overjoyed that the entire estate would now be hers.

The prisoner was then asked whether he had any final words. "Water," he muttered in a barely audible voice.

They brought him some water. One of the officers explained that he had been drinking water throughout the day but had not uttered a single word.

Then they led him to the foot of the scaffold. He was supposed to climb up a set of stairs.

The police turned him over to the Chief Executioner and his assistants, and then stepped aside.

Until that moment, the young man seemed to be sleepwalking, but he suddenly noticed the stairs up to the scaffold. He seemed to be taken by surprise, although they had been right in front of his eyes. He began to shudder violently and recoiled in horror.

At that moment, the Chief Executioner – the enormous man from Said – grabbed him by the neck and, with the help of his two assistants, lifted him up the steps.

When they tried to hook the noose around his throat, the young man resisted again.

The Chief Executioner bent down and whispered something to the prisoner.

The young man instantly relaxed and let them secure that lethal rope.

The captive stepped onto a spring, and the planks beneath his feet gave way. His body plunged down, dangling in midair as his limbs convulsed horribly.

That torment lasted almost two minutes.

The government physician was standing beside the hanged man. He felt his wrist, dropped his hand, and pronounced, "He is dead."

An official telegram was dispatched to the Khedive declaring that justice had been served.

The crowd of five to six thousand people began to disperse. And we went to a Greek café on the banks of the Nile, ordered a couple of beers, and tried to forget our ordeal.

Once the executioner had fulfilled his duties, he too stopped by the café to take a break from his labors.

The executioner represents the authorities of Egypt. And, in that capacity, he is the object of great deference.

As soon as he entered the café, we invited him over to our table, which he graciously honored with his presence.

I was curious to learn how he had helped the prisoner relax in his final moments.

"It is a trick. I use it every time. And it works every time," he replied.

"What kind of trick?"

"Those poor souls," continued the executioner. "When the time comes to place the noose around their necks, they completely fall apart. They either resist with all their might, or they cry, plead, and kiss our hands not to hang them. At that moment, I whisper into their ears. I tell them that I have made special arrangements for their release; that I have rigged the noose not to choke them; that they must pretend to be dead, until all the government officials have dispersed; and that, afterwards, my assistants and I will smuggle them away, and so on. To gain their trust, I also tell them that they will have to pay me some random amount of money for rendering this service…"

"And they believe all that?" I balked.

"When they are that desperate, when all hope is lost, the poor souls do believe it. And as they cling on to that last hope, they let me ring the rope around their necks. Maybe they die feeling reassured, perhaps even at ease."

This executioner from Said was genuinely humane. His innocent lie was meant to comfort his victims in their final moments.

In the meantime, the scaffold was taken down, and its planks and beams lay on the ground.

At that moment, something truly bizarre attracted our attention. A group of Arab women had been standing nearby. And, suddenly, they began jumping over the beams as though they had all lost their minds.

I asked about the meaning of that strange performance.

"These women are infertile. That is why they are jumping over the beams," explained one of the locals.

This superstition is apparently so deeply rooted in Arab culture, that even wealthy women make the long trip to jump over the scaffold's beams.

"That is the only reason that some of these women have come all the way from Cairo," said the local.

It is worth noting that Europeans, especially the French, also place great value on the hanged man's rope. They consider it a talisman that can bring fortune and success.

The next day, Faraskur suffered the woeful consequences of this spectacle. About ten very young *fellah* boys got together, found a rope, and tried to reenact the previous day's events using a tree for a scaffold.

They chose their respective roles as prisoner, executioner, policeman, and so on. The boy pretending to be the condemned man was led to the tree, where they had tied a noose to a branch. He was instructed to stand on a chair. The noose was fastened to his neck. And the chair was kicked away from his feet. The innocent "convict" began to choke. Panicking at the sight of his horrible convulsions, his friends ran away. A minute later, the poor little boy was dead.

Those young, unwitting murderers were not made to pay for their crime, because the oldest member of the group was only nine years old.

***

At the end of September '97, Arpiar Arpiarian left London for Egypt.

When I learned that he was in Alexandria, I immediately left Sharabas and went to see him.

It was the first time I was seeing him since leaving Constantinople. And my heart was pounding with joy. As I noted earlier, Arpiar's letters were full of grievances about his circumstances. And he was prepared to turn his back on the confining world of the revolution.

I had accordingly assumed that once in Egypt – where his brother, Dikran Arpiarian, I, and several of his other friends now lived –, we could free him from this career in political activism. It did not suit him at all, and he openly disparaged it.

The main concern was finding a source of income. But that did not seem to be too challenging. H. Alpiar and Dikran Arpiarian were publishing *Paros* three times a week in Cairo. It was gaining in popularity and, with Arpiar's collaboration – his paid collaboration, of course –, it could truly shine. In addition, *Mshag* was always willing to pay for his articles. He could have earned a modest income from these two jobs. And we could have found some temporary bookkeeping work for him as well.

Dikran and I had planned everything before Arpiar even arrived in Egypt. We had decided that we should spare no effort to make him withdraw from the revolutionary movement.

Arpiar was already waiting for me at the station when I arrived in Alexandria. We met some friends for lunch and then retreated for a more private meeting in his hotel room.

As soon as I broached the topic of our arrangements, he stopped me.

"Don't waste your breath," he said.

"Why?"

"Because there are some new projects in play, new plans have been devised, things are moving in a new direction, and so on, and so forth."

And that same Arpiar – whose letters to me conveyed nothing but his exhaustion with party politics and his desperate need to leave that world behind – had suddenly become a staunch revolutionary.

"But you said you were fed up with your comrades, the revolutionary world, and not to mention, your lifestyle."

"True. But now everything is settled," he replied. "I have no reason to complain anymore. Finally, we are getting down to some serious work."

"What kind of work?" I asked skeptically.

At which Arpiar opened his bag of miracles. First, in addition to *Henchak*, the revolution's official publication – whose name they were now finally allowed to use again –, they were going to publish a literary bimonthly in London under Levon Pashalian's directorship. He had already decided to leave Paris for London. Moreover, a group of wealthy, capable individuals in Paris had founded a committee, which was prepared to support the party with a contribution of up to 50 liras. Finally, a militant wing of the revolution was in the works. Sustained efforts were already underway to secure the necessary resources for its foundation in a largely Armenian-inhabited region.

I could not check my amazement at Arpiar's naïve excitement, as he relayed all this with utmost conviction and faith.

It was now quite clear that what Dikran, I, and his other friends had planned would not be put into effect. And Arpiar would remain a Henchag, more fervently than ever.

"So, why did you come to Egypt?" I asked.

"Because the Delegates are meeting in Alexandria this time," he replied.

The following day, we went to Cairo together. We were welcomed by Dikran Arpiarian, Sarkis Svin, Setrag Davitian, H. Alpiar and several others.

They, too, had assumed that Arpiar had come to settle in Egypt and to withdraw from the party. But Arpiar quickly made it clear that they were wrong.

They were bitterly disappointed, as was I, and, even more so, his brother Dikran. Dikran had a tendency to cup his ears or run out of the room every time Arpiar got talking about the revolution.

Chapter 5

There was a wonderful circle of Armenians in Cairo back then. And every couple of months, I took a week off from Sharabas to enjoy their delightful company.

In addition to the people I have already mentioned, there were several other Bolsetsis who had settled there, including the renowned – now deceased – dentist, Dr. Esmerian. He was a jovial, sincere man among close friends. Dr. Yetvart Masis was also pleasant in good company. And there were several others, who were in Cairo temporarily.

We usually met at Dr. Esmerian's place in the evening before going out to dinner. After dinner, we moved on to the home of Mr. Lekejian, Bishop Ormanian's uncle and Cairo's most renowned photographer.

This circle of acquaintances pleased Arpiar to no end after his lonely life in London.

He kept telling me, "I feel like I'm back in Constantinople." He was truly blissful, since all he ever dreamt of was Constantinople.

Shortly after arriving in Egypt, he spent a month with me at the Sharabas farm.

He spent his days gorging himself on fruit.

Arpiar was susceptible to just one deadly sin: he was an incorrigible glutton. He had an insatiable appetite for fruits and confections. And he could be moved to genuine ecstasy over a delectable meal.

The farm provided an abundance of fruit. Sweets, on the other hand, were in short supply.

So, to satisfy his cravings, I attempted to make a cake one day.

I mixed butter, sugar, flour, and eggs and briefly cooked them on the stovetop. Then, I splashed in some liquor to leaven the dough. But the alcohol caught fire and burnt the top of the cake.

Even the most undiscerning palate could not be tempted to eat it.

I tasted it and realized that I was a worthless cook, despite my good intentions and sincere efforts. I was about to throw that appalling excuse of a pastry away. But Arpiar stopped me. His reasoning was, "It contains nothing but the most delicious ingredients: butter, sugar, flour, and fresh eggs. And since no Tashnags were involved in its preparation, how could it not be appetizing? Do not throw that cake away. I will eat it."

And he snacked on that atrocious thing for the rest of the day, enjoying every bite. His only suggestion was, "You should have added some fruit. Then, it would have been truly outstanding."

We slept in the same room. And for the first time in my life, I noticed that Arpiar talked in his sleep, loud and clear. The subject always concerned the nation's political future. This is what tormented his mind even while he slept.

"Long before the Berlin Conference, Patriarch Nerses once said that…"

Or "Khrimian told Salisbury in London that…"

And so on, and so forth. These nighttime ravings were hardly any different from his daytime rants.

Aside from Arpiar, I also hosted the Reverend Nshan Keshishian at the Sharabas farm for about a month. He had also left Athens and was living in Cairo. A man by the name of Yeginian – a former Henchag activist turned baker – was putting him up.

The poor Reverend was growing weaker by the day. He could feel death drawing near. As I noted earlier, he had an illustrious revolutionary background as one of Kalousd Arkhanian's guerrilla fighters. This group was actively pursued by the authorities and eventually had to disband. The Reverend had several close calls but managed to escape. But Arkhanian was ultimately arrested and sent to the prison in Yerznga, where he was still serving time. This fact broke the Reverend's heart, since he practically worshipped his former comrade.

While he was at the farm, I insisted that he pen his memoirs. This proved to be an extremely arduous process, taking up his entire time at Sharabas. When he died just a few months later, those notebooks were given to Arpiar, who edited, arranged, and published them in *Nor Gyank* as a series of installments entitled, "Pages from Contemporary History: The Memoirs of a Guerrilla Fighter."

The poor Reverend suffered a devastating disappointment in the final months of his life, one which may have hastened his death.

While I was in Alexandria, murmurs began to spread in Mansheya Square that "Kalousd Arkhanian had arrived!"

Kalousd Arkhanian! That noble man from Armudan who had sacrificed his life and his fortunes for his people's liberation and who had been wasting away in prison for these many years.

The news travelled fast, hitting Cairo like a lightning bolt. And the Reverend sped immediately to Alexandria.

Arpiar wrote a very moving account of this incident in one of his installments for "Life in Our Times."

Chapter 5

Rural Egypt. Odian worked at a plantation for almost two years.

The Reverend arrives at the station. His voice trembling with excitement, he asks every Armenian he meets, "Where is he? Where is Arkhanian?"

"He's here. He's not going anywhere. Take a moment to catch your breath. You're as white as a ghost. Otherwise, you might drop dead."

"Drop dead?" Oh, every second that postponed his embrace with Arkhanian was the death of him.

"One and the same heart was beating in these two sons of the same land as they fought in the mountains of Armudan. They had gone forward hand in hand as brothers of the light,[*] marching towards the glowing flame that would announce their homeland's Resurrection."

The Reverend is beside himself trying to find Arkhanian.

He eventually receives the address of a *han*. Groping his way up the staircase, he enters a dark room and calls out, "Kalousd, my dear."

A weak voice replies, "I'm right over here."

He walks towards that voice and embraces his Kalousd with the strength of a man possessed. Then, they take each other's arms and walk down the stairs together.

---

[*] From the Armenian, "*lousyeghpayr*," referring to one's companion on the pilgrimage to Jerusalem. (Tr.)

"You're so thin, brother. But Lord knows what you have been through…"

As they reach the light by the door, the Reverend is suddenly taken aback.

This was not Arkhanian.

He was now more heartbroken, desperate, distraught, and devastated than ever. The poor man came to Mansheya Square to tell us about this heartrending misfortune.

"Such a cruel lie! Life means nothing to me now… It was not him."

And he began to weep.

We tried to soothe and console him. We, too, had been fooled. But our deception was nothing compared to his disappointment.

Yet, despite his dejection, the Reverend also felt sorry for the fake Kalousd.

"Such a pitiful soul," he said and told us the story.

That parched, starving Kalousd shows up in Alexandria, finds an Armenian-operated hotel, and orders some food. They ask for his name. He replies, "Kalousd."

"What was I supposed to do?" the poor wretch tells the Reverend. "My name is Kalousd. Was I supposed make up another name? But then I noticed 'Arkhaniants' written next to it. I didn't know why. 'Mr. Arkhaniants this, Mr. Arkhaniants that,' they said and passed me around. They gave me a room, they gave me some food, they made a big fuss over me. They kept calling me 'our comrade' every time they introduced me to someone. I didn't know why. I had nothing to do with these people. But they kept calling me their 'comrade.' A man came to see me. He told me his name, but I didn't recognize him. Not that I know anyone here. He put out his hand and said, 'our hero.' Anyway, I told myself that maybe God was taking pity on me and putting an end to all my misery. Until, suddenly, you showed up. What was I supposed to do? I didn't want any of this."

The Reverend then sighed and said, "Ah, I thought my longing would finally be quenched. But it torments me now more than ever. I cannot stand much more of this. Such overwhelming joy only to discover that he is not the real Kalousd – something deep in my heart has been irreparably crushed."

Sure enough, weary and depleted, the Reverend died a short time later.

***

The appearance of this fake hero was nothing unusual in Egypt. Back then, these sorts of heroes turned up in Alexandria every month. Some people were naïve enough to welcome them with open arms. But these heroes were frauds trying to exploit popular sentiments.

More often than not, they claimed to be one of the heroes who had stormed the Bank.

A friend of mine had compiled a list, by name and date, of everyone claiming to be one of the revolutionaries who stormed the Ottoman Bank. Over the span of two years, their number surpassed two hundred.

Then we got several impostors pretending to be Minas Oghlu, that brave commander who had led Samson and Sivas to great victories, saving countless Armenian lives and arousing the terror and dread of savage bandits.

At one point, after several impostors had come and gone, two Minas Oghlus were left in Alexandria.

They both insisted that they were the genuine article and accused the other one of being a phony.

Whom were we to believe? "Which to keep and which to forsake?"

Many people dubbed them both phonies. But the rest were divided into two competing camps claiming its Minas Oghlu was the real deal. Naturally, the two conmen exploited these passionate disagreements to secure all kinds of favors from their zealous followers.

In amongst all of this, the authentic Minas Oghlu arrived with a reference letter and several official documents that finally put an end to this tedious farce.

The real Minas Oghlu – whom I had the pleasure of meeting – was a tall, slim individual with distinguished features and a modest, dignified bearing.

Contrary to the phonies – who spent their days sitting in the corner of some café, regaling their listeners with their fantastical feats –, Minas Oghlu never discussed his past exploits, despite our persistent efforts to make him talk. Like other such heroes, that man could barely hold a conversation and seemed disdainful of talk.

He was also noble to the extreme. During his long stay in Alexandria, he never once spoke of his financial circumstances. So, we were all under the impression that he had some source of income. But purely by chance, we learned that this man was practically starving. And then we realized that none of us had ever seen him at a restaurant.

The Church tried to offer him some financial assistance. But he declined.

"If you have a job for me, I'd rather work," was his response.

So, he was appointed caretaker of Haig Effendi Ekizleri's farm in Cairo, where, I believe, he remained for some time.

***

Arpiarian was still in Egypt when the first issue of *Nor Gyank* appeared on January 1, 1898 under Levon Pashalian's directorship. He had left Paris and settled in London for the sole purpose of assuming that task.

The first issue contained several literary pieces: a lullaby by Arshag Chobanian addressed to Mother Armenia; an installment of Arpiarian's new series, "Pages from Contemporary History;" a piece by me entitled, "Bloodstained Memories," under my penname, "Vahram;" and last but not least, one of Levon Pashalian's enduring masterpieces, "Christmas" (signed L. Zartoumian).

From the outset, *Nor Gyank* received an overwhelmingly positive response from all the Armenian emigres. The *Hayrenik* of Constantinople was reborn, absent Shahnazar.

Arpiar was over the moon. A longstanding dream – one of the three projects that kept him tied to the Henchag party – was finally coming true.

The Armenians of Egypt gave an especially warm welcome to this journal dedicated to the three stated themes of nation, literature, and politics. And I think that, once the first several issues of *Nor Gyank* had appeared, its collective number of subscribers in Cairo and Alexandria reached three hundred. This was an extraordinary feat for an Armenian periodical.

But there was a day when the entire Armenian community of Alexandria was up in arms, when a veritable crisis erupted over *Nor Gyank*.

What happened?

The October issue began printing a novel with the modest title of *Mardig Agha* and signed with the name, "Barouyr."

The first installment was well-received for its elegant style. And many people were soon curious to know which prominent author was hiding behind that penname, "Barouyr."

Even Arpiar and I were left in the dark, because the text was sent directly to Levon Pashalian. And yet, this was no amateur's work.

"It must be Dikran Gamsaragan… No, Arpiar must be the author… Maybe it's Odian…"

There was a dizzying whirlwind of speculation.

After several more issues, the novel began to depict an Armenian salon in Alexandria, frequented by numerous prominent members of the émigré community. The men as well as women were caricatured in intricate detail. No one was spared. They were all stripped down to expose their most ridiculous attributes. Their faces, bodies, speech, dress, everything was laid bare with utmost irreverence and mischief.

See below, for instance, on how several extremely well-known bigwigs were depicted:

> Sarkis Effendi, the wealthy merchant from Constantinople, and his wife. A very compatible couple. The man is squat and chubby with a massive, craggy head and a stubborn boulder for a brow. A thick drooping moustache, a hooked, suspended nose, and something of the sluggishness, awkwardness, and stubbornness in his physical movements and the cadence of his thick, fleshy voice, which one typically finds among animals that chew the cud. His shoulders provided the frame for his head – not unlike that of an ox –, which nestled like a burden between the gulf of his broad, protruding shoulders.
>
> The woman at his side was his veritable pair: similarly fat, with bloated cheeks, a double-chin, plump breasts that lay like parcels of meat on her distended abdomen, and hands folded over her chest. Her movements and tone have a strangely haughty air of "no one but me." And when she speaks, wrinkles of condescension appear around her lips. A woman who is constantly bragging about herself and her house with the irrepressible boastfulness and upturned nose of a poor girl married to a rich man.

And, another portrait, Kafafian and his wife:

> Yet another fatty, this one. A cross between a bear and a boar. His most protuberant feature was his head – an ample, voluminous head, shaped like a watermelon, attached with his virtually absent neck onto his sizeable, stubby body, which carried the formidable load of his barrel-shaped gut. Bushy eyebrows, a shaggy moustache, a broad, paunchy nose, gaping puffy eyes with bulging eyeballs, a face ravaged with wrinkles, and a voice

befitting of all that. His wife shares nothing in common but his name. That heavyset, brutish pile of corpulence is married to a flimsy bundle of nerves, a body that vaguely resembles a woman, a slightly spoiled beauty, restless, energetic, fluting and flickering around that gross drum, that beast.

And so, one by one, Barouyr describes the notable Armenians of Alexandria with bitter and relentless disdain.

Although the names have been changed, their representations are so accurate that no one could mistake them, and no one could claim to be unmarked by his observations.

A terrible tempest swept through the city. People in every home, café, and park, were obsessed with *Mardig Agha*. Those who had not yet made their appearance in the novel awaited their turn with tremulous hearts. Meanwhile, those who were already caricatured consoled themselves that "their turn was over."

And yet, no one was willing to forgive Barouyr, whose identity remained unknown.

One day during this uproar, I left Sharabas for Alexandria to visit Arpiar. He was preparing to return to London.

The poor man had gotten into trouble over *Mardig Agha*.

Levon Pashalian had discreetly divulged Barouyr's identity to Arpiar, while requesting that he reveal it to no one but me. Meanwhile, Levon Mgrdichian – a Henchag leader – had contacted London to get the author's real name. But Pashalian had refused to divulge it. Mgrdichian had demanded that they stop publishing the novel. Arpiar and Pashalian had resisted. Mgrdichian had sent a telegram with another directive to stop publishing the novel. But they had persisted. In response, Mgrdichian had threatened to resign and withdraw from the party.

What amused us most was that the novel's hero, Sourian, – who was supposed to be a Tashnag – was actually a recognizable Henchag activist. This did not lessen the scandal among party members who were well-aware of what was at play.

As I noted earlier, when I arrived in Alexandria, the Armenians were up in arms. H. Alpiar had almost gotten a beating, when he had recklessly declared, "Only I could have written a novel like that."

The day after I arrived, we were sitting in Mansheya Square when Arpiar told me enigmatically, "Come on, let's go meet Barouyr."

"Why, where is he?"

"I gave him a rendezvous. He's looking forward to meeting you. But you must promise to keep his identity a secret."

I promised, and we went towards Sherif Pasha Street. Then, we took a side street and stopped in front of a confectionary shop called "Zola."

(Arpiarian had a habit of arranging rendezvous at confectionary shops.)

We went in and saw a thin, pale kid sitting in the corner.

"Barouyr is right over there," Arpiar said.

"But, what's his real name?"

Mikayel Giurjian.

We sat down and got to talking. We felt an instant connection, and, over time, our affection slowly grew to become a firm, untainted, platonic love.

As I noted above, Giurjian was a thin, pale kid back then. He could easily have been mistaken for a consumptive.

Mardig Agha gave a description of his features too.

Below is his self-portrait:

> And there was also a 19 – 20-year-old young man, pale, thin, sullen, with cadaverous features. He had a long, sharp nose, curly sprouts of facial hair, the vague shadow of a beard around his lips, and dark ugly brows above his dull, faded eyes. Whether he was alone or among friends, his eyes directed at the sky or at a book in his hands, this kid always paraded the flaccidity of his clumsy silhouette, walking through crowds of people with an uncertain gaze and an ungainly gait. Despite all this, and, to the great dismay of many who thought he was a certifiable imbecile, he had gotten a decent job as a civil servant. His name was Kourchian, a moniker that encapsulated his person and personality rather well.

Nor Gyank's enraged readers had read these lines referring to Barouyr and realized that Kourchian was Mikayel Giurjian. "That wicked boy!" they said. "Who would've expected it from that harmless Mikayel, placid, docile, too timid to break a heart…"

And yet, the scandal around this novel grew so great that ultimately, *Nor Gyank* had to wrap it up by abridging whole chapters. As a result, only about half of it got published. What *Azk* republished several years ago in the United States was this incomplete version.

While I was in London, whenever we felt despondent, Levon Pashalian and I would take out the unpublished manuscript of *Mardig Agha* and read it aloud to amuse ourselves.

The Armenian community of Alexandria never got over their anger at Barouyr even after many years had passed. When his real identity was eventually revealed, Mikayel Giurjian was harassed mercilessly; in fact, things got so bad that, in order to regain some semblance of peace, he was forced to make a public declaration that, "I was simply putting on literary airs by writing *Mardig Agha*. And I have since come to regret all of it."

Chapter 6

Jangiulian in Egypt. – He is eagerly sought after. – "Masked Men." – An incident. – Imprisonment and fine. – The Delegation's decisions. – Diran Arpiarian's homesickness. – He returns to Constantinople. – The Tower of Galata and the Eastern Question. – Dikran Yergat in Egypt. – Khazhag. – Friar Goundzig. – Departure from Egypt. – The desperate Italian. – Mgrdich Portoukalian.

At about the same time, Mr. Haroutiun Jangiulian was released from the Fortress of Akko and came to Alexandria as a political refugee.

His arrival had a powerful emotional effect on all the revolutionaries.

"Jangiulian is back from Acre…"

The new crop of revolutionaries was curious to know, "Who is Jangiulian?"

So their veteran elders elaborated that Jangiulian was a revolutionary; that he had taken part in the protest at the Patriarchate of Koumkapou – the first revolutionary demonstration in Constantinople; that he had stomped on Abdulhamid's portrait; that he had put Patriarch Ashukian in a cab and attempted to take him to the palace; and that he was eventually arrested and sentenced to death, but that his death sentence was commuted to a life sentence.

All this excited the hero-worshippers who began swarming around the new émigré.

And then the Henchags and Tashnags started fighting over him, trying to appropriate the new arrival, to have that hero all to themselves. Jangiulian was a former Henchag, but that was no assurance that he was still a Henchag. And conversions were known to occur frequently in prison. Some men had entered prison as Henchags only to be released as staunch Tashnags, and vice versa.

That is why, with their hearts pounding in their breasts, the revolutionary adversaries were anxious to learn which group their new hero would embrace, and which he would rebuff.

Finally, Levon Mgrdichian, Mihran Damadian, and several other important Henchag activists succeeded in winning Jangiulian over.

And to glorify this victory, they organized a rally – on Levon Mgrdichian's initiative – where Mr. Jangiulian was presented to the public through various speeches – including one made by Mr. Jangiulian himself

— spoken in that uniquely grandiloquent style typical of revolutionaries when they extol their birthplace. Such speeches are still occasionally made in the National Assembly.

But, alas, Jangiulian's Henchag days did not last for very long. One day, we learned that our hero had fallen into Tashnag hands thanks to the efforts of our Baba Kasbari; or, as we called him in Egypt, Mr. Babayantsi; or, as he is now known, Mr. Khazhag.

Mr. Jangiulian was not content with being a docile, discreet Tashnag. On the contrary, he published a diatribe entitled, "Masked Men," where he attacked all the Henchag leaders who had been active during his incarceration and whose transgressions he had discovered strictly by word of mouth from several different sources. Although that pamphlet contained some factual claims, it also levelled numerous unfounded charges. What substantiated them, of course, was his good standing. We all considered Jangiulian to be a man of integrity back then.

I got a hold of that pamphlet while I was in Alexandria. I read it with interest — I sometimes did stupid things like that — and realized that Jangiulian's series of brazen charges included some delusional statements about my brother.

I knew the circumstances of my brother's escape from Constantinople intimately well. So, I could not remain passive to these distortions.

I went to dinner at a beachfront restaurant run by a couple of revolutionaries — Andon Rshdouni and Comrade Vahakn. They were renowned among gourmands for their olive oil-brazed stuffed eggplants.

I told Rshdouni that I intended to demand an explanation for what "Masked Men" said about my brother.

"Don't take it too seriously," Rshdouni advised me. "He wrote some things about me too, but I..."

At which point, Mr. Andon Rshdouni resorted to a somewhat crude expression, which it would be indecorous of me to reproduce in writing.

What a pity that I did not follow that sage advice once I left the restaurant. Mr. Jangiulian was sitting at a table in Mansheya Square. Someone pointed him out to me since I had never seen him before. I approached him, introduced myself, and said, "Mr. Jangiulian, I read your 'Masked Men.' It contains a number of charges against my brother. I also read your introduction, which claims that you can provide both written and verbal proof for the list of charges enumerated in your little pamphlet. I hereby request that you furnish said proof."

"I was in prison at the time and had no idea of what was going on," replied Jangiulian. "When I got out of prison, our comrades told me what had happened. All I did was write down everything I heard from them."

"Which comrade told you the things you wrote about my brother?" I asked.

Jangiulian gave me a name. I forget what it was, Margos or Krikor perhaps. And added, "He told me!"

"Is that man here?"

"No, he's gone. He went to Russia."

"Is that all the proof you have?"

"Yes."

"Well, then, allow me to respond to your proof."

And I raised my hand to slap him. But as soon as I did, Jangiulian stood up and began to scream at the top of his lungs that he was being beaten to death.

A police officer was patrolling the square and sped to the scene. Many of my acquaintances who had been sitting nearby also ran over to us. We were all taken to the Mansheya garrison and questioned. But given the trivial nature of this incident, we were soon released.

But things did not end there. It was past midnight. And Parebashd – who had left Athens for Alexandria – was accompanying me back to the Hotel Bonnard. As we were approaching the entrance, three people suddenly ambushed us from a dark alleyway and began to beat me with a club.

Parebashd rushed to my side. And a huge commotion broke out in the middle of the street.

The police arrived immediately. But not before one of the assailants had already made a swift getaway through an unlit backstreet. Meanwhile, Parebashd, the two other assailants – including Jangiulian –, and I were escorted to the garrison.

"We were wondering when we'd be seeing you again," said the smirking officer.

"Why is that?" I wondered.

"Because these men" – pointing at Jangiulian and his friend – "were following you when I was doing my patrols."

"Well, since you already know that we haven't committed any crime, could you please let us go home?"

"No," he replied. "You must be questioned. But it's too late now, two o'clock in the morning. You'll have to spend the night in jail. They'll deal with your case first thing tomorrow."

Parebashd and I tried to insist. But there was clearly no other way, and we had to comply.

Jangiulian's friend took an American passport out of his pocket and declared that he was an American citizen.

So, he was immediately released. But they led the rest of us downstairs to the garrison's holding cell. It was full of thieves, drunks, tough-guys, and drug-addicts who had been brought in earlier that night.

Jangiulian had a small scratch on his forehead. That was the only injury he'd sustained during the attack and altercation. It was barely visible. Even he hadn't noticed it. But once he was in the holding cell, Jangiulian suddenly noticed that scratch and began to claw at it with both hands. He clawed and clawed until dawn, by which time, this tiny, insignificant scratch grew into a positively bloody wound. And his pretty little mug now looked absolutely hideous with that painful lesion on his face.

Jangiulian faked this impromptu injury to request medical assistance. He told the guard that his wound was unbearable.

So, a doctor stopped by and saw to it that the "wounded man" was transferred to the hospital "for treatment."

Of course, Mr. Jangiulian's epic wound was contrived to cause a huge headache for the rest of us. If the police physician decided that the wound inflicted by us, the alleged perpetrators, needed at least fifteen days to heal, then we would be charged with a criminal offense and tried in the Criminal Court.

Fortunately, this ingenious tactic failed. And the physician reported that, contrary to what the victim of this injured forehead claimed, it was not a club that had inflicted this wound, but rather a mauling.

Regardless, this incident meant that instead of being released in the morning, we had to stay there until nightfall, because we needed to go through the whole interminable series of official procedures and interviews.

It was not until Reyizian Bey vouched for us that Parebashd and I were finally released from jail – and even then, with no shortage of difficulty.

Nevertheless, I still could not shake off this ordeal.

I returned to the farm the very next day. And a month later, I received a court summons to return to Alexandria.

The General Prosecution had charged all of us with "disturbing the peace at night and inciting public disorder."

A return trip between the farm and Alexandria in addition to several nights' stay would have been a huge expense.

I asked Mgrdich Effendi Antranigian for advice. What he counselled me was, "You don't have to go anywhere. They can sentence you *in absentia*. They'll probably fine you a few hundred kurush, but that would still be less than what you would pay if you went."

I followed this counsel and did not reply to the two summonses.

At the trial, the defendants who had appeared in court received a fine of one lira. I, on the other hand, received a two-month prison sentence for failing to appear.

Arpiar sent me a telegram conveying this news.

I had to leave Alexandria the very next day. And I also had to find a lawyer, file an objection to the verdict, and demand an appeal.

I stayed there for two weeks and had to make several court appearances. The prison sentence was overturned, and I was instead fined to pay 400 kurush.

The incurred costs of the trial, the lawyer, the fine, the trip, and various other expenses came to a sum of 25 – 30 liras. But I was finally free of this ordeal. And I swore that I would never again trust anything that appeared in writing – be it in print or handwriting –, especially if it had any direct or indirect relevance to me.

My first retelling of these events appeared in *Jamanak*, where I had been publishing a series of instalments from my memoirs as an émigré. I took great pains to record every single factual detail, without the slightest deviation from the truth. I had set my mind to telling the truth and nothing but the truth throughout my narrative.

And then, lo and behold, what should come out after my publication but the *Memoirs* of H. Jangiulian, where his fifth instalment, chock full of shameless lies, gives a completely distorted version of this same incident.

Many of the witnesses to these events are still very much alive today. And I could have easily proven which of the two stories was true. But I couldn't be bothered with such trifles. I have now given a more detailed account, because this man, who mauled his own face to elicit a harsher punishment for his opponents, dubbed himself "An Eminent Hero." This I could not accept.

If a hero is capable of such "self-sacrifice," then he is also capable of calling black, white and white, black whenever it suits him.

***

I mentioned that Arpiar made his first trip to Alexandria for a conference of Henchag delegates.

That conference was taking place in Alexandria, and all the delegates had arrived. Simon Manigian, the representative from Greece, was among them. I mentioned him earlier.

One evening, I met Manigian for dinner.

He looked content and satisfied that day, despite his usual melancholia. And I soon learned that he had achieved a great feat during their meeting.

"What did you get up to today? It was a long meeting," I observed.

"We wrapped up an important item of business," he boasted cheerfully.

"What kind of business?"

"You're known to have a loose tongue, my friend. I can't trust you with anything."

"I promise to take the secret to my grave. And, if you say the word, even to the afterlife."

"It's not a big deal. It's just that we're sworn to confidentiality."

"That's all well and good. But you can trust me."

Eventually, after repeatedly swearing me to secrecy, Manigian told me, "*Janum*,* one of the agenda items was to take a vote on whether to buy Arpiarian a couple of pairs of flannel underwear and a winter coat. There were 'yays' and 'nays,' and the whole thing grew totally out of proportion. But today, the representatives of Bulgaria and the United States sided with us, and the assembly finally decided to go ahead with the purchases..."

"Are there enough funds in the treasury for that?" I asked in earnest.

"No," he replied. "But Levon Mgrdichian agreed to give us a loan."

---

* Turkish, commonly used to mean "my friend" or "my dear." (Tr.)

"Well then, Armenia is saved."

Some of my readers might be tempted to assume that I am exaggerating, that I am distorting contemporary Armenian history. But all the witnesses to these facts are fortunately still alive and well. And, if need be, they can vouch that my reminiscences are entirely devoid of exaggeration. Yes, I repeat, in 1898, during the Conference of Henchag Delegates in Alexandria, one of the most pressing items on the assembly's agenda was whether to procure a couple of pairs of underwear and a winter coat for Arpiar …

And to think that poor Arpiar had placed all his hopes for the liberation of Armenia on that political party.

Placed his hopes?…

To this day, I fail to make any sense of it. And I probably never will.

I cannot believe that Arpiar was so naïve as to serve a political party that spent several entire days arguing about buying a winter coat and some underwear during its annual conference of delegates.

I found this so incredible that I went against my word to Simon Manigian never to divulge these details. Several days later, when I saw Arpiarian outfitted in a new coat, I could not help but blurt out, "Well now, you have truly liberated Armenia!"

"Pardon me?" Arpiar asked, looking puzzled.

I pointed out his new coat. He was clutching it jealously, like a beloved old friend.

Arpiarian quickly got my drift and replied, "What could I do, Yervant? If I pull out now, then a bunch of madmen will take over. And they'll rush headfirst into decisions that, I have no doubt, will instigate even more massacres. At least, if I stay on board, I might be able to stop that from happening."

He was so right that I was lost for words. It was through just such anti-revolutionary rationales that Arpiar justified his decision to remain a revolutionary until the very end…

Imagine a political leader who, despite opposing his own party, stays on for no other reason than to neutralize its policies.

***

Homesickness…

An illness, which was often evoked in my presence, although I had never met anyone struck by that affliction.

It was not until I went to Egypt that I first encountered a man who had caught that disease.

That sick man was Dikran Arpiarian, the elder of the Arpiarian brothers, who had settled in Cairo. Despite his enviable position, he spent his days dreaming of nothing but Constantinople, and he did everything he could to hasten his return.

We tried in vain to convince him that it would be sheer idiocy to abandon his perfectly good circumstances and return to the inferno of Constantinople. But none of the sound advice and encouragement of his brother's friends and supporters made a jot of difference to him. Dikran Arpiarian had decided once and for all to return to Constantinople.

"I am going to die if I stay here any longer," he repeated over and over.

And it was true that his melancholy made him gloomier by the day. His life revolved around his memories of Constantinople and nothing else. That was the case until the very end. He would go to the Post Office several hours before anyone else whenever the postman from Constantinople was due to arrive. He would wait outside, trying to be first in line so that he could pick up all the correspondences and newspapers sent from Constantinople.

One day, he decided once and for all that he had to leave, regardless of the potential risks.

But he wanted to take some precautions before his departure. So, he consulted with Mrs. Lekejian. He asked that she send her brother, Bishop Ormanian, a letter apprising him of his imminent return to Constantinople and asking for his feedback.

The reply took longer than expected to arrive. Dikran ran out of patience, packed his bags, and left Cairo to take the steamship from Alexandria.

I set out from Sharabas to see him off. Arpiar was also there. We both made another last-ditch attempt to dissuade Dikran, but it was all to no avail.

"I don't care if they send me to a labor camp. I'm going to Constantinople," he insisted adamantly.

Despite that, he kept out of trouble by not appearing with his brother in public. And whenever he would find himself accidentally privy to a discussion about revolutionary matters, he would instantly cup his ears.

"They may decide to torture me in Constantinople, and I may end up blurting out everything I know," he would say.

One day before his departure, Mrs. Lekejian received a reply which suggested that Bishop Ormanian was dubious about his return to Constantinople. He advised him to stay in Egypt.

Not even that letter helped remedy his homesickness.

"I'm going, no matter what," he maintained. And, the next day, I went to wish him farewell as he boarded one of the Khedive's ships. As for Arpiar, he decided to play it safe and stayed out of sight.

As soon as Dikran reached Constantinople, he was taken to the police station. He was jailed there for about two months, until Bishop Ormanian eventually intervened to secure his release.

***

When I returned from the port, Arpiar said, "That crazy idiot! He just couldn't wait another measly couple of months for things to settle down so that we could all go back to Constantinople together…"

This was one of Arpiar's recurring fantasies. He maintained that the Armenian Question would be resolved in a matter of months, and that we would all be able to return to Constantinople triumphantly.

The most insignificant telegram about a trifling political matter could embolden his hope and excitement. That is how he sustained himself. He would draw the most outlandish conclusions from a totally worthless piece of news or a crumb of highly unreliable information.

One day, we were at Mansheya Square, and I had to leave him briefly to sift through the daily telegrams at the Restaurant Louvre.

Nothing of any importance had arrived.

When I got back, I knew full well that Arpiar would insist on knowing what the telegrams reported. So, I decided to make something up, a lie which could not possibly spur any political speculation.

"What's new?" he asked as I approached.

"Nothing, nothing at all."

"No telegrams from Constantinople?"

"There is one, nothing important…"

"Come on, tell me. What does it say?"

"There was a crack in the Tower of Galata. And they are going to use some metal rings as reinforcement to make sure that it doesn't collapse," I rattled off indifferently.

"Really?!" Arpiar exclaimed with a great show of excitement.

"Yes, the tower has cracked. What's so important about that...?"

"Well, if that is true, then it is very important indeed. It bodes incredibly well for our cause," Arpiar enthused.

"You're talking crazy. What does a crack in the Tower of Galata have to do with the Armenian Question?" I retorted.

But Arpiar was already predicting major consequences.

"The crack in the Tower of Galata," he declared, "will put an end to German influence in Turkey and make way for a British takeover."

"But, how...?"

"Just wait. I'm about to explain. You know that the German king visited Constantinople recently. And to mark the occasion, the newspapers announced that the German flag would be raised next to the Turkish flag on the Tower of Galata in honor of Kaiser Wilhelm. Presently, when the Tower of Galata suddenly cracks right after they raise the German flag, the ignorant populace will predictably blame the flag. This will precipitate an upswell of anti-German sentiment among the Turkish masses. And since Abdulhamid is terrified of popular sentiment, he will be forced to yield by reversing his pro-German stance. Meanwhile, Britain, which has been waiting eagerly to exploit any opportunity to reclaim its status..."

And so, Arpiar went on and on for a whole hour, speculating on the potential political outcomes of a crack in a tower. Then he went off to read that news for himself, because he planned to write a commentary about it for *Nor Gyank*.

What a pity that the tower had not actually cracked, and that German influence remained completely intact.

***

Towards the end of 1898, an extremely frail Dikran Yergat arrived in Egypt.

That ruthless disease – tuberculosis – had already advanced, and the poor man could barely walk.

He had spent several months in Cairo and then gone to Alexandria. He had intended to leave for Greece, but he had taken to his bed shortly before his departure.

The Armenians of Alexandria showered that brilliant patient with all the care and compassion they could muster.

Despite being bedridden and the debilitating pain in the joints of his hands and feet, he continued to write for *Revue de Revue*. Those articles inspired great admiration.

His analyses on Turkey were so well-received that France's Minister of Foreign Affairs, Mr. Delcassé, sent one of his aides to ask the *Revue*'s Director whether Hanotaux had penned those articles.

As soon as he had made a modest recovery, Dikran Yergat prepared to leave for Athens after his protracted stay in Alexandria. But, alas, he could not afford to travel in comfort.

Galata Bridge, Constantinople.

That is when an anonymous admirer unexpectedly gifted him with a first-class ticket for a steamship headed from Alexandria to Piraeus.

We later learned that Dikran Gamsaragan was this anonymous admirer.

Yergat's insufferable pain led to months of hospitalization in Greece. He then returned to his parents' embrace in Constantinople. But he eventually lost his battle with that ruthless disease. And he died towards the end of 1899 on the island of Halki.

Dikran Yergat – or Garabed Bilezikjian by birth – was a genuinely extraordinary individual. Unfortunately, today's younger generation never had a chance to know him. And he remains mostly unknown to the Armenians of Constantinople.

He grew up in France. That is where he received his education and took his first steps towards a lifetime of political activism. His first language was, therefore, French. Regardless, the rights of his nation had a profound impact on his intellectual formation. And he burst onto the scene to carry out his exquisite efforts towards that end when the massacres broke out. He began collaborating with various French periodicals while he was in Constantinople. And, as I noted at the start of my memoir, he also had a brief stint as a bona fide revolutionary. He was the one who drafted the memo addressed to the various Embassies in Constantinople, arousing the surprise and amazement of many a prominent diplomat.

One of his close friends, the scholar Maurice Barrès wrote the following words about him in *Journal*: "A prominent writer, a patriot, a young Armenian who signed his many superb articles in the *Revue de Revue* as Dikran Yergat."

At his core, he was a truly formidable writer, on a par with some of the best-known figures of modern French literature. It is a pity that he could only express his talents in French. His Armenian was extremely limited. He started learning it later in life, but he could never fully master it.

He contributed several loving and compassionate pieces for *Hayrenik*'s series, "Childhood Souls," and he oversaw their translation into Armenian. They remain some of the most poignant contributions to Armenian literature.

When he died, Levon Pashalian penned a beautiful eulogy in *Nor Gyank*. I have provided an excerpt below:

> At his core existed a great writer, whose exquisite prose could fill countless pages. But his life was cut too short to reach his full potential. Hardly had he embarked on the heroic task of advancing his nation's cause, when he was seized by that ruthless, unsparing disease. In an ironic paradox, his physical frailty was equal to his inner strength. His chosen penname[*] reflected the true nature of his soul: he possessed a steely, unyielding power. As an advocate of the national movement, he encouraged unreserved, unstinting effort, urging us never to lose hope, never to give in, and never to take our eyes off the great mission ahead.
>
> Our magnificent friend can no longer partake of those hopes. Tender hands took him from Egypt – where he went to alleviate his agony – to Constantinople, whence comes the news of his death. He labored for our cause until his very last breath. The

---

[*] "*Yergat*" means "iron" in Armenian. (Tr.)

Revue de Revue published one of his most recent priceless analyses – "Can Turkey Stay Alive?" – in its July 15 and August 1 issues. Our comrades read all the praise showered on those articles in various American monthlies and referred them to us, unaware that this unknown author was one of their own compatriots.

He fought the good fight at our side. But he, too, has fallen. One of our most precious, irreplaceable men, we shall stoke the agony of that loss for all time to come.

***

I met Khazhag – or as we called him back then, Babayants, the current principal of the school in Psamatia – for the first time in Egypt.

Khazhag was a dedicated representative of the Tashnag party. And although the Henchags had a stronger presence in Egypt at that time, he somehow managed to win everyone over, even some Henchags who became his good friends. He had an irresistibly chatty, witty, and charming personality.

His predecessor's – whose name eludes me – caustic zeal had fomented a great deal of strife within the party, ultimately destabilizing it. This was a man of such unfathomable ignorance that when he noticed a town by the name of San Stefano in Ramle near Alexandria, he assumed that was where the Russo-Turkish Treaty was signed. When Arpiar learned of this, he dubbed him Idiotov and promptly made him the subject of several satirical pieces for *Nor Gyank*.

Coming back to Khazhag, he was a justifiably renowned orator. And no one could find a Henchag to rival him in debates. That is how he succeeded in leading so many into the Tashnag fold.

I believe that Khazhag spent one year in Egypt. He then returned to Constantinople and resumed his work for the revolution.

In the winter of '96, Friar Goundzig – Shahrigian by birth – came to Egypt. He died shortly thereafter. As a gifted boy hailing from Tamzara, he had spent several years studying at the seminary in Armash. Unfortunately, he could not truly accept the Christian faith. So, rather than becoming a phony priest, he chose a well-trodden path and left the monastery once he had completed his higher education.

Shahrigian used the penname Friar Goundzig to publish some of his articles on religious topics in *Hayrenik*. They drew a great deal of interest.

Eventually, once Arpiar and Levon Pashalian had escaped, he succeeded them in becoming *Hayrenik*'s permanent editor.

When Shahnazar went to prison, *Hayrenik* was closed down again – this time, permanently. I went to Constantinople, and Shahrigian stayed here. At that point, he had also joined the Henchag party and was even appointed a member of the Acting Committee.

Shahrigian was already in the ruthless grip of tuberculosis, although he never suspected the speed with which the disease was hastening his death.

Friar Goundzig was a cheerful, smiling, good-natured, honest young man. He inspired everyone's love and affection.

During his brief engagement as a Henchag – a brief but tumultuous time –, the poor soul was overcome with intense anxiety and dread, and his condition worsened considerably.

Eventually, remaining in Constantinople became impossible. He and some of his friends decided to flee. But they lacked what they needed most and above all for their escape: money.

So, our hotheaded juveniles came up with a plan to get their hands on some cash – a plan that was most certainly ill-advised but that was understandably entertained as a viable option under those dire circumstances.

One of them pretended to be sick and bedridden. Another two hid themselves in a cupboard. And the last one went to summon a well-known doctor to treat his friend.

The completely unsuspecting doctor speeds to the designated address. But as soon as he enters the room, two of the guys emerge from the cupboard, and the patient throws off his blanket and jumps down from his bed.

The doctor instantly realizes what is afoot and starts negotiating with the boys. He manages to save his skin with a ransom in the amount of 200 liras.

The five or so young men pocket that amount and prepare to flee Constantinople with Friar Goundzig in tow.

But whereas the others – who were shrewder – manage to board the steamer, Friar Goundzig is apprehended on the docks. He is taken to jail and then to the hospital, where they keep him for an indefinite period of time.

Chapter 6

Once he is able, Hovhannes Shanazar arranges for him to leave on a steamer heading for Egypt. And he is put in the care of the young Henchag, Miss Kristiné.

After a difficult journey, he arrives in Cairo in such a terrible state that none of the hotels offers him board. He spends the night on the streets and is then admitted to the German hospital. He remains there for several months, until he eventually succumbs.

During both his journey from Constantinople to Cairo and his illness, Miss Kristiné devoted herself wholeheartedly to caring for that young man. She never once left his side.

***

After almost two years on the farm, I had had enough. And, one day, I handed in my resignation and left Sharabas for Europe.

I arrived in Alexandria in January 1899. I stayed with some friends for a few days. Arpiar was also there. But he intended to move to London several months after wrapping up the Conference of Delegates.

I left Alexandria for Marseille on the Messageries' steamer, *Saghalien*.

A terribly catastrophic event unfolded on that steamer, which was destined for Marseille. My thoughts often return to the indelible memory of that heartbreaking ordeal. I was traveling in second-class. My roommate was a Frenchman. He had been globetrotting with less than 10 paras in his pocket. He had made a little bit of extra money by selling colorful postcards, reciting poetry, making decorative vignettes out of cardboard, asking strangers for donations – of course –, or making himself a nuisance to the French Consulates.

He had thus succeeded in spending two years traveling across all of Europe, Asiatic Turkey, the Sudan, and Habeshistan on foot. He had eventually made it to Egypt, which he was leaving for Marseille, whence he intended to walk to Paris, where he would supposedly receive an award of 10,000 francs for achieving this feat.

He had met an Italian family in Alexandria. They had also boarded our steamer, although they were traveling in first class. They were a young couple. She was a woman of exceptional grace and beauty, and he was no less attractive.

The French globetrotter – who had availed of their assistance in Alexandria – would not leave their side and eventually introduced me to them.

Odian left Egypt for Marseille on the Messageries' steamer, *Saghalien*.

The couple, who had been married for several years, behaved as though they were newly in love.

The woman seemed extremely petulant and spoiled, making constant demands on her husband. And the latter obliged her every whim with the utmost obedience.

The Italian woman found the Frenchman's wit extremely entertaining. She had him carry on for hours. And, in return, she kept ordering her husband to buy us another round of drinks. Drinks were a wildly extravagant purchase on the ship.

The Frenchman and I did not make too much of it and respectfully indulged in our drinks, since, according to my roommate, the Italian was a man of means.

And yet, one night, the day before I was due to arrive in Marseille, I saw the Italian standing on the bridge. His wife had retired to their cabin. He approached us and, looking agitated, said, "My friends, I must make a request."

"Of course," said the Frenchman.

"If my wife decides to order you more drinks, I would greatly appreciate it if you would firmly decline…"

We were dumbfounded by this odd and tremulously spoken request. We failed to grasp why he should be telling us this.

"We promise from the bottom of our hearts to fulfill your request," mumbled the Frenchman. "Only, I hope you believe me when I say that your words…"

"I know, I know," interrupted the man. "My words must come across as very strange. But I will explain everything."

And the man began to recount his terrible story.

Apparently, he had once owned a factory in Italy. It produced matches, the kind that we would call *Shamali kibrit.** Gradually, in a period of several years, a sequence of failed ventures, unemployment, financial crises, competition, and so on drive the man to bankruptcy. He barely manages to salvage 30,000 francs from that pile of total ruin with which to try to rebuild his life elsewhere. He decides to seek his fortunes in Egypt, where he has some friends from the good old days.

He conceals these series of misfortunes from his young wife, who continues to believe that she is married to a wealthy man.

"My wife delights in the lavish lifestyle of pleasure, recreation, and luxury," he told us. "And I know that were she to discover my ruin, she would suffer terribly. And since I absolutely worship her, I could not countenance such a turn of events. It may have been best, perhaps, to explain my situation to her at the outset. But once I had deceived her in the hopes that I could put my business back on track, I was compelled to keep up the charade."

His former friends in Egypt – who knew about his bankruptcy – turn their back on him. His wife, meanwhile, continues her profligate lifestyle in Cairo. And soon enough, the 30,000 francs are all used up.

One day, his wife finally discovers the shocking news that her husband is in financial need. She questions him.

But her husband denies everything and tells her that she must be misinformed. And, to convince her, he shows her some forged bank statements supposedly revealing his substantial account holdings.

His wife – who had apparently been reduced to a state of sheer panic – calms down and cheers up. But she becomes even more demanding.

They finally arrive in Alexandria with only a few thousand francs to their name. They rent a hotel room for two weeks. And when the man

---

* Turkish name for Damascene sulfur matches. (Tr.)

realizes that they barely have enough left to cover their travel expenses, he immediately purchases two tickets to Marseille.

"After paying for the hotel expenses and tickets, I had barely a few hundred francs left," confessed the man. "I thought we wouldn't have to spend any more money on the steamer. But suddenly, here we are, three days later, and I have spent 60 francs on drinks. I won't have more than a few francs on me when we get to shore. Now that I have revealed my situation, I believe that my request does not seem so strange…"

This story made us both feel so terrible that we had no idea what to say.

I briefly considered paying the man back. But I got the sense that he would be awfully offended. So, I refrained from suggesting it.

"Very few people have suffered so bitterly," the man went on. "If only I had told my wife early on, I could have easily rebuilt a new life. I'm confident, young, healthy, educated. I could have taken up any profession, succeeded, and reestablished myself. But that would have required a period of sacrifice, frugality, and scarcity. And I could not inflict all that upon my wife. It would have been far too embarrassing. It would have been humiliating… I think that if she ever witnessed my poverty, I would lose her love. She would feel nothing but contempt for me. I'm petrified by the very thought of it. I can feel it reducing me to nothingness. I had friends in Egypt who offered me some modestly paid work earning 500 – 600 francs a month. But I could not, I did not want to accept it. My wife believed that she had married a wealthy factory-owner. How could she suddenly be the wife of a petty salaried employee!"

"So, what are you going to do in Marseille?" we asked.

"There is one last semblance of hope," he replied. "I have a rich friend there. He might agree to loan me a substantial amount of capital for a new business venture, one that might generate at least 2,000 francs per month. If that happens, I can tell my wife everything. But under my current circumstances, that would be simply impossible…"

We did not enquire about alternatives were that plan to fail. But he promptly added, "If my hopes turn out to be in vain, I intend to kill myself…"

The Italian uttered these words with such conviction that we shuddered.

We arrived in Marseille the following day.

Before leaving the ship, the French globetrotter and I went to bid the Italian couple our farewells.

Chapter 6

In Marseille for three days, Odian met with Armenian friends and exiles, including the veteran revolutionary Mgrdich Portoukalian.

The young lady greeted us with a warm smile.

"We are staying at the Hotel de Nouailles," she said. "We will be expecting you for dinner tonight."

"I am starting my walk to Paris in an hour," announced the Frenchman. "So, unfortunately, I cannot accept your invitation, much to my chagrin."

"And I am leaving on the express train this evening," I replied in my turn.

We parted from them with exceptionally heavy hearts.

The wife continued to smile as she shook our hands warmly. The husband, meanwhile, appeared too embarrassed to look us in the eye. He felt utterly humiliated by his confession.

When I walked onto the docks in Marseille, I met Kegham Barsamian, whom I had not seen since leaving Constantinople.

We lunched together. And then we went to see the Director of *Arménia*, Mgrdich Portoukalian, whom I was meeting for the first time. I found him to be extremely despondent and disillusioned back then.

I could not believe that I was in the presence of a revolutionary pioneer.

His tone, expression, and gestures exuded profound bitterness. Portoukalian left me with that impression.

Two or three days later, I left Marseille for Paris on the morning express train. I had picked up several newspapers to occupy myself during the trip.

As I began to browse through the pages, I could not suppress an audible cry. In the space of several brief lines, the paper reported that an Italian man had committed suicide. He had shot himself with a revolver. The Italian and his wife had arrived from Egypt several days earlier on the steamship *Saghalien*.

It was our friend the factory owner, whose ultimate hopes were evidently dashed.

Chapter 7

Arshag Chobanian's room. – The enemy of Sahag and Mesrob. – One way of solving the Armenian Question. – Andronik Ianesco. – We leave together for Vienna. – Ianesco's dictionary. – The Vienna Mekhitarists. – Several small incidents. – Rupture. – London. – Mrs. Raffi. – Arpiar in London. – Ohanchan's linguistics. – A duel that does not take place. – The prerequisites for unity.

I arrived at the Gare de Lyon in Paris on a cold, snowy February morning.

The first thing I did was hire a cab and make my way to No. 14 Rue Royer-Collard – an address that Arpiar had given me, where I was supposed to meet Vahé Arzouyan.

Vahé was still in bed when I knocked on his door.

He got dressed immediately, and we went out for breakfast.

I rented a room in the same hotel. At some point or other, all my friends and most of the Armenian emigres in Paris stayed there.

And then I went to see my brother, as well as Arshag Chobanian, Dr. Kololian, Minas Cheraz – in short, all my friends and acquaintances.

Chobanian lived on the top floor of a hotel on Place de l'Odéon, in a cramped, dirty room packed full of books and newspapers.

It was almost impossible to move around in his room. He had at most a couple of chairs. And when a handful of us would get together – which was not unusual –, half of us would have to sit on the bed.

Arshag Chobanian had not started publishing *Anahid* yet, did not have a reliable source of income, and his financial situation was far from splendid. Nevertheless, he persevered undaunted by these obstacles. On the contrary, he was constantly hatching up big plans. And he worked tirelessly every day to achieve them. One of those plans was to publish an Armenian journal in Paris with the Armenian nation and its literature as its focal points. It did not take too long for him to do just that with *Anahid*.

He also worked towards the creation of an Armenian school, an Armenian union, a coalition of Armenian revolutionary political parties, and other similar initiatives geared towards the nation's advancement.

Arshag Chobanian's room on Pl. de l'Odéon was an unofficial meeting point for all the Armenian bohemians. They assembled there almost daily to talk, sometimes even over coffee – that is, if anyone ever got their hands on enough money to buy some coffee, sugar, and alcohol to light the lamp.

Mrs. Zabel Yessayan – formerly, Miss Hovhannesian – Dikran Yessayan, Vahé Arzouyan, Adom Yarjanian – presently, Siamanto – Onnig Kharibian, Vahram Svajian, I, and others usually gathered there.

A few months after I arrived in Paris, Chobanian told me about a strange man he had just met.

"I think he is totally daft. But it was still worth meeting him," he said. "I was thoroughly amused."

"Who is he? Where is he from?" I asked.

"Apparently, he is a Romanian-Armenian. Andronik Ianesco by name..."

And Arshag Chobanian described their meeting.

The minute Ianesco enters his room, he starts damning Saints Sahag and Mesrob to hell, denouncing them as frauds and declaring that those two exalted men are responsible for all the misfortunes afflicting the Armenians of today. Their alphabet caused a rift between Europe and the Armenians. If we had adopted the Latin script instead of Mesrob's invention, we would have joined the ranks of civilized European nations; we would have enjoyed their sympathy and protection just as the Greeks and Romanians now do, and so on.

"To prevent any further harm from Sahag's and Mesrob's evil invention," continued Chobanian, "this man intends to create a dictionary – which he has been preparing for the past twenty years – illustrating how the world's languages branched off from Armenian. Ianesco is convinced that the Armenian Question will finally be resolved when he publishes this dictionary, thereby convincing European scholars that Armenian is the mother of all languages. He thinks Europe will feel an enormous debt of gratitude towards a nation that has given birth to its myriad tongues."

Chobanian added that in a few days, this man would be returning to Vienna to continue his projects there and that, in the meantime, he had requested his help in finding someone to assist him on the dictionary.

"I thought of you. Would you want to go?"

"Of course I'll go," I said.

"In that case, come round to my place tomorrow morning so that I can introduce the two of you, and we can negotiate the terms. Only," Chobanian added, "if you want this to work out and you want to win him

Chapter 7

Paris, the scene of many colorful encounters.

over right off the start, then I'd recommend taking aim at Sahag and Mesrob with everything you've got."

"I'll damn them both to hell," I said emphatically.

Early the next morning, I went to Chobanian's place. We were joined by Andronik Ianesco – or, in Armenian parlance, Antranig Hovhannessian – shortly thereafter.

He was about sixty years old, a thin, sickly old man with an arthritic right leg, the look of a Polish Jewish moneylender, and an extraordinarily enormous nose that drooped down the middle of his face.

He was indisputably hideous, and my first impression was terribly unfavorable.

On the other hand, I could not be too selective, given my financial situation. I had to seize this opportunity.

Chobanian introduced us. I thought that perhaps my name would ring a bell with Ianesco, since I naively assumed that being an Armenian philologist, he would know something about contemporary Armenian literature. But the man was completely ignorant. As far as he was concerned, there were only a handful of Armenian writers: Apraham Ayvazian, who had made a compilation of Ankara's provincial Armenian dialect; Smpad Tavitian, who had published the Armenian terms of Agn in *Piuragn*; and several provincial Armenians, who had prepared similar wordlists for various daily newspapers. To his knowledge, there were no other Armenian writers.

In any case, our meeting got underway. Chobanian pointed to me and said, "Mr. Odian is a fierce critic of Saints Sahag and Mesrob…"

"Those men are our nation's worst traitors," I exclaimed passionately.

Ianesco looked at me in agreement and replied, "It will be our mission to rectify the consequences of their evil deeds, to expose their treachery, and to prove that the Armenian script consists of more or less corrupted versions of the Greek and Phoenician alphabets."

I am, of course, relaying the overall sense of his words. Ianesco spoke an extremely garbled and incomprehensible Armenian, so we had to deduce his meaning.

His native language was Romanian. He had taught himself Armenian much later mainly by relying on dictionaries. So, he would use the oddest terms for the simplest things.

He would say, "wrist bone" for "handkerchief";[*] "work glove" for "glove";[†] "guard" for "waiter;"[‡] "headdress" for "hat";[**] "sandal" for "shoe;"[††] and *"gsba"* for "clothes."[‡‡]

Ianesco explained that as his employee, my responsibilities would be more of a patriotic rather than professional nature. So, I should keep my expectations regarding the terms and conditions relatively modest. The moral compensation would more than make up for the financial shortfall.

Back then, my monetary difficulties compelled me to happily accept any arrangement.

And so, we came to an agreement. I would receive 120 francs per month. He would also cover the costs of my food and board. In return, I would spend eight hours a day working on his philological dictionary.

"Have you made much progress on your work?" I asked.

---

[*] *Tasdarag* instead of *Tashginag*. (Tr.)
[†] *Tatban* instead of *Tsernots*. (Tr.)
[‡] *Poushdiban* istead of *Sbasavor*. (Tr.)
[**] *Pagegh* instead of *Klkharg*. (Tr.)
[††] *Soler* instea of *Goshig*. (Tr.)
[‡‡] This word does not appear in any of the numerous Armenian dictionaries I consulted. The only word that bears some resemblance to *"gsba"* is the verb, *"gsbil,"* referring to the damage occurring to a piece of cloth exposed to but not burnt by fire. (Tr.)

"We're still at Ա,"* he replied.

"But didn't you just say that you've spent the past twenty years on this project?" I wondered.

"Yes, but making a dictionary isn't like eating pudding!" replied Ianesco.

This was his favorite expression. And he frequently said things like, "All you Bolsetsis do is eat pudding."

"So, what you're saying is that you will never be able to finish this dictionary," I persisted.

Ianesco used another one of his favorite expressions to reply, "I can able, young man, I can able."†

He always had an unshakeable faith that "he can able." That faith emboldened him to work tirelessly day and night to create a dictionary, which, twenty years on, had not even gotten to the letter Բ.‡

We agreed to a rendezvous at his room on the Avenue de Versailles the following day. I met him there promptly. His niece was accompanying him. He introduced her as Mrs. Marie Enfiyejian. She was on holiday from Constantinople.

Naturally, our conversation turned to languages, and we spoke of Sanskrit, Avestan, Chaldaic and Old German. We had a mutually good understanding of these languages.

"You seem like a nice kid," Ianesco said in appreciation of my philological skills.

And then he added, "Gather your cassocks,** throw them into your sack,†† and be at the knot‡‡ first thing tomorrow morning."

I surmised that "knot" meant station. So, I met him and Mrs. Enfiyejian at the Gare de l'Est at the appointed time.

Arshag Chobanian and his nephew, Ardavan Hovveyan, came to see me off.

---

* Ա is the first letter of the Armenian alphabet, equivalent to A in the Latin alphabet. (Tr.)
† In the original Armenian *"Gi garnam, dgha, gi garnam."* (Tr.)
‡ Բ is the second letter of the Armenian alphabet, equivalent to B in the Latin alphabet. (Tr.)
** *Gaba.* (Tr.)
†† *Makhagh.* (Tr.)
‡‡ *Hankouyts.* (Tr.)

It was a difficult separation, at least for me. After several meetings with this diminutive man – who was quite simply a dimwit –, it was clear to me that I could not tolerate him for very long. Fortunately, our contract stipulated that should either one of us be dissatisfied with the arrangement, he would pay for my return trip to Paris.

There was another thing, which made me apprehensive. Ianesco was rich. But despite his arthritis, he only traveled in third class, even during winter.

When I commented on this, Ianesco replied, "Imperators get first-class, bankers get second-class, and people like us get a couple of benches."

"But I almost always travel in second class," I said.

"You Bolsetsis grow up on pudding," he replied.

I got the feeling that my boss would be a real miser, and this was terribly distressing. But then I realized that Ianesco was no miser. On the contrary, he was extremely generous when it came to others. But he was always stingy when it came to his own person.

When we arrived in Vienna, I spent my first night in a hotel room. The next day, I moved into his home on Lerchenfelder Strasse.

Ianesco got straight to work. He buried himself in three hundred dictionaries but gave me several days to rest.

Finally, a week later, once Mrs. Marie Enfiyejian had returned to Constantinople and it was just the two of us, we got down to do some serious work.

Ianesco first explained his method for rendering any foreign word into Armenian.

Then, he gave me a Romany-French dictionary written in the Latin script and instructed me to use his method to Christen every word as Armenian in origin.

It was a fairly mechanical process devoid of any intellectual effort.

A month later, all the words with Romany roots had been returned to the bosom of their Armenian forebear.

While I worked hunched over my desk day and night changing Romany words into Armenian, Ianesco hunched over his well beyond day and night, regularly burning the midnight oil or staying up until dawn to convert Arabic words into Armenian. He often fell asleep at his desk, pen in hand, over a partly converted half-Armenian, half-Arabic word.

I refused at the outset to work in the evenings, explaining that my eyes were not accustomed to writing by gaslight.

"I understand," said Ianesco. "You Bolsetsis grow up on pudding…"

But he did not insist and gave me the evenings off after seven.

Yet, I could not take advantage of that freedom, because I did not know German and could not spend much time outdoors.

In addition to working on his dictionary, Ianesco was also trying to reform the Armenian alphabet by simplifying it to resemble – or, more accurately, to be identical with – the Latin script.

Zabel Yessayan.

I was tasked with assisting him on this process of butchering and dismembering the heads, arms, feet, torsos, and backs of our ill-fated Mesrobian letters.

While we were miles away from doing serious, legitimate work, I nonetheless felt some respect for the old man, who ignored all his ailments and steadfastly poured all his energies into completing his project.

In Paris, he had told me that he would be returning to Russia a month after our arrival in Vienna. He had to attend to some business on one of his farms and expected to be away for approximately two months.

"I'll explain everything, so you can continue in my absence," he said.

It was this prospect specifically that had encouraged me to join him. And I waited anxiously for the moment of Ianesco's imminent departure, when I would finally be left alone and in peace.

I would ask him now and then when he intended to leave for Russia.

"I'm waiting for a letter," he would reply.

One day, a letter arrived from Russia. I delivered it to him in high spirits hoping that this was the letter he had been waiting for.

The old man was neck-deep in dictionaries. He put the letter aside, unopened, and continued to write.

Then, he briefly put down his pen to roll a cigarette. And at that moment, he opened the envelope and began to read the letter.

I noticed that his expression suddenly darkened. And I gathered that he had received some terrible news. But I was reluctant to pry.

He read the letter again very carefully. Then he folded it, inserted it back into the envelope, and said, "My whole farm has burned down."

"How can that be!" I exclaimed.

"Yes," he went on. "The losses amount to approximately 10,000 gold rubles."

He lit his cigarette, drew on it several times, and then said with a peculiarly cheerful tone, "Now, I don't have to go to Russia! We can continue our work without any disruptions..."

He picked up his pen and added, "Check the Sanskrit dictionary for the meaning of the word *atavara*."

Ianesco was simply incredible at that moment. What a shame that he was not more serious about his work. His objective was primarily to mislead all the European scholars.

"To blindfold them," as he used to say.

Once the European scholars had fallen for the idea that all the world's languages were derived from Armenian, our work would be accomplished.

As I said, Ianesco was convinced that this was the only way to resolve the Armenian Question.

He too was a revolutionary, in his own way. The difference was that instead of arming himself with grenades or dynamite, he reached for dictionaries to solve the Armenian Question. At least he could not be blamed for occasioning more pretexts to massacre Armenians. But he did massacre the Armenian language.

***

My greatest pleasure in Vienna was visiting the Mekhitarist Monastery, which, as I mentioned, was not far from our apartment.

That is where I met Father Dashian, whom I admired greatly. But I found one thing to be somewhat disappointing: namely, the fact that this magnificent and imposing scholar was a fervent antisemite. His hatred for the Jews rivalled that of the most bigoted Catholics. The Dreyfus Affair was already underway. And everyone was embroiled in arguments about his guilt. In Vienna, where the antisemitic current was especially intense, everyone except the Jews was against Dreyfus. Father Dashian and the entire Mekhitarist congregation were, alas, among his opponents. Whenever I went to the monastery, there were two chief topics of conversation: the Dreyfus Affair and daft Ianesco.

The poor Mekhitarists found themselves in a delicate position vis à vis Ianesco.

Of course, the naive old man held the Mekhitarists in extremely high esteem. And he wanted to attract their interest in his farfetched dictionary.

He did everything in his power to win them over. When I was there, he gifted them with the entire collection of the Larousse Encyclopedia, valued at 800 – 1,000 francs. Moreover, he had willed his entire library – which, if I am not mistaken, was also worth a great deal – to the Mekhitarists.

In return, Ianesco wanted the monks to appreciate his work and even to collaborate with him. This expectation was a little too optimistic.

On the one hand, the Mekhitarists did not wish to dismiss him completely. On the other, they hesitated to discuss the dictionary, whose significance they had gone out of their way to appreciate.

They visited him often and would enquire briefly into the status of his project.

"I can able, I can able," Ianesco would reply. "The section on the letter *U* is almost complete…"

I believe that the poor man was still a long way from "the letter *U*" when he died. And Garabed Pasmachian swallowed all the other letters whole.

Aside from this taxing project, Ianesco also took on the household chores. First thing in the morning, he would grab the broom and sweep all the rooms.

Ianesco claimed that this was a beneficial form of exercise. But the truth is that for a whole month, we were unable to hire any maids, because no one wanted to work for us.

We had applied to several agencies, all of which dispatched several maids over the course of one day. But as soon as they would walk in, they would all turn right back around and flee, yelling, "You're Jews! We don't clean for Jews!"

I would make the sign of the cross to prove, in vain, that I was Christian. But Ianesco's seemingly Jewish features kept giving us away.

And it was a cruel fact that this man, who had found a way to transform all of human language into Armenian, had nonetheless been unable to alter his face to look more Armenian.

Finally, in our desperation, we asked one agency to send us a Jewish maid.

Unfortunately, the day that a daughter of Israel finally appeared at our doorstep, we were in the midst of eating ham. As soon as Rebecca, Judith, or Rachel saw this, she cried, "Oh no! You're Christians!" and fled.

Whenever we went out to buy a dictionary – since Ianesco never left the house otherwise –, we were usually met with hostile glares. We often heard people use pejorative terms like "*Jude*" as we went by. We feigned not to hear that term meaning, "Yehudi."

One day, we went to a bookseller on Stephansplatz looking for a dictionary of Dahomese.*

Ianesco had such an off-putting, down and out appearance that when we entered the bookstore, the apprentice presumed that we were Jewish beggars and tried to turn us out.

Ianesco, who spoke German, hurriedly told the apprentice that we were not beggars, but rather customers who wished to purchase a book.

"Which book are you looking for?" asked the apprentice as he blocked our way into the shop.

Ianesco gave the name of a Dahomese dictionary.

Meanwhile, the shop owner arrived. His greeting exuded nothing but disdain.

When he heard the title, his expression changed to exasperation and he exclaimed, "The book you're looking for consists of three large volumes!"

"I know," mumbled Ianesco, holding his hat respectfully.

---

* This language does not appear in any Armenian dictionaries or other sources. The likeliest candidate is Fon, a language spoken by the Dahomese of the Kingdom of Dahomey in modern-day Southern Benin. Dahomey was well-known enough at the time that the Belgian composer, August de Boeck (1865–1937), had composed his "Dahomese Rhapsody" (*Rhapsodie Dahoméenne*) in 1893. A French grammar and dictionary of Fon or Dahomese was published in 1895, and it is possible that Odian and Ianesco were attempting to acquire a copy of it. See A. Bonnaventure, *Éléments de Grammaire de la Langue Fon ou Dahoméenne* (Paris: Henri Charles-Lavauzelle, 1895). (Tr.)

Chapter 7

Odian was in London for less than a year. He lived in much squalor, like other Armenian exiles and revolutionaries.

"We only have one copy, and it is bound."

"Even better. I was looking for a bound copy," stuttered Ianesco.

"We don't sell the volumes separately. You must purchase them as a bundle."

"I need the whole series anyway."

"Each volume costs 50 florins…"

"Very well."

"Will you be paying up front?"

"Of course."

And Ianesco immediately pulled out his wallet. It was always full of banknotes worth at least 700 – 800 gold rubles.

His thick wallet instantly worked its miracle.

Shocked, the apprentice stepped aside to let us in, and the owner made such a deep bow that he almost snapped in two.

"Do please come in, my lord," he mumbled, bewildered…

We strode in calmly and relaxed into a couple of armchairs.

The dictionary Ianesco had requested was so rare that it took half an hour for them to find it.

Meanwhile, the bookseller bent over backwards to appear as deferential as possible.

We finally made our purchase and left.

Despite being a man of means, Ianesco had clownish habits that often caused a great deal of embarrassment.

Whenever we dined out, the servers would greet us with the customary, "Good morning, my lord," or, "Good evening, my lord."

The patrons would usually nod in response.

Ianesco, on the other hand, would jump to his feet, put down his fork, knife, or spoon, doff his hat, and reply with great deference, "Good evening, Madam."

You can imagine how this exaggerated civility embarrassed all the patrons, especially since this scene would recur three or four times over the course of a single meal.

While Ianesco insisted that I eat and drink to my heart's content, he adhered to the strictest regimen. He always took his meals during the day. This normally consisted either of soup or fish. And, in the evenings, he was contented with several cups of tea, which he preferred to prepare himself.

He never consumed alcohol. And according to his linguistic analysis, "*alcool*" meant "dampness, sickness, contamination, debauchery, etc."

Still, a month and a half in, I realized that I could not continue living with Ianesco.

That senseless work to which we were devoting every hour of every day became absolutely unbearable.

I could tell that being around that eccentric, naïve old man all the time was slowly sapping my good sense. At times, I would find myself believing that I was actually doing scholarly work and that every word in the world was indeed derived from the root, "av," just as Ianesco claimed.

One night, we had an argument about how to stitch the notebooks. (We used to make our own notebooks. Ianesco had a special method for stitching pages using a fine thread and that did not require any knotting. He taught me this method. But I was unpracticed, and sometimes failed in my task.)

That night, none of the notebooks I threaded came out right.

Ianesco complained.

Since I had already run out of patience, I replied a little too curtly. An argument was suddenly underway, one that got more acerbic and caustic as it went on.

"I have had enough of this idiotic project!" I shouted.

But I did not feel that I had gone quite far enough. And I launched into a long lecture telling Ianesco that instead of wasting his life on a project that would turn him into a laughingstock, he would do better to retire into a life of leisure which he could clearly afford.

I concluded my speech by yelling, "You are out of your mind!" at his face.

Of course, I should never have treated him that way. And I regretted everything almost instantly. But after my stimulating life in Paris, being confined with him in the same place for almost two months had taken a toll on my nerves. And I was almost at my wits' end.

Minas Cheraz.

Ianesco did not reply. He realized that this was a decisive rupture. And after a moment of silence, he said, "Our contract already stipulates that if you no longer wish to stay here, I am obliged to send you back to Paris. I will, therefore, pay what you are owed."

And he immediately took out his wallet and gave me the money for my fare.

It was six o'clock in the evening. I went directly to my bedroom, packed my bag, and came out to bid him farewell.

One day, just to seem like a great admirer of his work, I had told him that I had prepared a collection of provincial terms. Ianesco asked to see it. I told him that it was in Paris among my other papers. Ianesco insisted that I write to Paris and ask them to send that notebook. I pretended to write a letter and claimed that I never received a reply.

There I was, holding my bag, almost feeling guilty and definitely regretting my incivility. When I went to bid him farewell, Ianesco stood up respectfully, accompanied me to the door, and said, "If you can able, send me your collection of provincial terms. I'll pay whatever you want."

"I can able," I said and left.

I caught my breath at the Mekhitarist Monastery, where I explained my situation in not so many words.

The monks said, "We figured you'd get fed up with that man pretty quickly."

My greatest wish when I arrived in Vienna was to meet the Mekhitarist Abbot, Father Arsen Aydunian – that extraordinary scholar who had written a critical grammar of the vernacular and to whom every living Armenian writer owes a tremendous debt, one way or another. Unfortunately, that venerable elder was ill at the time, and my wish could not be fulfilled.

On my last visit to the monastery, I again voiced my wish to see Father Aydunian.

"The doctors have proscribed all visits," replied the monks. "All the more so, since the patient cannot help drawing these visits out."

Then, I requested that they at least escort me to his room and allow me to glimpse the great elder through the doorway. Surely, they would not refuse me that. And so, I was able to see the author of *The Critical Grammar* from a short distance as he lay asleep in his bed several weeks before he died.

I went from the Monastery directly to the station and left Vienna that night. I arrived in Paris via Switzerland three days later.

This time, I stayed in Paris for a couple of days, then continued my journey to London, where I tracked down Arpiar and Levon Pashalian.

Need I describe how I looked when the train pulled into Victoria Station, and I walked out onto the sprawling intersection holding my bags?

I had apprised neither Arpiar nor Pashalian about my arrival. So, no one came to greet me.

I showed a policemen the address of *Nor Gyank*'s office.

The man said something in English. But when he realized that I was a foreigner and could not understand a word, he decided to escort me there. Fifteen minutes later, he passed me over to another policeman, who walked with me for a while, before passing me over to a third policeman, and so on like a series of *giro* transfers. Finally, after two hours, I arrived, exhausted and spent, at a small house.

"This is the address you asked for," said the last policeman as he gave me a salute and left.

I knocked on the door, and a young English girl opened it.

She realized straightaway that I was Armenian. She invited me in and led me to the ground floor. This was the location of *Nor Gyank*'s printing house – or should I say with all humility, a dark, dirty, basement, which contained several cases of Armenian type and seemed to be haunted by the wandering spirit of a wan and scrawny typesetter.

I introduced myself and asked to see Arpiar.

"I've been waiting for him as well. He was supposed to bring me some manuscripts this morning, but he still hasn't showed up," he replied.

Mrs. Raffi (Anna Hormouz)

And then he added, "Do you need me to typeset a manuscript?"

Arpiar arrived a little later. He was surprised to see me there.

He had assumed that I had settled in Vienna permanently.

Once he got over his surprise, he asked me the same thing as the typesetter, "Do you need us to typeset a manuscript?"

"No."

"Then why did you come all the way over here?"

We left together to pay Levon a visit. I had not seen him since leaving Constantinople. And then we quickly found a room for me not far from the printing house, on Saint Mary Road, where Pashalian and Arpiar had been living in separate accommodations.

At that time, *Nor Gyank*, a biweekly, was one of several other papers in circulation, including the Henchag party's official organ, the monthly *Mard*. It took a lot of work to solicit manuscripts, copyedit, write out addresses, stuff envelopes, and post everything for both of these publications. The three of us were barely managing. And *Nor Gyank* generated scarcely enough to keep us three and the typesetter afloat, even with the most austere measures to economize.

There was a relatively big Armenian community in London consisting mainly of laborers and students.

The two children of the renowned novelist, Raffi, were among those students. They had settled in London with their mother, Mrs. Raffi, several years earlier. And, I believe, they still live there to this day.

Raffi's home was a central meeting place for the Armenians of London. And we frequently went there for tea.

Mrs. Raffi was a very active woman. And it was practically on her initiative that The Union of Armenian Laborers and Students in London was founded. Its mission was to organize various lectures and presentations to help assemble the Armenians of the British capital in one place. Professor Hagopian was elected as the Union's President, Levon Pashalian as its Chairman, and I as its Secretary.

Members of the Union paid a small monthly fee, which enabled the organization to rent two halls and distribute several newspapers.

I should add that Mrs. Raffi collected that amount for the rooms she was renting to us on the ground floor.

We used to take turns presenting every week. The audience was given an opportunity to pose their questions in response to the speakers' presentations. And these frequently generated valuable debates, which proved to be salutary for everyone in attendance.

I remember giving several talks on Jewish philosophy and crowd psychology. They were well-received.

***

Arpiar lived like a veritable dervish in London. He would retreat into his room at night to write his articles. Then he would get up early in the morning and rush over to the public Reading Room, where he would have to stay standing in order to peruse the newspapers mounted on the bookstands. So, Arpiar would often be on his feet for four to five hours at a time. He had learned quite a bit of English and had no difficulty understanding what he read, but he could barely speak the language. After his reading session, he would go to lunch – if he had the means. Otherwise, he would content himself with some tea, deriving consolation from the fact that he could rely on dinner at Levon's place. Dinner, at least, did not depend on his financial circumstances.

The Transvaal War had been raging during my time in London. Every day, the newspapers reported more losses for the British, who were greatly agitated, very much contrary to their usually placid mien.

Unfortunately, Arpiar's dark complexion, long hair, and broad-rimmed felt hat made him look like a Boer. So, he attracted a lot of unwanted attention whenever he stepped out, especially since he was one of very few disheveled men on the streets of London, and even fewer dark-skinned people.

Kids would shout, "Black man, black man," at him and run away. And be it from patriotism or too much drink, some Englishman would take him for a Boer and wave their fists in his face. They almost beat him up on a train one day.

He delighted in spending his days reading books or newspapers in Hyde Park or Kensington Gardens.

He also loved going for long walks. He would walk every day all the way from our place in Notting Hill to the City just to buy a copy of *Matin* or *Journal*. And this trip would take him four hours.

I had just arrived in London when, one morning, he decided to give me a tour. We went well beyond his usual route and suddenly found ourselves in an unfamiliar neighborhood on the other side of the Thames.

Arpiar, who liked to boast that he knew London like his own pocket – which did not amount to much, considering the state of his pocket – refused to ask for directions back to Notting Hill.

"How can I claim to be a revolutionary leader if I can't even find my way around London," he said.

And we continued our aimless meanderings. Until, by chance, we arrived at a familiar square whence we could easily retrace our steps back home.

When we arrived at Pashalian's place, it was already past eight o'clock at night.

We had walked nonstop for eleven hours.

***

Ardavazt or Artiur Ohanchan was also in London during my time there. I spoke of him earlier in this memoir.

Artiur had married an English widow, the mother of several children, and lived in our neighborhood. He often spent his evenings with us. He had dropped out of the Henchag party, but still took a great interest in its dealings. This often led to heated arguments with Arpiar.

Artiur struggled greatly to earn his keep. Nevertheless, he always dressed like a perfect gentleman, complete with a black suit, polished shoes, gloves, and hat (*haute forme*).

His primary occupation was teaching Russian to an affluent English aristocrat, who was going to assume a diplomatic post in Russia. He also translated various Oriental languages into English. This second job took on a somewhat strange and amusing character.

London hosts numerous translation bureaus for every conceivable language. Let's say, for example, that you receive a letter written in Japanese, but you do not know the language. You immediately apply to one of these bureaus to translate your letter into a language of your choosing.

However, these organizations never employ permanent staff to translate less common languages. Individuals with proficiency in such languages must register at the bureaus. They are then notified whenever an opportunity presents itself. And they are paid an amount that is commensurate with the requirements of the assignment.

Artiur Ohanchan had registered at these bureaus, claiming to be fluent in Russian, Armenian, Greek, Serbian, Bulgarian, Turkish, Persian, and Arabic. The fact is that he was proficient only in the first two and had set his hopes on his friends' assistance for the rest.

Sometimes he received assignments for translations from Arabic, Persian, or Turkish. Ohanchan would come round to ask for our help with his documents. But unfortunately, Arpiar's, Levon's, and my combined knowledge still proved to be insufficient to fully puzzle them out.

One first had to determine whether the document was in Arabic, Turkish, or Persian. Only then could one attempt to deduce its contents.

Artiur could often get a general sense of the contents from the employees by posing a few incisive questions.

"It appears that the gentleman's Arab friend has sent him a letter congratulating him on his recent wedding. He would like a verbatim translation of the letter," says the employee.

That would make our job a lot easier. All we then had to do was to narrate something on the order of *The Thousand and One Nights*, along the lines of, "Oh exquisite, divinely inspired flower of bliss and glory," etc.

And that gentleman would probably assume this was part of Arab epistolary custom and show that letter's translation to his friends.

One day, Ohanchan brought us an antique tray with Arabic engravings.

This was an especially difficult puzzle to solve. All those flourishes made it impossible for us to figure out the words in that archaic calligraphy.

"What could it be saying?" Artiur asked as he anxiously rubbed his brow.

"I think they usually cite phrases from the Koran," replied Arpiar.

That was our solution.

The inscription said, "*La ilaha illa Allah.*"*

The next day, Ohanchan received two pounds sterling for that fake translation.

***

While I was in London, I almost got into a duel with Mr. Minas Cheraz, although, ultimately, it did not take place.

One day, I received a letter from Ardavan Hovveyan apprising me that some strange rumors were going around about me; that word had spread of my meeting with Ahmed Jelaleddin Pasha during his stay in Paris; and that he had probably repaid me for my unrestricted services.

However ridiculous they were, I could not help but take these rumors to heart, especially since I knew full well how easily such slander could spread its roots among our circles.

I immediately asked Ardavan for further details. He replied that Ardavazt Hanumian had relayed the nature of those rumors. He was one of my very close and very dear friends, who had studied chemistry and worked as a teacher in an Egyptian public school. Ardavazt Hanumian is also one of our best poets, although he remains completely unknown to Constantinople-Armenian literature. His poetry only ever appeared in the expatriate press.

I wrote to Hanumian. He replied that the source of this rumor – which he did not believe for an instant – was Minas Cheraz, who had conveyed it to several other people.

As far as I could tell, that must have been the source of the slander. So, I immediately drafted a highly combative letter addressed to Mr. Minas Cheraz. In the meantime, I also asked Dr. Boghos Kololian and Vahé Arzouyan – both in Paris at the time – to confront Cheraz and demand an

---

* Arabic meaning, "There is no God but Allah." (T.r.)

explanation. I told them to challenge him to a duel on my behalf if he failed to provide an adequate response.

There were numerous protracted discussions, until finally, Mr. Minas Cheraz declared that he had heard this rumor from Dr. Robinson. The latter had sworn that he had witnessed my visit with Ahmed Jelaleddin at the Champs Elysées Palace with his own eyes.

I realized that Mr. Minaz Cheraz was entirely innocent in that defamation campaign, although he had been all too willing to believe it by foolishly trusting Dr. Robinson's firm testimony.

And I quickly worked out how that slander must have taken root…

One day, while I was still in Paris – before my departure to Vienna –, I ran into Diran Kelegian along the Boulevards. I had not seen him for years, namely since leaving Constantinople. We embraced and went to a café to catch up.

Kelegian explained that he had come from Constantinople to accompany Ahmed Jelaleddin. They were leaving for Contrexéville on the recommendation of several physicians. The pasha was in Europe to find a treatment for his ailment.

Kelegian told me that Dr. Hekimian – a family friend through my father – was also with the pasha.

He also added, "Your father asked Dr. Hekimian to meet with you no matter what and bring him your news."

"All right, where can I meet with him?" I asked.

"Come to the Champs Elysées Palace in the morning. You'll definitely find him there," he said.

The next morning, I went to the Champs Elysées Palace. Several Turkish political refugees were waiting at the entrance. They probably wanted to initiate discussions or negotiations with the Pasha for their safe return to Constantinople.

Dr. Robinson was among them.

I asked a butler for Ahmed Jelaleddin Pasha's apartment. Kelegian had told me that the pasha was renting an entire apartment of that exquisite residence to accommodate him and his entourage.

The butler led me upstairs. Several Turkish servants were on call. I told them that I wanted to see Dr. Hekimian, and they led me directly to him. And then I went to see Kelegian. I spent about an hour there and then left.

On my way out, I noticed that the Young Turks and Dr. Robinson were still waiting.

I visited Kelegian at the Champs Elysées Palace twice more after that. And on both occasions, I saw Dr. Robinson at the entrance, still waiting for a meeting.

It seems that these visits – which did not even grant me a distant fleeting glimpse of Ahmed Jelaleddin Pasha – became fodder for the ensuing slander.

Here is the funny part. A year later, the Tubini crisis broke out. And France sided against Abdulhamid's government, sending battleships into Midilli to display its willingness to use force. It also expelled all the spies working for the Turkish Embassy in Paris.

That list of spies – which was later printed in London's *Daily Mail* – included the name of Dr. Robinson. Nevertheless, after being escorted all the way to the station, the doctor had worked something out at the last minute so that he could remain in Paris. So, my defamer ultimately received his just deserts.

***

We had been in London for five or six months, when one day, suddenly, Hovhannes Shahnazar showed up and tracked us down.

He had come from Italy, via Geneva and Paris. And so, the entire *Hayrenik* cohort briefly regrouped in London after a separation of three or four years.

Shahnazar had come to London with a special task, namely, to unite the Tashnag and Henchag parties.

This unification of the political parties had turned into something like the quest for the *philosopher's stone* or *the eternal mover*, a quest that many men pursued to the point of exhaustion, but to no avail.

Many both before and after Shahnazar had tried their hand at forging this unification. And they had all failed.

The creed, "let us unite to liberate Armenia" was such a common revolutionary refrain that, one day, Souren Bartevian, made the following plea in *Vaghvan Tsaynu*: "For the love of God, would you please unite and liberate us from your lot already."

One should add that back then, Bartevian was not a *Hunchag* or a *Reconstructionist* or a *Constitutional-Democrat* or a *Resigned Constitutional-Democrat* or a *Tashnag*, where the "Current" eventually carried him.

But Shahnazar was not on a revolutionary mission. He was neither Henchag nor Tashnag, but rather, a patriot, who wanted to perform a good deed – an innocent pretension harbored by many a patriot.

It seems that he had first stopped in Geneva to get a better sense of the mood in the Western Bureau.

The Bureau was only too willing to unify, provided that its conditions were met. Only then, and, in the name of patriotism, would it risk any sacrifice to bring that unification about.

Shahnazar had communicated those conditions in London. The priorities included the following:

a. Arpiar's withdrawal from the party

b. Vahé Arzouyan's withdrawal from the party

c. The cessation of all Henchag publications in London

d. The elimination of the name, "Henchag," and the resumption of all activities under the "Tashnag" banner

Clearly, what the Tashnag party meant by unification was actually assimilation.

Need I add that no such unification occurred? Shahnazar left London for Manchester.

While in London, Shahnazar apparently thought he would be returning to Paris fairly quickly – presumably on the assumption that the discussions for unification would be successful. Accordingly, he had purchased a return ticket.

He held on to that ticket when he decided to stay in England. I thought it would be a shame to waste it, so I took it off his hands and left London for Paris.

Chapter 8

The Armenians and the Dreyfus Affair. – French fervor and British sobriety. – Guidon Lusignan and his dictionary. – The Prince's medals. – A lucrative trade. – Miss Marguerite. – The various branches of the Lusignan tribe. – Prince Vitanval. – Queen Wilhelmine of Holland and the Melusinian sash. – The open-mindedness of Prince Lusignan. – The Egyptian-Armenian knight. – Rupture and trial.

I returned to Paris during the most heated period of the Dreyfus Affair.

Every day, there were demonstrations, disturbances, and beatings in the streets.

We Armenians almost unanimously supported Dreyfus, but we were also cautious about taking part in demonstrations, because the French government immediately deports any foreigners who interfere in its domestic affairs. But several Armenians were beaten by the mobs for raising their voices in defense of Dreyfus.

At the time, there were more than a hundred Armenian street vendors making their living selling pistachios and *cacahuetes* (American peanuts). Among them were graduates from Getronagan, revolutionary activists, former terrorists, future members of parliament, explorers, and so on. They earned ten to fifteen francs per day for that work. The Jews got into that line of work later as well, but the Armenians had invented that occupation.

The French, who were not in the habit of snacking in cafes, eventually warmed up to the idea. *Cacahuetes* even began selling out. Some French ladies bought dozens of packets just to feed their parrakeets.

But one day, a nationalist newspaper printed an editorial claiming that the *cacahuete* sellers were all Jews, and it urged people to stop buying from them.

In that hotly anti-Dreyfus environment, this piece was instantly effective. As though losing customers wasn't bad enough, now the general public was hurling abuse at the vendors.

Many of them were friends of mine. They brought me their grievances and pleaded with me to find a solution.

I went to *Libre Parole*'s office and met with Edouard Drumont. I explained that the *cacahuete* vendors were Armenian – in other words, Christians who bore no resemblance to the Jews apart from their noses.

Edouard Drumont – a hotheaded Catholic and a fervent antisemite – was, nonetheless, a great Armenophile, who always defended our cause against Abdulhamid.

He was profoundly sympathetic and took my complaint on board. The very next day, he printed another piece rectifying the error and urging people to stop insulting the *cacahuete* sellers, who belonged to a martyred Christian race.

That put an immediate stop to all the persecution…

***

One night, a rally in support of Dreyfus was held in the grand Freemason auditorium on the Rue Cadet. Pressensé, Pierre Quillard, and several others were expected to speak.

Many Armenians attended the event. They knew that Quillard would mention the Armenian massacres in his speech.

After the rally, the dispersing audience was met with a huge and vociferous anti-Dreyfus mob outside.

I was exiting with Setrag Ambarian. The speeches had left a profound impact on him. So, he could not hold himself back and roared, "*Vive les Youpins!* [Long live the Jews!]."

Not even the most fervent Dreyfus supporters were that audacious back then.

Sure enough, twenty or so enraged antisemites began rushing at us from across the road, waving their batons.

I, who had wisely held my tongue, was about to suffer the consequences of my friend's unwarranted display…

Driven by an instinct for self-preservation, I lunged at Setrag, slapped him twice across the face, and yelled, "*Sal juif!* [Dirty Jew!]."

This was followed by the proverbial "*Vive l'armée!* [Long live the army!]" at the top of my lungs.

My somewhat roguish tactic saved my skin. On the other hand, Setrag suffered several blows to his head.

Gradually, the majority of people became Dreyfus supporters and dominated public discourse. And we could finally read newspapers such as *Aurore* and *Droit de l'Homme* out in the open, on the streets or in cafes.

Until then, we had to exercise extreme discretion to avoid coming under suspicion.

It is difficult to imagine the violent fanaticism to which that affair had driven one segment of the French population.

By contrast, in England, such scenes would simply not occur under any circumstances.

Even in the most highly polarized situations, the British do not lose their cool.

While I was in London, I and Pashalian or Arpiarian would often spend our Sundays in Hyde Park. Confrontations were common between opposing political parties or the representatives of hostile denominations. Yet, they never erupted into out and out violence.

There were Methodists, Anglicans, Evangelicals, Sabbatarians, Presbyterians, and the Commander of the Salvation Army. Each would take his turn standing on a chair to deliver a series of disputations and criticisms. All this was done face to face and with perfect composure. The assembled crowd, meanwhile, listened intently with a similar show of equanimity.

One day, an American atheist was among those religious preachers. He stepped up to a small pulpit – which he had brought – and loudly proclaimed, "There is no God! There is no God! There is no God!"

He instantly caught the attention of several Protestant pastors as well as the congregation, which had assembled to hear the various sermons.

Again, the man proclaimed, "There is no God…!"

"But what sort of proof do you have?" asked one of the Protestant pastors.

"I shall provide proof without delay," replied the atheist and took out his watch.

He presented his watch to the congregation and said, "Behold! It is ten past ten. I shall give God – if he exists, that is – until twenty past ten – that's ten minutes – to show himself and strike me down on this very spot…"

He put his watch on the pulpit, folded his arms smugly, kept one eye on the minute hand, and waited.

The assembly kept still and calm.

When the ten minutes were up, the man announced triumphantly, "There you have it, you see? God does not exist! I've shown you my first proof. Now, let's get started on the other ones…"

He went on for a full hour, refuting every one of the assembly's beliefs and convictions.

And not one person attempted to silence the speaker.

There was another occasion, when the Boers were trouncing their enemy, and every British patriot felt the painful sting of temptation. An English orator spent two hours telling a thousand-strong crowd in Hyde Park that the British had lost every battle they had ever fought, except for a few measly victories over some savage Zulus and Sudanese dervishes, etc.

The crowd listened patiently. Only one man spoke up to say, "I believe that we did subdue the French during the Battle of Trafalgar…"

"Thanks to some blind luck and the French navy's incompetence," replied the unyielding critic.

Imagine a Frenchman insulting the army or navy in a time of war, or even peace. He would be beaten to a pulp within seconds.

I have noticed another contrast in their national dispositions.

Whenever throngs of people clogged the streets of Paris during major congestion, they would deploy thousands of policemen to maintain order. And when there seemed to be too few street patrollers, they would even send in the mounted police. Whereas, in London, one rarely saw more than a few dozen policeman among hundreds of thousands of people.

For several months during the Transvaal War, Queen Victoria holed up in Windsor Castle and avoided going into London. The Queen's visit to London was announced only once the British had broken their series of losses with a major victory.

On the day of her visit, innumerable crowds flooded the procession route from Paddington Station to the Royal Palace. The streets were so full that the coaches and trams had no room to operate.

There was no military or police presence. And when the Queen's carriage came into view, guarded only by two cavalrymen, the crowd parted spontaneously to make way for the royal cavalcade.

There were no accidents, incidents, or fights in that enormous turnout of more than one million people, according to some newspaper reports.

By contrast, in Paris, such occasions – including the funeral of President Félix Faure or the visits of Colonel Marchand and the Transvaal President Kruger, both of which I attended – always involved collisions, accidents, and even deaths, despite widespread police measures.

***

Shortly after my return from London to Paris, I met Mr. Dikran Doghramajian – or as we called him, Dikranig Agha – in a restaurant one evening. He was the chief typesetter for Prince Guidon Lusignan. And he asked me, "Would you like to be Prince Lusignan's secretary?"

"What would the job entail?"

"Working on a French-Armenian dictionary and proofreading the drafts."

"What else?"

"Responding to correspondences from His Royal Highness."

"Does he receive many correspondences?"

"Scarcely a few every month."

"Where would I work?"

"In his villa, where you would be given special accommodation."

"All right, I accept the offer."

"In that case, we will go meet him together tomorrow morning, so that we can finalize the terms and conditions."

It was going to be my first audience with Prince Lusignan. Although I had often heard of him, I never had the opportunity to meet him.

In the morning, Dikranig Agha and I proceeded to the Prince's residence on the Avenue de Neuilly.

It was a two-story flat of about six rooms in a large building.

Leading into the building was a small garden consisting of several trees.

A wooden sign announcing "Villa Lusignan" hung above the garden gate.

The Prince's office was located off the garden through a connecting door.

Dikranig Agha led me that way into the office where the elderly Prince was seated at a large but modest desk.

When we entered, a fair-haired young woman – quite lovely and full-figured – was administering his medicine in a cup.

I later learned that this woman was Miss Marguerite de Beaudoin, the Prince's secretary, housekeeper, cook, Keeper of the Seals, and Chancellor.

It did not take long for us to agree upon the terms and conditions, and I began my employment the very same day.

The Prince had prepared his French-Armenian dictionary in 1876, but it was still just a draft. Only after receiving a generous contribution from Mrs. Lambert to underwrite the whole project did he initiate its publication. This required thorough revision, which we would undertake together.

Before me, the Prince had employed several other secretaries of both sexes, among them Mrs. Arshagouhi Teotig, Mrs. Zabel Yessayan, Mr. Hrachya Ajarian, and so on.

When I met him, half of the first volume was already in print, and the second half was already complete. So, we began revising the second volume.

It was a mechanical process that needed minimal mental effort. And I quickly got the hang of it, especially since it was a much more intelligent project than Ianesco's.

The Prince had been using several sources to prepare his dictionary, including Flammarion's eight-volume encyclopedia – which contained the etymologies of French words and listed their Latin or Greek roots –, as well as Norayr's, Nubarian's, and Demirjibashian's dictionaries, Alishan's botanical dictionary, and Kachperuni's two-volume scientific dictionary.

Although the Prince had no philological training, he demonstrated extraordinary discernment and expertise in rendering his elegant neologisms, many of which can still be used today.

That illustrated, costly publication was financed entirely by, as I mentioned earlier, Mrs. Lambert, to whom the dictionary is dedicated.

Apparently, that Lady was a friend of Princess Marie, namely the wife of Prince Lusignan, who was many years deceased and whose watercolor portrait decorated the villa's reception hall.

The Prince had lived a most eventful life. He and his brother received their education in the monastery in Venice, where they were ordained as the priests Ambrosios Kalfayan and Khoren Kalfayan. The brothers had accompanied the teacher-monk, Gabriel Aivazovsky, to Paris, where he was to run the Mouradian School. And then, all three had quarreled with the Mekhitarist Congregation and returned to the bosom of the Armenian Church. But, whereas Aivazovsky and Khoren Kalfayan had remained priests, Ambrosios had tossed his calpac away and become Mr. Kalfayan.

During that time, he had met the mistress of a very wealthy baron and become her lover.

Ambrosios and his brother had eventually changed their last names to Narbey and then to Lusignan. And he had changed his name, Ambrosios, redolent of the priesthood, to the more noble-sounding, aristocratic moniker, Guidon, in addition to dubbing himself Prince.

Upon his death, the old bachelor baron had left all his fortunes to his young mistress.

At this point, the mistress marries her lover and becomes Princess Marie Lusignan. Thanks to her fortunes, the married couple adopt a truly aristocratic lifestyle in Paris, eventually building an illustrious circle of relations.

The Princess had inherited an enormous house from the baron. Victor Hugo was her tenant. And the Lusignans had therefore gotten to know him intimately well. Princess Marie – youthful, beautiful, intelligent, and an incredibly talented pianist – had charmed the great French poet, and the Prince and Princess often attended his literary evenings. After Victor Hugo's death, the government purchased his residence from the Lusignans and, I believe, transformed it into a museum dedicated to the renowned poet. It also renamed that street Avenue de Victor Hugo.

To prevent their brilliant royal name from falling into oblivion – *la noblesse oblige* –, Princess Marie had lavished her wealth on various philanthropic and religious organizations as well as on expensive functions. As a result, at her death – Marie had died more or less young –, she had not been able to leave very much behind.

It was said that she had bequeathed her remaining wealth entirely to her son, whom she had conceived with the baron and whom Lusignan had adopted and legitimized with his own royal name. However, the Princess had obliged her son to pay the Prince a monthly allowance until the end of his life. Lusignan's primary income was that monthly allowance.

When I met him, he was leading an extremely modest lifestyle. His only luxury was a one-horsed carriage which he took out for visits and excursions.

But, apart from that fixed income, he also generated a round sum from trading in medals and decorations of honor.

There were two categories: the "Order of Melusine" and the "Order of Mt. Sinai and St. Catherine." The former was meant for members of royal or aristocratic families; and the latter was granted to common mortals. Melusine was the guardian spirit of the Lusignan line. The other order was born from a tradition according to which the Lusignans had founded the Convent of St. Catherine on Mt. Sinai.

Like all self-respecting orders of honor, these were divided into five ranks.

It might seem strange to the reader to learn that it was commonplace for both Frenchmen and foreigners to submit requests for medals of honor and other such decorations.

By law, the sale of such decorations constituted extortion. So, the Prince avoided doing business with Frenchmen or would simply bestow them as gifts. But it was a different matter with foreigners. Hailing from distant lands – usually emigres from South America, Egypt, or Africa –, they could not jeopardize the Prince, all the more so, because everything was orchestrated expertly.

Let us say, for instance, that an Argentinian *rasta*[*] who adores such decorations pays the Prince a visit. The coachman, Basil, opens the gate and asks almost too deferentially, "What can I do for you, sir?"

"I desire a meeting with His Highness the Prince."

"Have you already requested an audience with him?"

"No, sir."

"In that case, I regret to inform you that the Prince cannot receive you. Kindly take heed of the above notice…"

And Basil duly shows the man the above disclaimer, "Requests to meet with the Prince must be made in advance and in writing with an explanation as to the purpose of the visit."

"I apologize. I was not aware," he replies. "I shall do as I am bid. Farewell."

---

[*] Spanish, short for "*rastacuero*," meaning nouveau-riche. (Tr.)

"Farewell, sir."

The next day, a letter arrives in more or less the following tone: "Having heard my Argentinian compatriots, who have had the honor of being admitted into St. Catherine's Order of Knighthood, speak of Your Royal Highness with such profound awe, I wished to take advantage of my stay in Paris by requesting an audience with Your Royal Highness in order to express my deepest reverence. I hope that Your Royal Highness will not deny me this favor."

There is no ambiguity about the man's true intention, which is to submit a request for a medal of honor.

Miss Marguerite replies accordingly and grants him an appointment on behalf of the Prince.

When the Argentinian raps the garden gate the next time, Basil swiftly invites him in and escorts him to the Prince's office. Miss Marguerite greets him there soon thereafter, introducing herself as, "The Personal Secretary of His Highness, de Beaudoin."

The man bows so deeply that his head nearly touches the floor.

"Although the Prince is feeling somewhat ill today, he will nonetheless receive your visit," she explains.

"I am much obliged, Miss."

"I should add that the doctor has proscribed long, exhausting conversations. I would therefore like to request that if you have a specific message for His Highness, you relay it to me…"

The man replies somewhat flustered, "The thing is, Miss, I was encouraged by the goodwill he had shown some of my compatriots to request a favor of him…"

"What sort of favor? It is important, sir, that you tell me."

"I would like to request a knighthood in the Order of St. Catherine."

"I do not believe that the Prince will have any reservations compelling him to deny you that request, especially if you can provide letters of reference from our knights."

"Of course I can, Miss."

The man removes several letters from his pocket and hands them to the young woman.

"Of course, these are worth a great deal," continues Miss Marguerite. "But they will not suffice. There are a number of formalities that must also be observed."

"What sorts of formalities? I am prepared to fulfill all the requirements."

"First, you must present your request for a medal of honor in writing. You must attach a short biography presenting the accomplishments for which you feel entitled to receive admission into the Lusignan knighthood."

After this preliminary meeting, he is escorted to the adjoining reception hall, where the Prince has already made himself comfortable in an armchair.

Marguerite performs her routine as mistress of ceremonies, briefly introducing the visitor and explaining the reason for his visit.

The Prince enquires after his knights in Argentina, and the meeting concludes.

"I believe you left a good impression on His Highness," whispers the young woman as she escorts the visitor to the door.

"Do you really think so, Miss?"

"I am absolutely certain of it. Do send the request soon, and I will see to it that it is fulfilled."

"Oh, Miss, I am eternally grateful."

The petitioner leaves, and a few days later, he returns to submit his request along with a biography introducing himself and listing all his admirable achievements and attributes – such as being a devout Christian, protecting orphans and widows, putting his own life at risk to rescue two children from a fire, fighting a duel to defend a maiden's honor, his military feats, and so on.

Some days later, the man receives another letter from Miss Marguerite, composed in the following tone:

> The Chancery of His Royal Highness has the honor of informing you that it has submitted your petition and all attached documents to the Prince's review. And His Highness has graciously accepted the petitioner's request.

In conveying this happy news, we also request that you appear on such and such a day at such and such a time at the villa of His Highness to finalize the outstanding formalities.

The medallion collector makes yet another trip all the way to the Avenue de Neuilly, in a neighborhood outside the city center and well beyond the Paris gates.

Marguerite greets the visitor alone and announces the same news verbally, hastening to add, "Although the Prince tends to be very selective regarding medals of honor, he has nonetheless made a very rare exception in granting his approval, thanks to the references that you had procured from his other knights."

"May I be so presumptuous as to request admission into the Order of Melusine?" asks the man timidly.

"I am afraid that would be impossible. That honor is granted exclusively to members of royal families with an ancient lineage. The Prince even refused to approve the application of King Alexander of Serbia, despite his countless attempts, objecting that his lineage simply did not reach back to the Crusades…"

Arshagouhi Teotig.

Marguerite rolled out such grandiosity so easily and spontaneously that it was impossible to question her honesty.

And she continues, "Therefore, I am afraid that you will need to wholly resign from the idea of the Melusinian order."

"Very well, then. Since that is impossible, I will be most contented with the order of St. Catherine of Mt. Sinai. However, I do wish to obtain admission into the highest rank."

"The highest rank? Yes, why not. But that rank requires significant responsibilities."

"What sort of responsibilities, Miss?"

"Naturally, you will be knighted for your qualities and not in return for any financial contributions. But, in principle, you must make a gift to the convent of St. Catherine on Mt. Sinai, since you will be named that institution's Knight-Protector."

"I will gladly submit that gift as an expression of my sacred duty."

"We have no doubt that you will. Presently, dear sir, the value of the gifts is determined according to rank. If you enter the highest rank, you must pay a sum of 2,000 francs to the convent, where more than 400 maidens currently reside…"

"Two thousand francs!" exclaims the man.

"Yes, sir. But why insist on the highest rank? You may request a lower rank, and you will still attain the title of a Lusignan knight."

"What are the other ranks worth?"

"The second rank requires a gift of 1,000 francs; the third, 500; the fourth, 300; and the fifth, only 200."

The man rubs his brow as he briefly gives it some thought.

"Would it not be possible to enter the second rank for 500 francs?" he finally asks.

"That would be impossible, sir. That amount is not deposited into the Treasury's account and we, therefore, cannot offer a discount. It will be transferred directly to the convent on Mt. Sinai."

If the prospective knight happens to be rich and generous, he makes no objections and consents to "paying" the named sum. Otherwise, he tightens his resolve and starts to haggle. He stubbornly resists giving more than 800 francs for a second-rank knighthood.

The moment has arrived to seal the deal.

"I do not have the authority to make a unilateral decision, but I will relay your request to His Highness," says the experienced young woman.

She disappears momentarily and returns to tell him, "The Prince has accepted your offer. However, so as to offset any potential shortfalls affecting the convent situated under his auspices, he instructed me to contribute 200 francs out of his own coffer."

And so, for all intents and purposes, the Prince appears to be not only innocent of receiving payment for the conferred knighthood, but rather even generously out of pocket.

After repeatedly expressing his gratitude, the man takes out his wallet and places the 800 francs on the table with one more question, "When may I receive the edict of knighthood?"

"When the Prince admits you into the order," Marguerite replies seriously.

"Meaning?"

"We will convey the time and place in writing. I should add that you must appear in formal, namely black-tie attire on that day."

"Naturally, Miss."

The man leaves. And several days later, he receives an invitation to attend the "conferral ceremony."

That day, Prince Lusignan greets the prospective knight in the great hall, donning the sashes of the orders of Melusine and St. Catherine of Mt. Sinai, in addition to several Russian, Romanian, and French medals of honor.

Soon, Miss Marguerite enters holding a silver tray carrying the edict. She appears profoundly solemn as she presents it to the Prince.

The knight-to-be follows their instructions and kneels.

At this point, the Prince takes the edict from the tray and addresses the novice with a series of grave pronouncements enumerating the duties of a Lusignan knight. The man kisses the Prince's hand and with a show of profound reverence, accepts his edict.

That concludes the ceremony.

The man has attained his dream and become a knight of the Order of St. Catherine of Mt. Sinai.

But there was one more thing. He had received the edict, but there were no decorations as yet.

He parts from the Prince and as Miss Marguerite is showering him with congratulations, the novice knight mumbles, "But, Miss, I believe that the Prince forgot to confer the medal along with the edict…"

"No, sir. Nothing has been forgotten," Marguerite replies with a lovely smile. "The Prince grants edicts. If you would like to receive a decoration, you will be able to do so by presenting this edict."

"Where may I obtain one?"

"I will provide you with an address. But you must make a special payment."

"A special payment! But haven't I already paid what was due?" the man complains.

"Meaning that you contributed a gift to the convent of St. Catherine, whose difference the Prince made up. And the Prince also freely granted you with knighthood. How can you expect him to simply give you the decoration? ... One must understand that the Prince is not a reigning prince. His estates in Cilicia, Antioch, Jerusalem, Cyprus, and so on, were seized from him. Under these circumstances, how can you expect him to shoulder such exorbitant expenses? As for the medal, you may purchase it from Mr. So and So... My Chancery does not occupy itself with such services and has no share in those transactions."

"And how much is a medal worth?"

"A second-rank medal of honor for the order of St. Catherine of Mt. Sinai costs 50 francs, I believe."

The man then takes the medallion dealer's address and sets off to see him.

Do I need to underline the fact that the Prince was making respectable profits from his medallion business?

Of course, this transaction did not always go as I have described. But usually, the bargaining process would take place more or less in the same fashion with some minor differences.

Prince Lusignan had secured a considerable annual income from this ingenious medallion scheme. And I must confess that if those sums were not transferred to St. Catherine of Mt. Sinai, they were all nevertheless spent on gifts.

Whoever made an appeal to the Prince never left emptyhanded. They received at the very least a quarter of the requested amount. And this did not only apply to Armenians. Numerous French men and women would appeal to his coffer, and he would contribute as much as possible to every one of them.

In addition, he had also allocated contributions to several French newspapers, which ostensibly protected the royal interests of the Lusignan clan and occasionally demanded that Cyprus and Antioch be returned to Prince Guidon.

One of these newspapers also protected the interests of Napoleon, because it could not sustain itself solely on demanding the return of Cyprus to the Lusignans. That paper – which was published in Bordeaux – was a weekly called *L'Aigle*. Every issue contained a passage in support of Prince Lusignan. One day, it attacked the Austrian kaiser, proclaiming that Franz-Josef had no right to list "King of Jerusalem" as one of his many titles, because it officially belonged to the Lusignan line, a royal lineage, whose last living descendant was Guidon Lusignan – that valiant nobleman who awaited an opportune moment to draw his sword from its sheath and defend his rights on the strength of his honor.

On another occasion, it attacked the British government, calling it a thief and a predator for its occupation of Cyprus. By law, the island should have been returned to Guidon Lusignan, who was its rightful heir through the generations. "But," the subsidized paper added, "England should know that thousands of Lusignan knights are watching and will not allow the knavish Albion to rest its paws on the estates of the valiant Prince." More often, it took aim at Abdulhamid, who had deposed the Prince of Cilicia and the Taurus Mountain range …

"Draw your sacred sword and march forth!" it urged Prince Lusignan. This was at a time when he was struggling to stay alive. He could only breathe thanks to a nargileh-like contraption that administered oxygen through a tube.

Down-and-out French poets – much like the genius, the down-and-out poet has no homeland –, often received gifts in the amount of 40 – 50 francs in return for their interminable epics. These depicted Prince Lusignan leading his knights to fantastical victories against no less fantastical foes.

Marguerite read these rhapsodies aloud to the Prince, commenting with feigned childish gullibility, "*Mon petit prince, est-ce que vraiment vous avez fait tout cela?*" (My little prince, did you really perform such deeds?).

"Perhaps," the old man would reply solemnly.

I derived much amusement from the fact that many of Guidon Lusignan's French acquaintances believed he was an actual Prince; that, after a fierce battle – against Abdulhamid, of course –, he was forced to abdicate his throne and take refuge in Paris – where all dethroned sovereigns eventually settled.

The elderly Marquises or Baronesses who visited him regularly would ask with fluttering hearts, "Any news from the enemy?"

Abdulhamid was "the enemy." Those poor souls believed that the dethroned Prince had been at war with that tyrant for the past twenty years.

Lusignan salvaged the situation by proffering some ambivalent response or other, and thus perpetuated their delusions.

How those aristocratic hags would urge him on with their heartfelt exhortations.

"Dear Prince, you must not lose heart. God is on your side," they would repeat on every occasion.

There was perhaps some degree of self-interest or vanity in their exhortations. The old hags could hardly wait for "the ultimate triumph" so that they could attain their places of honor in the court of Lusignan.

***

As I already mentioned, the Prince had inherited a son from Princess Marie, whom he had adopted and named Prince Levon Lusignan. He was a broad-shouldered, handsome, kind man who would occasionally pay his father a visit.

He lived on a farm near Paris with his wife and children. I believe that Prince Levon once also resided in Constantinople and that his wife is Armenian, a family relation of His Holiness Narbey.

He is a man of simple, peasant tastes, who gives no credence whatsoever to his royal title, having apparently learned the true nature of its worth.

Whenever Prince Levon Lusignan would visit, Marguerite would tell me, "You have to work in the room upstairs, because the Crown Prince will be visiting over lunch."

Marguerite demonstrated tremendous deference toward "The Crown Prince," especially since his pockets were always full whenever he visited.

Chapter 8

One day, a scrawny, very elderly woman with bleached blonde hair stopped by.

I could not help but notice that she was welcomed with an unusual degree of deference, although it was the first time I was seeing her on the royal estate.

After she left, I asked Marguerite who she was.

"That is Princess Henriette," she replied.

"Which Princess Henriette?" I asked, mystified.

"Princess Henriette de Lusignan."

"Where in the world did she come from?"

"She's from the English branch of the Lusignan clan."

I then learned that the Lusignan clan also had branches in Russia and Italy.

***

During my tenure, another Prince came to light in Paris. This was Prince Léon de Vitanval, a young charlatan who knew our Prince well. They had exchanged several medals of honor like a couple of allied sovereigns.

Prince Vitanval was also in the business of selling decorations, but he plied his trade out in the open. This ultimately led to his demise. He was arrested and jailed for extortion and fraud.

This charlatan had extraordinary nerve and wit.

During his trial, two Frenchman whom he had knighted and decorated, testified against him.

As their testimonies concluded, Vitanval – who was entirely unfazed by their devastating accusations – stood up, put on a tone of royal grandiloquence and addressed them, "Gentlemen, I am deeply aggrieved to behold that you were not deserving of my medals of honor. And I hereby strip you of your decorations this very instant. Henceforth, I forbid you to wear them…"

Vitanval had sent Prince Lusignan a letter from prison requesting financial assistance.

That letter was dated thus: "17 December, the first year of our captivity."

St. Louis had dated his prison letters from Mansour that way when he was captured by the Arabs.

The arrest and trial of Léon de Vitanval really distressed our Prince.

That scandal had spurred one newspaper to observe that Lusignan was also known to grant such decorations. The police opened an investigation and even questioned Miss Marguerite several times. But they could not prove that the Prince had accepted payments in return for these decorations. So, it all came to naught in the end.

But for several months thereafter, there were no more knighthoods for the order of Mt. Sinai and St. Catherine.

However, one day, a Frenchman appeared just when the Prince had gone out in his carriage. Miss Marguerite was in Paris to conduct some errands. So, I was tasked with greeting this guest.

"I would like to see the Prince," said the man.

"Unfortunately, he is not in at the moment."

"May I see his secretary?"

"I am his secretary."

"Very well, then. I can discuss the issue with you."

I led the man to the small office on the ground floor.

The guest began to explain, "I would like to ask the Prince for a large sash from the Melusinian order as a gift."

I replied, "I believe that those sashes are only granted to members of royal families."

"I know."

"In that case, I do not believe that you will be able to obtain one, unless, of course, you can provide evidence of your royal lineage."

"The sash is not meant for me," said the man with a smile. "I do not harbor such grand pretentions. I would like to request the large sash for Holland's Queen Wilhelmine."

I stared at the stranger in stunned silence.

"Are you making this request on behalf of the Queen perhaps?" I asked.

"No, not at all. I am making a personal request. I also wish to present the sash in person as an Envoy Extraordinary."

The man realized how odd his words sounded.

"Let me explain. There is a mine in the Dutch colony of South Africa that currently belongs to the Queen. I would like to monopolize it. I have already tried to do so by using various means. But that has merely resulted in further obstructions and intrigues to undermine me. Some of my friends advised me to find some way of meeting the Queen in person. That is when

I hatched this plan to present her with a large sash from the Melusinian order on behalf of Prince Lusignan and as his Envoy Extraordinary. I am not averse to large expenses. And I am prepared to make any sacrifice to perform my duties as an envoy flawlessly. I have already wasted 20,000 francs to secure that monopoly. And I have no issue whatsoever wasting just as much if it will ensure my success."

"Very well," I said. "I will present your request to the Prince. Please be so kind as to provide me with your name and address."

The man removed a calling card from his pocket and handed it to me.

Then he asked, "As far as you are aware, how much does the large sash of the Melusinian order cost?"

"The decoration is free of charge, of course," I hastened to reply. "But I believe that one must make various gifts, which probably will not exceed a sum of 5,000 francs. In any case, I cannot speak with any authority on the matter. I am merely the Prince's office secretary. The secretary of the Chancellery handles all matters pertaining to medals and decorations…"

And the man left.

When Miss Marguerite returned, I immediately told her about this conversation and gave her the calling card.

She read the name and said, "But I have heard of this man. He is a wealthy contractor."

"I had the same impression," I replied.

Two or three days later, I saw from my window that this man had returned to the villa.

He must have received a written invitation.

I learned later that the negotiations had proceeded very smoothly and that the man had smugly set off for the Dutch capital with the Melusinian sash and edict in hand.

The problem was that, alas, Queen Wilhelmine refused to accept both him and the Lusignan decoration.

His monopoly on the mine went practically down the drain.

**

As I noted earlier, while Prince Lusignan exploited human vanity on the one hand, on the other, he was as generous as his coffer would allow to all who appealed to him.

One day, he received a letter from an Armenian returning from America. It stated that he was a carpet restorer and that financial difficulties had forced him to leave America and return to Paris. He hoped to resume his trade here. But, alas, this was presently impossible. He asked that the Prince allow him "to restore the carpets of the royal palace" in return for a modest compensation.

"Tell him," replied the Prince wryly, "that the carpets in our palace do not need to be restored."

Nonetheless, he placed a 500-franc note in the envelope.

To cover the extra charges associated with their registration, Armenian students from poor families could always count on the Prince's coffer, as much as his means would allow.

If anyone returned emptyhanded after an appeal, he could be sure that it was because the Lusignan treasury was completely empty.

Despite his previous life as a cleric, Guidon Lusignan was extremely open-minded, almost an atheist.

When he learned that Mantashian wanted to make a large donation to build a new church in Paris, he exclaimed, "Idiot! What do we need another church for! He should spend that money on building schools and educating people."

This criticism was perhaps a little too rash. After all, the late Russian-Armenian philanthropist had also made huge contributions to schools and sponsored hundreds of Russian and Armenian university students.

***

As we approached the new year, the Prince, who was pleased with my work, said, "I would like to offer you something for Christmas. Do you prefer a monetary gift or would you rather become a knight of Mt. Sinai and St. Catherine?"

A tricky question, in fairness, which I had to think over before replying.

"Prince," I mumbled, "of course, it would be a great honor for me to join the ranks of our knights, but I do not consider myself worthy of such distinction and…"

"I understand," said the Prince cutting me off.

On Christmas, I received a monetary gift. But Marguerite apprised me that the Prince was extremely disappointed by my response.

"If you had chosen knighthood, you would have also received a monetary gift," she said.

"Alas," I cried.

***

There were many Armenians among the knights of Mt. Sinai. Two Egyptian Armenians – whose names I forget – accepted their knighthood during my employment there.

Marguerite was ill at the time. So, the Prince instructed me to sign the edicts as "de Beaudoin" on behalf of the Chancellor.

I declined to perform that harmless act of forgery.

"If you like, I can sign them as Yervant Odian," I said, "but not as de Beaudoin."

In the end, the coachman Basil signed those two documents.

Haroutiun Alpiar.

When I returned to Egypt a year later, Alpiar had resumed his publication of *Paros*. He showed me one of the knights, who was wearing his Mt. Sinai badge in his buttonhole for all to see.

"He's been impossible to talk to since he was knighted," Alpiar said.

So, I told him about how his edict of knighthood was actually signed.

"I beg you to write that up for *Paros*," said our witty friend. "I will reward you with a feast."

I got to work immediately. That article, "Comic Knights," was published in two instalments in *Paros*. I recounted the aforementioned episode and also divulged the true worth of Lusignan's decorations.

H. Alpiar kept his word, and we went out together for a "feast."

As we were leaving the restaurant, someone at another table stood up and charged at Alpiar.

"That's the knight of Mt. Sinai," muttered the director of *Paros* and braced himself for a punch-up.

The knight was wielding a fork instead of a sword. Swearing loudly at Alpiar, he stood right up to him and demanded an explanation for the article about the Lusignan orders of merit.

Several people stepped in to keep them from coming to blows. The furious restaurant manager dragged the knight outside and disarmed him, namely by snatching the fork out of his hand.

"I'll be seeing you again," shouted the man as he glared at Alpiar. The latter replied coolly, "Let's arrange a rendezvous at the convent of St. Catherine on Mt. Sinai."

Imaginary portrait of Guy of Lusignan.

My article nonetheless compelled that man to remove the badge in his buttonhole.

It was, admittedly, meanspirited of me. That decoration had made the poor man truly happy and proud.

***

I worked for the Prince for a year and a half. One day, Marguerite suddenly told me, "The Prince will be spending a couple of months in the country to get some fresh air. He needs to pause your work on the dictionary. You will resume in two months."

"Great!" I exclaimed overjoyed. "So, I'll get to enjoy two months of holiday…"

"I believe you misunderstand me," said the lady. "The Prince advises you to seek alternative employment for those two months."

"What for? Won't I be paid during his absence?"

"No."

"But that is simply unfair," I cried. "In that case, you should have given me at least one month's notice and an hour-long break every day so that I could apply for another job. That is stipulated by law."

"That is just how the Prince works."

I rushed over to the Prince. He was lying on the sofa and looked extremely unwell.

I realized that he was in no state for a long-drawn-out discussion. Marguerite requested that I let him rest and convey any complaints I may have separately in writing.

Infuriated, I left the villa and sent him an acerbic letter the very next day. I did not receive a reply.

I filed a lawsuit with Neuilly's Justice of the Peace and sent the Prince a summons addressed to "Mr. Ambrosios Kalfayan (known as Prince Lusignan)."

In Paris, lawsuits concerning 1,000 francs or less must be addressed to the Justice of the Peace. And one may defend one's own case without legal representation.

I finally had my day in court. An attorney and Miss Marguerite stood in for the Prince.

The trial was a veritable farce.

Every time I spoke, I addressed the Prince as "Mr. Ambrosios Kalfayan." His attorney, on the other hand, referred to him as "His Highness Prince Lusignan." The exasperated Justice of the Peace eventually crowed, "Would you please make up your mind about the defendant?! Is it Mr. Ambrosios Kalfayan or Prince Lusignan?"

"Yes, my dispute is with Ambrosios Kalfayan."

"And whom do you represent?" the judge asked the attorney.

"Prince Lusignan."

"Prince Lusignan is Ambrosios Kalfayan's pseudonym," I said.

The attorney objected.

On that, I took out Ambrosios Kalfayan's Armenian-French pocket dictionary, presented it to the judge, and said, "Could you kindly ask the attorney whether or not his client is this dictionary's author?"

The judge repeated my question.

"Yes, Prince Lusignan is the author of that dictionary," replied the attorney.

"All right then," I exclaimed, "the author's name here is Ambrosios Kalfayan… See! That name even appears in French."

"True," admitted the Justice of the Peace.

Then he turned to the attorney and added, "How do you respond?"

"That's simple," replied the attorney. "*Kalfa* and Prince mean the same thing. The word '*kalfa*' is the same as the Arabic '*kalifa*,' which means prince or nobility."

"No," I said. "The word '*kalfa*' is Turkish and refers to the supervisor of a construction site or a junior architect."

The attorney attempted to prove the contrary, while I insisted otherwise.

The Justice of the Peace lost his patience and bellowed, "I am not an Orientalist! I cannot be wasting my time on the intricacies of language. Now, let's get back to the real issue."

I presented my dispute, and the judge ruled that I was entitled to a half month's wages.

And that is how I parted ways with the Prince.

Chapter 9

Ianesco again. – My provincial dialect. – Chobanian and his opponents. – The Pashalian event. – Souren Bartevian's speech. – Arpiar and Vahé Arzouyan. – Bartevian takes over *Nor Gyank*. – Chobanian against Arpiar. – *Azad Khosk*. – Arpiar comes to Paris. – An innovative *poghacha*. – Chobanian's three projects and the ivory mines. – The fair and its victims. – The Persian Shah's bird-keeper.

One day, Arshag Chobanian ran into me on the Boulevards. "Brother, I've been looking for you for two weeks," he said. "I couldn't find you anywhere."

Curious, I asked, "Why, what's wrong?"

"Ianesco sent me three letters back-to-back asking me to tell you that you should send him your collection of provincial words without delay."

Confused, I asked, "What collection of provincial words? I have nothing like that in my possession."

"Apparently, you compiled that collection. That's what you told him when you were in Vienna… The man is prepared to remunerate you for it, if need be. But he wants to receive it as soon as possible."

And then I remembered that on several occasions, I had tried to ingratiate Ianesco by mentioning this imaginary collection, which I had supposedly forgotten in Paris.

I told Chobanian the whole story.

"Pity," he exclaimed, "now that poor man is going to be terribly disappointed!"

"Maybe I *should* send him a collection of provincial terms?" I said with a chuckle.

"How can you do that if you don't have one in the first place?"

"I'll just make one up… I'll invent a bunch of provincial terms and their meanings off the top of my head… I know the kind of thing he goes for…"

Chobanian thought it was a brilliant idea.

"Go ahead! Let's have ourselves a good laugh," he said. "That way, he'll stop sending me more of his letters."

"I'll post it to him first thing tomorrow," I decided.

And we parted.

I immediately purchased a notebook for one sou. Then I went to a café on Boule-Miche, asked for a pen and some ink, and got to work.

Just two hours later, the notebook was full of provincial terms.

I can provide some examples, if you like.

Brjoug: A swelling that grows on the backside of a horse's leg (dialect of Arapgir).

Chmpouloug: A leafless, yellowish spring wildflower native to the province of Vaspurakan.

Gmbosh: A vessel for making bread dough (dialect of Yevtokia).

And so on in that vein to the tune of one-hundred and twenty words, which spontaneously sprang forth from my mind complete with their meanings and etymologies.

I put the notebook in an envelope, wrote out Ianesco's address, dropped it off at the post office, and did not give it another thought.

One Sunday morning, about two weeks later, I was in bed reading a newspaper.

There was a sudden knock at my door.

"Who's there?" I asked from my bed.

"The postman," shouted a voice from the door.

Back then, the postman only knocked to deliver certified mail.

But I was not expecting a delivery. Surprised, I jumped out of bed and went to open the door.

"Are you Mr. Yervant Odian?" asked the postman.

"Yes, sir."

"Then, please sign this document."

He opened the satchel hanging from his neck and began counting some money.

Money? What a miracle!

I signed the document at a glance and returned it to him.

The man counted seventy-five francs and handed them to me, saying, "Is that the correct amount?"

"It is," I said automatically.

Then, unable to contain my curiosity, I added, "But who sent this amount?"

"Did you not read the document? It's from Vienna," he replied with some suspicion. "Are you not Mr. Yervant Odian?" he asked a second time.

"Yes, I am," I replied immediately…

The word Vienna explained it all.

"Was it perhaps Mr. Ianesco who sent this money?" I added.

The postman glanced at the signed document and said, "Yes, it is from Mr. Andronik Ianesco."

"I had to wait three whole days to receive this amount," I replied.

And the postman left.

This was my payment for the collection of provincial terms.

But this farce was not over yet.

A month later, I saw the latest issue of the Vienna Mekhitarist Monastery's *Hantes Amsorya* on Arshag Chobanian's desk. I picked it up and began browsing through it.

You cannot imagine my shock when I saw the provincial terms that I had coined on the pages of that prominent scholarly journal. They were accompanied by the following attribution: "A selection of provincial terms taken from Yervant Odian's collection."

Since then, some of those words may have been consecrated for use in the Armenian language. Naturally, this gives me a tremendous sense of honor, one which I share in great part with Ianesco. Without his persistence, I would never have imagined that I could endow the Armenian language with one-hundred and twenty neologisms.

I hasten to add that Vienna's Mekhitarist fathers are entirely innocent of this harmless act of linguistic fraud. And this joke can never obscure their undeniable authority in the field of Armenian philology.

I confess that, despite much financial hardship, I spent a wonderful three years in Paris.

We were a big bunch and practically lived together. Arshag Chobanian, Edgar Shahin, Dr. B. Kololian, Yervant Manvelian, Maksoud Mihrtadiants, Souren Bartevian, Adom Yarjanian, Zabel and Dikran Yessayan, Ardavazt Hanumian, the Fndklian brothers – including Dr. Krikor Fndklian as he is known today –, among some others, represented the core constituent.

But that group was doomed to shatter rather violently.

That event merits recounting.

Souren Bartevian was already publishing *Vaghvan Tsaynu* in Manchester and had mounted a fierce campaign against Arshag Chobanian.

Ceasing the publication of *Vaghvan Tsaynu* (which came to five issues anyway) made no difference in Bartevian's profound antagonism for Chobanian. The former was not alone. He was backed by an entire group of Chobanian opponents consisting of Adom Yarjanian, Ardavazt Hanumian, and Maksoud Mihrtadiants. After *Vaghvan Tsaynu*, he started publishing the periodical, *Zhoghovourtin Hamar*, whose leadership consisted of Souren Bartevian and Maksoud Mihrtadyants.[*] This periodical was also hostile to Chobanian, but not to the same extent as *Vaghvan Tsaynu*.

Of course, Chobanian – who had pretensions of exercising some sort of pontifical sovereignty over all young intellectuals – did not take very kindly to those who not only rebuffed him but also begrudged him any genuine talent.

And there was an incident, moreover, which exacerbated these tensions.

Levon Pashalian, who had been living in London for several years, came to spend some time in Paris.

On Souren Bartevian's urging, the young Armenians of Paris decided to demonstrate their solidarity with Levon Pashalian.

They organized an event in the auditorium of the Armenian Students' Association. The program included a reading of Pashalian's best literary pieces followed by a speech from Souren Bartevian elucidating Pashalian's significance for Armenian literature.

As it later came to light, this event's actual purpose was to strike at Chobanian through a celebration of Pashalian. What was shockingly wicked was that they asked Arshag Chobanian to chair the event.

Chobanian had his suspicions about this event. He had heard that Souren Bartevian was going to make an homage to Pashalian. So, his response to Adom Yarjanian's invitation was, "And will I be the object of any criticism?"

---

[*] This sentence is taken from the original 1914 publication. It appears to have been mistakenly skipped in the 1922 edition. (Tr.)

"How can you even think that?" Siamanto replied. Back then Levon Pashalian had christened him as Adom Mirza, which is what most of us called him.

"In that case, I graciously accept your invitation," Chobanian said, "especially since Levon Pashalian is one of my best friends. It would be my pleasure to preside over an evening in his honor."

Souren Bartevian kept his speech a secret from all of us until the night of the event.

Whenever we asked him about it, his response was, "I haven't prepared anything yet. I don't know what I'm going to say."

"Are you going to say anything about Chobanian?"

"Not at all. I'm just speaking about Pashalian."

The day of the event finally arrived.

I met Souren Bartevian in the afternoon at Café Soufflé on the Boulevard St. Michel.

"You've obviously prepared your speech by now. What are you going to say? Tell me," I asked.

"I wrote a bunch of things today," he replied. "I haven't gone over it yet. We can go over it together, if you want."

"Go on, read it."

Bartevian began to read his speech. Along with completely valid praise for Levon Pashalian's literary merits, it was also replete with caustic criticisms of Chobanian.

"Brother," I said, "you're just laying a trap for Chobanian, pure and simple. If that's the sort of speech you had in mind, you should never have invited him to chair the event."

"I didn't invite him. Adom did."

"Yes, but he did it on behalf of the Students' Association. And he even assured Chobanian that he would not be publicly criticized."

"That assurance was a personal gesture. I hadn't prepared my speech yet. He couldn't have known what I was going to say."

"If you ask me, this is completely out of line."

"I haven't named any names. He doesn't have to take it personally."

"But how can he not take it personally, when the comments are so obviously aimed at him?"

Eventually, after a protracted argument, Bartevian claimed that he would expunge the speech of any barbed comments.

"You can rest assured that, if you stick to what you wrote, Levon Pashalian will be terribly upset by your speech."

Then, we went to the auditorium of the Armenian Students' Association. All our friends were already there.

Arshag Chobanian took his seat next to Levon Pashalian.

He made some opening remarks complimenting Pashalian and his work. This was followed by readings of Pashalian's best works presented by Adom Yarjanian and others.

Then, Arshag Chobanian finally announced, "And I now give the floor to Souren Bartevian."

Bartevian got up, stood in front of the Chair, and proceeded to read his speech.

He had not expunged a single word. In fact, I believe that he may have even added some things at the last minute. And a veritable barrage of the most trenchant, venomous, relentless abuse was launched at the defenseless Chobanian, as he just sat there and took it all.

Most of the audience was equally sympathetic to both Pashalian and Chobanian. They did not enjoy what they were hearing. And some became downright indignant at this diatribe, which clearly sought to calumniate Chobanian rather than to praise Pashalian.

But some did applaud passionately each time Bartevian reached into his arsenal and tossed yet another dynamite at Chobanian.

Several Chobanian supporters lost their patience and left the auditorium. Others remained in their seats, trembling with rage. And Levon Pashalian was visibly upset.

The speech ended. Pashalian said a few words of gratitude, and that concluded the event.

Chobanian was truly heroic and remained in his seat until the very end. But this assault he did not forget.

In his very first issue of *Anahid*, he published "The Pashalian Event," where he launched his own fierce attack against Souren Bartevian, Adom Yarjanian, and even Levon Pashalian, who he believed took part in this treacherous conspiracy.

Souren Bartevian retaliated to *Anahid*'s attacks with a diatribe entitled, "Whip." It is a genuine masterpiece of the genre, where even I got worked over thoroughly for supporting Chobanian.

"Whip" demolished Chobanian's literary reputation. And its effects have been demonstrably permanent.

Chobanian gave up writing original works of literature after that, devoting himself instead exclusively to translation and interpretation.

Arshag Chobanian.

***

Arpiar was in London this whole time. He was publishing *Nor Gyank* and leading the Henchag party.

Vahé Arzouyan – who was relegated to the party's margins for a time – had been rehabilitated as an active member thanks to Arpiar's efforts. One of the consequences was that Vahé went to Constantinople to carry out a mission. A French woman was accompanying him. But Vahé was arrested in Constantinople, whereas Zareh Kochian managed to escape to Paris and then went over to London.

After several months in prison, Vahé was eventually released thanks to his American passport and his French fiancée's interventions. The police paid for his expulsion from Constantinople, and he came to Paris.

At the same time, Kochian, who had fallen out with Arpiar, also returned from London.

Vahé and some of his loyal collaborators had reached their limit with Arpiar, who kept frustrating their audacious plans. They wanted him out, or, at least made editor of *Nor Gyank* so that he would have to resign from his position in the Central Bureau. I should add that the Henchag Central Bureau was something of a peculiarity. It had one branch in London, another in America, a third in Cyprus, a fourth in Paris, and a fifth in Egypt.

In any case, Arpiar had sympathetic supporters from various branches in America. And only the Americans ever sent any money to the political party. So Arpiar was often heard saying, "If Christopher Columbus hadn't discovered America, the Henchag party wouldn't exist today."

Vahé and I were on very close terms back then. And I shared all his views on Arpiar. Arpiar could not lead a revolution, of this I was already convinced many years ago. Arshag Chobanian was of the same opinion.

So, the three of us had no difficulty whatsoever in conspiring to topple Arpiar.

I was sure that my involvement in this conspiracy would ultimately be for Arpiar's own good. Once he lost his position in the Central Bureau, he would devote himself entirely to *Nor Gyank*. And this would therefore spare him a lot of financial hardship and various other difficulties. He would also have more time to write literature. Besides, Arpiar himself had repeatedly said that he was sick and tired of the Central Bureau. But his friends kept insisting that he stay on, because none of them was in any position to quit his day job, move to London, and manage the party's finances.

As I mentioned earlier, the American branches were staunch Arpiar supporters. So, we had to convince them above anyone else if our plan was to succeed. That would have been impossible to achieve by correspondence alone. So, we decided that Vahé should pay the branches a personal visit.

America's Henchags knew Vahé well and had tremendous respect for his audacity, thanks in great part to Arpiar. He took every opportunity to raise Vahé's standing both in his correspondences and on the pages of *Nor Gyank*. Although they were ultimately unsuccessful, Vahé's most recent exploits had also helped to spread his name.

Entering Constantinople despite extensive police restrictions, moving around the city for several weeks, ending up in prison, and then being released, were not run of the mill experiences.

But we lacked the means to wage this war, namely the money for a ticket to America.

Chobanian managed to raise the required amount. And Vahé left for the United States.

His mission was crowned with success. And several months later, Vahé returned triumphantly to London as a full-blown member of the Central Bureau. Arpiar even left London and relocated to Brighton, where he continued to edit *Nor Gyank*.

But once he had firmed up his position, Vahé decided that *Nor Gyank* needed a new editorial direction, namely, in keeping with his personal vision. This was what ultimately led to his rupture with Arpiar. And, of course, Arpiar would not stand for that sort of censorship, so the paper was handed over to Vahé.

Arzouyan came to Paris to find a new editor for *Nor Gyank*. He offered that position to me first. I declined. So, he took Souren Bartevian to London covertly to replace Arpiar.

Until then, every one of Souren Bartevian's writings and speeches had mocked, criticized, and attacked the Armenian revolution and its adherents. This was such common knowledge that when Souren Bartevian suddenly disappeared from the cobblestoned streets of Paris, no one could conceive that he, of all people, was off in London to edit a revolutionary newspaper.

This editorial shift at *Nor Gyank* led to the discontinuation of my satirical novel, *The Propagandist*. Vahé had decided against publishing satire.

Chobanian was outraged beyond words when the identity of *Nor Gyank*'s new editor was revealed.

Bartevian had just published "Whip," which had gouged deep wounds into Chobanian's breast. Those wounds were still throbbing. And after plotting so intimately together to topple Arpiar, he could not conceive how Vahé could then appoint Souren Bartevian as his replacement.

Nevertheless, Vahé somehow kept Chobanian on board by some ingenious design. Just how remains a mystery to me. Chobanian not only refrained from subjecting Bartevian to further attacks in *Anahid*, but he also did an about-face and initiated a series of violent attacks against Arpiar. He was evidently doing all he could to make a laughingstock out of him.

The anti-Arpiar opposition was so ugly, so uncalled for, and unjust that I could no longer bring myself to contribute to *Anahid*. That is why my novel, *Men of Action* – depicting various prominent figures from Constantinople – stopped appearing on its pages.

Two of my novels thus remained incomplete as a result of these various challenges.

The opposition to Arpiar – which went well beyond anything I could have anticipated – forced me to cut my ties with Arshag Chobanian and Vahé Arzouyan.

At about the same time, Levon Pashalian left London and settled in Paris.

That is when we decided to publish a short monthly, mostly satirical, to push back at our ideological adversaries. The printing costs for each issue – around 50 francs – would be covered by my brother, Hrant Odian, as well as Levon Pashalian, Dr. B. Kololian, Kalpakjian and one other person, whose name I forget.

The paper was called *Azad Khosk*. Arpiar, still in Brighton, was one of our collaborators. We even included an "open letter" to Agheksandr Mantashian in our first issue. We attacked him mercilessly for trying to make Armenians out to be a bunch of beggars. This was followed by sustained assaults on Arshag Chobanian, Minas Cheraz, Hakhoumiants, and so on.

From the outset, this publication received a very warm reception from the Armenian communities in Paris as well as much further afield. There is evidently always a market for ridicule, warranted or not.

Only four issues of *Azad Khosk* appeared in Paris. I had to return to Egypt, where I continued publishing it sporadically. There were 70 issues in total.

***

After leaving the Henchag party, Arpiar came to Paris towards the end of '91 [sic].* He was in terribly dire financial straits.

His dirty broad-brimmed hat and beard made him look so much like a dangerous anarchist that the hotel managers were refusing to rent him a room. We had to find him a guarantor so that he could have somewhere to stay.

I was residing in a small four-room apartment on Rue de Richelieu.

One of my acquaintances had rented and furnished that apartment but had to leave Paris suddenly. Since he still had seven months remaining on his lease, he sublet it to me.

The problem was that he had not paid his rent in full, so the doorman had claimed his furniture as collateral.

I had one vacant bedroom, so I sub-sublet it to Arpiar. That way, he would not have to pay for a hotel room.

---

* Probably 1901 (Tr.)

Arpiar settled snugly into that cramped apartment. The two blankets he had brought along with him were also claimed as collateral.

But shelter was not enough. We also needed to put something in our stomachs. So, we got to pawning off some of the little trinkets lying around the house.

We left home every morning wearing our bulky coats and returned home in the evenings with a very much lightened load. We discreetly pilfered utensils, books, bowls, small mirrors, plates, anything really, until, one day, the doorman noticed a grill hanging out of Arpiar's coat.

We smoothed the whole thing over by bribing the doorman with a large mirror.

Winter was upon us, and we were freezing in that house.

"We can't remove the furniture," I told Arpiar, "but they can be put to very good use right here."

"How?"

"By helping us keep warm."

"Didn't they make an inventory of all the furniture for collateral?"

"No, not at all. All they said was that I'm not supposed to relocate or remove any of the furniture."

"So, there's nothing to stop us."

The first to burn as firewood were the chairs, then the drawers, and, eventually, just about every piece of furniture ended up in the fire – that is, unless a friend happened to drop by and offered to buy something at the landlord's stated price.

We struck a mean bargain. Once we had paid the rent in full, we still had 200 francs to spare.

As I mentioned before, Arpiar had an insatiably sweet tooth.

One day, he barged into my room overjoyed and announced, "Yervant, I made a brilliant discovery!"

"What? You figured out how to resolve the Armenian Question?"

"Something far more important than that!"

"Spit it out!"

"I found a *poghacha** shop!"

"Where?..."

---

* A stuffed pastry. (Tr.)

"Right in the heart of Paris, in Faubourg-Montmartre…"

"Really?"

"Get up, quick, I'll take you there. There's just one little hitch…"

"What little hitch?"

"The *poghacha* doesn't come with sugar."

"We'll just have it with the cheese stuffing."

"No. I tried a piece. It didn't have any cheese."

We went to the bakery. It was selling something that resembled *poghacha*.

"This *poghacha* looks really civilized," I told Arpiar skeptically.

"No," he replied firmly. "This is our very own authentic *poghacha*. I interrogated the man about it. The baker used to be the chef to the Ottoman Consul, Jemil Pasha. The Pasha took him to Constantinople with the express purpose of introducing him to *poghacha*. The only problem is that he doesn't have any sugar for the topping…"

This sugar problem was a veritable nightmare for Arpiar. But he eventually solved that problem as well. Every morning, he would put a raw sugar cube in his pocket and then go to the bakery to buy his pastry. And then, to live out his fantasy, he would alternate between the two, first taking a bite out of the pastry and then nibbling on the sugar cube.

***

Arshag Chobanian had set his mind to three major projects in Paris. In my humble opinion, as far as the nation was concerned, they were all outstandingly edifying, enriching, and noble.

The first project was to unite the Tashnag and Henchag parties. The logical next step was for him to become the President or Chairman of the unified political party.

To achieve this aim, he initiated a months-long epistolary campaign. He corresponded with everyone he knew across every continent, and especially those at the Western Bureau based in Geneva. But it all came to naught. A strongly worded letter from Geneva finally drove home the point that he should abandon his designs on the presidency.

Arshag Chobanian's second project was to establish an Armenian college in Paris. It would be funded by the donations of affluent Armenians. And it only made sense that he should assume the institution's leadership.

He bandied this idea in *Anahid*. And then he personally approached or wrote to several prospective donors.

This spurred me to write a fantastical little story in *Azad Khosk*. I presented a notable Armenian merchant in Manchester, Mr. Tokatlian. He was a well-known miser. The story had him supposedly donate 20,000 pounds for the construction of an Armenian college in Europe, and another 20,000 as a revenue-generating endowment. And then I went into some detail on how the revenue from the 20,000 would be used to purchase bonds in ivory mines.

To make things even more absurd, I included a bit about how elephants were once worshipped in India; how their bodies were buried in special graves; and how currently, those graves – whose locations I listed – were appropriated by a British company to profit from the elephant bones. These were the ivory mines, whose bonds supposedly yielded a 6% return.

In closing, I added that Tokatlian had given strict instructions that the college must be constructed in Germany and that its director must be German.

When he read that little fantasy – which no person in their right mind could take seriously –, Chobanian was completely taken in by the ivory mines. And, in the next issue of *Anahid*, he published a furious diatribe reproaching the imaginary philanthropist for establishing his college in Germany, rather than in Paris.

But Chobanian had not been the only gullible reader. The newspapers in Constantinople also announced the wonderful news that the wealthy M. Effendi Tokatlian from Manchester had donated 40,000 pounds to establish an Armenian college in Europe.

There was nothing for that poor man to do but to publicly deny that fake news, which was invented with the sole purpose of teasing Arshag Chobanian.

Since my collection of provincial terms for Ianesco, this was yet another one of my unintentionally succesful ruses, which had unexpected consequences for some eminent individuals.

Chobanian's third project was to create an Armenian General Benevolent Union with him at the helm, of course.

He shed a lot of blood, sweat, and tears to make that happen. He drew up the plans, created an administrative counsel, and successfully petitioned numerous people. But, alas, the will of providence prevailed, and that project was implemented instead by Boghos Nubar Pasha many years later in Egypt.

At some point, one segment of the Parisian Armenian community began to foment a campaign against Chobanian.

I hereby swiftly condemn the injustice of that campaign. Their charges against Chobanian were wholly unfounded and had no basis in fact.

I hesitate to rehash that sensitive topic here. But I will just say this much: that, despite being one of Chobanian's opponents, I nonetheless felt obliged to protect him from this unbridled slander. But it had grown to such proportions that a Court of Honour was convened to conduct an investigation and make a ruling on the charges levelled against him.

Numerous eyewitness testimonies left no doubt whatsoever regarding his innocence. But that Court of Honour – whose judges included several enemies of Chobanian – ruled only that the case was moot.

But this did not go far enough for Chobanian's opponents, who organized a rally to publicly denounce him. They rented the grand Freemason hall on the Rue Cadet.

The rally was supposedly meant to be a debate. And Chobanian's supporters were granted an opportunity to speak in his defense.

The popular actor, Arménian, who had been studying theater in Paris, spoke on behalf of Chobanian. He was followed by Krikor Kalfayan. But the entire audience started insulting and threatening the speakers. At one point, several men pulled out their revolvers. And the audience began to disperse as a result of all the commotion. But by that point, a vote had already been taken, and the majority had voted against Chobanian.

That was why Chobanian's third project – the Armenian General Benevolent Union – went down the drain.

He thought up new projects all the time after that, but none of them ever materialized.

Such was the fate of all beautiful ideas.

***

Numerous Armenians came to the 1901 Paris World Fair in search of fame and fortune. Several Armenian women were among them. They were hoping to get rich on their performances of oriental dances.

I remember that there was a pair of sisters from Egypt. They had arrived with a substantial amount of capital and high hopes.

Chapter 9

We already knew one another from my time in Egypt. So, I advised them to give up their lascivious dances. They had no novelty value in Paris.

But they were so full of themselves, so spoiled by their notoriety in Egypt that they rejected my advice. Instead, they rented an extremely expensive little auditorium at the World Fair to stage several performances.

Just next door was another auditorium, where a Parisian woman known as "pretty Fatma" was also performing her oriental dances. There was no contest. The Parisian was the overwhelming favorite. And those pathetic Armenians ended up performing in a virtually empty auditorium. They had spent everything they had and run themselves into debt. They went through quite an ordeal to make their way back from Paris.

Many Armenians had their hopes dashed at that fair. One had devised a get-rich-quick plan selling yogurt. He fell into total ruin. Another had set his hopes for the future on selling "*keten helvasi*."[*] He went bankrupt. And the list went on.

But the yogurt-seller was shrewd and resourceful. He did ultimately turn his misfortune around.

When the Persian Shah Muzafereddin visited Paris, he prepared a yogurt fit for royalty and personally delivered it to the Shah. The ruler of Iran was so delighted by this gift that he commanded his men to grant him a reward.

The Shah's attendant summons the Armenian yogurt-maker and says, "Our Royal Majesty was delighted by your yogurt and would like to grant you a reward of 500 francs."

"No," replies the cunning Armenian. "I am not after money. I wish to enter into His Majesty's service."

"What can you offer? Apart from making yogurt, do you have a profession?"

"I can do anything," replies the man with perfect confidence.

"All right, then. Come and see me tomorrow."

The next day, he presents himself to the Shah's attendant.

"Can you take care of birds?" asks the Persian.

"It is my expertise," replies the Armenian.

"Well, that is splendid," continues the attendant. "Our Royal Majesty has purchased a selection of exotic birds, which we are transporting to

---

[*] A sesame-based confection much like cotton candy. (Tr.)

Tehran. Each bird has a specific diet and requires special care. Since you are an expert, we shall name you Birdkeeper of His Majesty the Shah."

The Armenian thanks him profoundly and speeds over to us with this great news.

The self-proclaimed birdkeeper consults with all the bird-dealers, purchases the appropriate feed for each bird, and gathers all the information he needs to provide them with the best possible care.

"I suspect," I told him, when he came to bid me farewell, "that not one of those birds will reach Tehran alive."

"So do I," he replied, "because we have forty birds, and each one has a different diet."

The man left. Months later, I received a letter from him. He informed me that he had received a medal of honor from the Shah for his service as Birdkeeper.

And he apprised me of some further details.

On their long train journey, they stop at the Russian border for a transfer. In the process, he loses the entire case of special bird seeds. So, he resorts to feeding the birds breadcrumbs and corn kernels.

Sometimes, the poor birds do not even receive that much or any water to boot. Yet, they all reach the Persian capital alive.

This unexpected feat demonstrates the Armenian fortune-seeker's marvelous birdkeeping expertise.

The man remains in Tehran until Shah Muzafereddin's death. He then receives a royal edict dispensing him of his duties. And he parts with great pride at the medal of honor pinned to his breast.

Chapter 10

The Parisian Society of Christian Youth. – Cheap meals, cheap baths. – A reading of the Holy Bible. – A successful start. – The Society of Temperance and their president. – Drunk on water. – The newspaper *En Avant*. – The Salvation Army. – Its officers and soldiers. – News of a battle. – A gymnastics prayer. – A public confession.

One day, I was complaining about the exorbitant cost of dining out, when one of my friends in Paris, Mr. Setrag Ambarian, replied, "I have a feast every day for just ninety cents."

Ninety cents amounted to just four kurush. This sounded absolutely unbelievable.

"What do you eat for that amount?" I asked.

"First, some appetizers, and then a portion of meat and vegetables, then dessert, cheese, fruit, a glass of wine, and a cup of coffee…"

"You're joking!" I exclaimed.

"On the contrary, I'm being quite serious… and that's not all," he continued. "The establishment where I dine has a reading room, a games room, and a library at the patrons' disposal, all furnished magnificently and lit with bright electric lights."

"Is that right?"

"Just wait, there's more. The establishment also hosts multiple baths. For ten cents, you can have a glorious bath with hot water, but only if you agree to use the soap that they provide…"

"I cannot believe it. That's impossible. You're just pulling my leg."

"I'm not done yet," persisted Ambarian. "If you get sick, a physician treats you free of charge, and your medication is prepared on site in the establishment's pharmacy for seventy-five percent less than what you would pay at other pharmacies…"

"But won't you lead me to this promised land?!" I cried out in my excitement.

"I may take you there just once as my dinner guest, but I can't do that every day," Ambarian replied. "If you'd like, we can dine there tonight."

"But how is it that you can go there every day, but I'm only allowed there once?"

"Because I have signed up as a member of their organization," my friend replied proudly.

"Oh dear. Does that establishment belong to a specific organization?"

"Of course... The institution belongs to the Christian Youth, on Rue de Trévise, a gorgeous building, a veritable palace...."

"So, it's a Protestant institution?"

"From top to toe."

"But I thought you were Apostolic?"

"What difference does that make? All you need to do is ingratiate the Director of the organization. He's the one who decides whether to accept you."

"And how can one ingratiate him?"

"By abstaining from drink, gambling, lechery..."

"Is that all?"

"Apart from that, one must be a devout believer."

"In other words, attend the Chapel every Sunday?"

"Yes, if you are Protestant. And if not, you may attend your own church. They don't mind. They have only one condition for membership."

"What's that?"

"You must attend Bible study every Tuesday and actively take part in discussions."

"I'm joining the Society of Christian Youth this very day," I informed my friend. "But let's have dinner there first, so that I can sample their food. Do you think it'll be hard for me to get in?"

"I don't really know," replied Ambarian hesitantly. "These people are a little hard to please, and they only accept members after giving them a good grilling."

"I don't mind getting grilled," I told him confidently.

"Then, it would be best to go there for dinner on Tuesday night, so that you can participate in the Bible study session as a guest. If your participation goes well, and you leave a good impression on the Director, Mr. Pique, the whole process should be much more straightforward."

And, on Tuesday night, we did indeed go to the Rue de Trévise together, not far from the Grands Boulevards.

We entered a magnificent building crowned with the engraved inscription, "Society of Christian Youth." Then, we climbed a marble

Chapter 10

Paris.

staircase to the first floor, walked through a large corridor, and arrived at the dining hall, which was bathed in the glow of electric lights. More than forty young men between the ages of eighteen and twenty-five were already having their meals. We took our seats at a free table and joined them.

What struck my eye were the announcements, as large as theatre billboards, plastered throughout the dining room. They began with the words, "I denounce!" At the time, the Dreyfus Affair was still a hot issue, and Emile Zola had published his famous article, "J'accuse!" in *Aurore*. The posters adopted the style of Zola's article and pronounced:

"I denounce alcohol, which is the mother of all vices.

I denounce absinthe, which destroys one's health and leads one to a life of crime.

I denounce Picon Amer, which upsets the stomach.

I denounce wine, which destroys reason."

In short, the posters denounced all alcoholic beverages.

These were the only decorations on the dining room walls.

As for the dishes, they were generously portioned and truly delicious. My friend, Ambarian, was not exaggerating. The tables, plates, and utensils were immaculately clean, and the place felt like an upscale restaurant.

"So, we won't be able to have any wine?" I asked my friend.

"We are allowed one glass, but no more than that. You may also have a glass of beer instead of wine. But I abstain from both here. I just order a glass of milk."

"Why is that?"

"Milk drinkers gain more respect and trust…"

"Then, please order me a glass of milk as well… and feel free to drink it yourself."

After dinner, we made our way to the reading room, where several serious newspapers, respectable illustrated journals, and periodicals were on display.

The Director Mr. Pique stopped by briefly. My friend introduced us and told him that I would like to join the Society of Christian Youth.

"That's fine. But we'll discuss that later," he replied brusquely.

"My friend wishes to attend this evening's Bible study group," continued Ambarian.

"Very well. We would be pleased to have him as our guest."

"My friend has studied the Bible extensively," continued Ambarian to help pave my path to membership.

Looking skeptical, Mr. Pique smirked and said, "Sure, sure."

It was clear that he had little faith in my knowledge of the Scriptures. He figured that I wanted to join the Christian Youth more for its inexpensive food than to audit readings of the Bible.

After a little while, a bell sounded to let everyone in the reading room know that it was now time to get some spiritual exercise.

We proceeded to another large room. An extremely long table stood in the middle. It was draped with a green tablecloth. We huddled around the table, looking serious and pensive. I observed the faces of all the young men. They bore the deep impression of boredom. They were simply there for the cheap food, the baths, and the warmth provided by the various rooms. This weekly reading was tantamount to a Golgotha to which they subjected themselves in return for all the other benefits.

Mr. Pique came in holding a Bible and took his place at the head of the table. We all stood up and with eyes closed, listened to the Lord's Prayer, which the Director recited quietly in that lachrymose, monotonous tone typical of Protestants.

Then we took our seats, and Mr. Pique opened the book and began to read.

It was an excerpt from the Book of Kings, telling the story of how David's soldiers had stolen the burnt offerings of food from the temple, and how the Lord had meted out a punishment of death for this transgression.

After reading the entire chapter – to which maybe only a handful of people were listening attentively –, the Director closed the book and asked, "Did you listen to the story?"

"Yes, yes," everyone declared.

"Did you understand the moral of it?"

"Yes, yes!"

Mr. Pique turned to one of the listeners and said, "Mr. Jacques, please tell me what the moral of that story is?"

Mr. Jacques, who had most likely not listened to the whole story, lifted his head looking bewildered and timidly replied, "What David wants to convey with this story…"

"First of all, David himself says nothing at all," interrupted Mr. Pique, his voice serious and curt.

"I mean, what the Gospel wants to say is…"

"The excerpt I just read was not from the Gospels."

"The prophet means…"

"But, Mr. Jacques, it pains me to say that you have obviously not listened to a word of my reading," pronounced Mr. Pique, his voice still serious and solemn.

"I did listen. It's just that…" mumbled the young Christian looking bewildered.

Then, the Director turned to everyone and asked, "Who can tell me which book of the Scriptures I read from?"

One person shouted, "The Book of Genesis."

Another said, "The Book of Leviticus."

"The prophecy of Isaiah…"

Mr. Pique dismissed these responses with a wave of his finger.

"It is from the second Book of Kings," I replied from my seat.

The Director, who had been looking elsewhere, suddenly turned his head and asked, "Who said that?"

"I did," I replied.

Everyone was staring at me.

"Bravo!" said Mr. Pique. "That is correct."

And then he turned to the others, pointed at me, and said, "This gentleman is a guest, who is attending our gathering for the very first time. He is not even a member of the Society of Christian Youth. Nevertheless, you can see that he is much better acquainted with the Bible than you are."

At that moment, Setrag Ambarian's breast swelled with pride. He turned to his neighbors and whispered, "He's my friend. I brought him here."

"I am now going to ask you one more thing," continued Mr. Pique. "An almost identical story appears in the New Testament. In other words, the Lord does the same thing to two people – to be exact, a married couple – by punishing them with death for an act of theft. Can you tell me where that story appears?"

No one replied.

"I read you that chapter from the New Testament a couple of months ago," explained the Director. "And, surely, some of you must remember it. I beg you to collect your thoughts and try to remember."

"Judas, who betrayed his master for thirty silver coins," mumbled one young man just for the sake of saying something.

These words provoked a round of laughter.

"Silence!" commanded Mr. Pique. "Come on, try to remember."

The poor man was trying in vain to elicit a response.

Hopeless, he finally turned to me. "Sir," he said, "could you perhaps tell these gentlemen where this story appears…?"

"In the fifth chapter of the Acts of the Apostles," I replied.

"That is correct!" cried the excited Mr. Pique. "Yes, I was referring to the story of Ananias and Sapphira, which is told in the fifth chapter of the Acts of the Apostles. My compliments, my good sir."

Then several others read some essays about the Scriptures, and that was the end of the meeting.

When Ambarian and I approached Mr. Pique to take our leave, he said, "Would you like to join me for tea in my office?"

"It would be our pleasure," I replied.

As soon as I had made myself comfortable in an office armchair, Mr. Pique said, "Do you have any formal experience in Bible exegesis?"

"Since childhood, it has always been my favorite reading material," I replied. "And I've read it cover to cover maybe a dozen times or more. I've also consulted the works of various authorities on the Bible."

"That sounds about right," replied Mr. Pique.

"I think you would agree that my friend fully deserves to become one of our members," Setrag Ambarian chipped in, feeling much more emboldened to advocate for my membership.

"We would be lucky to have Mr. Odian among us," the Director replied immediately.

This was the moment to take full advantage of his goodwill.

"Would it be possible for my friend to receive a membership card straightaway?" Ambarian asked.

"Unfortunately, that would be impossible. First, Mr. Odian has to submit an application, and then the administration will make a decision… These are all basic formalities, and we don't anticipate any obstacles, especially since I will be supporting his nomination."

"We are deeply grateful for that. But those formalities normally take at least two weeks."

"We'll do our best to expedite matters."

And he took out an application form and filled it in. I signed and submitted it.

"Would it be possible to take my meals here before my official acceptance?" I asked.

Mr. Pique rubbed his forehead for a moment.

"That would contravene our rules," he said. "But it doesn't matter. We'll make an exception in your case…"

Then he reached into a drawer, pulled out thirty tickets, handed them to me and said, "Here's two-weeks' worth of tickets for two meals a day."

It was customary for diners at the institute of Christian Youth to purchase their meal tickets from the Director in advance. They had to give the server a ticket to receive their meals in the dining hall. Presently, I had to pay twenty-seven francs for the thirty tickets Mr. Pique gave me, an amount that I did not have.

"Sir," I said, "I would prefer to leave the tickets for another time, because I cannot make payment for them today."

"That's all right, entirely alright," exclaimed the man. "I'll handle all that. You can pay me back later."

"I am most grateful."

And so, the Prophet David's soldiers and Ananias and his wife paid for two weeks' worth of my meal tickets.

A week later, I was already an elected member of the Christian Youth thanks to Mr. Pique. He must have spoken very highly of my Scriptural expertise during their administrative meeting.

Every Tuesday after that, I gave further evidence of my religious expertise, so much so that some members of the Administrative Committee got curious and wanted to meet me personally. The other members of the Society seemed to look up to me, and on many Tuesday evenings, I was the one they came to for assistance.

When I used up my thirty tickets, Mr. Pique gave me another thirty, on credit as usual. And then another thirty and so on for more than two months.

Eventually, one day, Mr. Pique felt compelled to call me into his office.

"Sir," he said, "you now owe us one-hundred francs. We are not in the habit of granting tickets on credit, and we did so as an exception in your case."

"I know," I replied, "and I am most grateful for that."

"When do you hope to pay your dues?"

"As soon as possible."

"In other words…?"

"Mr. Pique, you realize that I am a political refugee. Abdulhamid has confiscated all my properties and sources of revenue. Under these circumstances, I find it difficult to tell you for certain when I will be able to repay you… If the political climate in Turkey were to suddenly change, then you could rest assured that…"

"I understand, I understand," the Director interrupted me. "It seems that everything is tied up with finding a solution to the Eastern Question."

Then, after thinking for a moment, he continued, "I already presented your case to the administration, who think very highly of you. They told me that if you find yourself unable to repay your debts to our institution, we may simply forgive them. As for the future, we may consider another arrangement."

"What sort of arrangement?" I asked, my curiosity piqued.

"An arrangement that will save you paying for your meals."

"And how might that work?"

"I will explain. First, I believe that you sincerely oppose the consumption of alcohol."

"Most certainly."

"Perhaps you yourself never consume any."

"Just a little wine over dinner… You know, the apostle Paul makes that recommendation to his protege, Timothy."

"Perhaps those writings attributed to Paul should be verified," replied Mr. Pique. "But that's not the real issue here. Do you think you can abstain from wine over dinner…?"

"Why not? If need be…"

"Then, please listen carefully. We have a Society of Temperance under our auspices in Paris. If you sign up as an active member, you make take your meals entirely for free in the Society's dining hall, which is located on the Rue St. Martin. Their meals are as carefully prepared and tasty as ours."

"Then, I will definitely sign up," I said firmly. "But apart from my consent, do they need anything else?"

"We have sung your praises so often to the Society's President that you may rest assured that you will have absolutely no difficulty in being admitted."

"And what must an active member do?"

"A very simple, enjoyable, and morally uplifting job," replied Mr. Pique.

"In what sense…?"

"For instance, let us imagine that you run into a drunkard stumbling along on the street. You rush to his side, greet him respectfully, and use some pretext or other to engage him in conversation. When you get the feeling that he is warming up to you, you gradually bring up the topic of alcohol. You mention their harmful effects, and you try to steer him away from his addiction."

"What if the drunk becomes belligerent…?"

"Even better. That is when you can really show your mettle by patiently fielding his insolence and responding to him with Christian forbearance."

"What if the man tries to attack me…?"

"Recall the torments of Christ and do not desist. But your work will involve more than drunks on the street. You will visit working class neighborhoods, you will enter their taverns, and you will strive to save their souls. Each time you successfully reform a drunkard and convince him to join your Society, you will receive a reward of fifty francs. Will you accept this sacred task?"

"Yes!"

"In that case, come round tomorrow, and I will take you to the President of the Temperance Society."

And the next day he introduced me to the President, a cheerful, kind old man. He was the patriarch of an enormous family. That man had already heard about me, and he immediately admitted me as a member and pinned a special membership badge to my buttonhole.

"Come to the dining hall on the Rue St. Martin tonight," he said.

When I went to the dining hall that evening, I saw that everyone had the same badge in their buttonholes, even the women and girls.

"Where is the President?" I asked the server.

"He'll be here in fifteen minutes," he replied.

I was reluctant to dine alone, so I waited for his arrival. Indeed, fifteen minutes later, the President arrived with his family of about a dozen individuals – from little girls to elderly women – in tow.

As soon as he noticed me, he approached me cheerfully, took me by the hand, and led me to his group.

"Here is our most recent prisoner," he told them as he presented me. "We captured him after a vicious battle with the army of addiction…"

They all shook my hand warmly.

The President turned to his younger daughter – who was a lovely fair-haired, blue-eyed girl, no more than seventeen – and said, "Adele, I hereby submit a fresh prisoner from our latest victory into your custody."

Following this ceremony, we gathered around a large table. I sat next to Miss Adele.

"Have you ever consumed alcohol?" asked the President.

"I did for a time, yes, but presently, no," I replied hypocritically.

"What pleasure did you derive from its consumption?"

"The pleasure of inebriation and cheer."

"But why turn to alcohol to derive such pleasures…? Man can get just as drunk and cheerful on water, given the right attitude."

"Water?" I exclaimed in surprise.

"Yes, sir," replied the old man cheerfully. "I get drunk on water every night."

And he called the server over. "Jean, we have a guest this evening. I would like to get a little tipsy before dinner. Bring us something to drink…!"

This order confounded me, and I cast a puzzled look at the young girl beside me.

"Yes," Adele said with a chuckle. "My father gets drunk every time someone becomes a member of the Society."

The server brought the beverage, which was nothing more than a bottle of water.

The President poured the water into our glasses and said, "To your health."

"And to yours," I replied, emptying my glass in one gulp.

"Aimless drifter!" shouted the old man angrily. "How can you drink this draught in one gulp?"

And he took a little sip, puckered his face like a true tippler, and set the glass down.

Then we continued our conversation about various topics. Meanwhile, the old man behaved as though he were drinking absinthe, sipping at his glass very slowly and acting tipsier by the minute. His performance was so convincing that anyone could be duped into thinking that he was drinking alcohol. By the time he emptied his glass, he was acting the perfect drunk.

"Let us eat," he said.

I had never seen such a jocular, cheerful man in my life. We had a wonderful time all through dinner.

"Is your father always this cheerful?" I asked Miss Adele.

"Yes, whenever he drinks," replied the young girl.

"But he's just having water."

"My father has such formidable willpower that whenever he pretends that his water is alcohol, he gets truly drunk… Fortunately, he only had one glass. If he'd had two glasses, you can be sure that he wouldn't have been able to sit still for very long."

"Does he often have two glasses?" I asked.

"Very rarely," replied Adele, whose lovely eyes were as intoxicating as any alcoholic drink… "That only happens when our Society wins a great and decisive battle."

"A great and decisive battle" caught me unawares.

"Excuse me, Miss," I said. "I am a novice among you, and I still do not fully grasp your meaning. Earlier, your father presented me as a prisoner of war. And just now, you mentioned a battle. What does all this mean?"

Miss Adele smiled and fixing her innocent eyes on me, she said, "Sir, it appears that you have never read our newspaper."

"I didn't even know one existed…"

"All right, then. It gets published every Saturday, which is tomorrow. You should pay the one sou [ten para] and purchase a copy."

"What is that paper called?"

"*En Avant* [*Forward March!*]," replied Miss Adele with the most serious expression on her face.

"And what does it contain?"

"The official reports of our battles."

These responses seemed so bizarre to me that I had no idea how to respond. Naturally, the young woman noticed my bafflement and, as though she meant to confuse me further, she said, "I can see that you truly are a novice. But don't worry, you'll soon figure it all out… Be here tomorrow at four, so that I can take you around our army headquarters and give you a copy of our newspaper. I'm also the newspaper's distributor."

"Tomorrow at four?" I mumbled. "But, Miss, I may not be able to come at that time."

"You are an enemy prisoner, and you are in my custody," replied Miss Adele suddenly looking stern. "You will therefore obey me and be here at the stated time."

"Very well, Miss," I promised her, realizing that I had no other choice.

The meal finally concluded, and the waiter served some oranges and apples.

"Bring us two bottles of champagne," ordered the President. "We are going to drink to our new prisoner!"

The server returned shortly, carrying two bottles that looked just like champagne.

"Hand those over! I am going to open them," declared our peerless President.

He grabbed a bottle and, as though it were actually champagne, he removed the metal wires and began to carefully remove the cork with his fingers.

There was a sudden pop, the cork flew out, and the foamy liquid was poured into our glasses.

There was no doubt about it. This had to be champagne.

"To your health," proclaimed the President, reaching over to me and clinking his glass with mine.

"To everyone's health," I replied.

And I brought the glass to my lips.

Alas! The champagne was nothing more than some kind of effervescent pear cordial.

And so concluded this first meal with the "Good Templars."

We bid each other goodnight when it was time to leave. And as she shook my hand, Miss Adele said, "I will be waiting for you here tomorrow at four."

Her voice was so commanding that I replied almost timidly, "Yes, Miss. I will be here tomorrow at four."

The next morning, I told my friends about my latest experience, and we had a good laugh.

"The poor girl set up a rendezvous for us this evening too," I said. "She's going to take me around the army headquarters and make me read their newspaper..."

Towards evening, a few us friends went to a café near the Boulevards. I had almost forgotten about the previous evening's events, when suddenly, I saw Miss Adele motioning to me from across the road.

They hadn't served our drinks yet. I got up instantly and told my friends, "Wait here. I'll be right back."

I went up to the young lady.

"I'll bet you forgot our rendezvous," she said.

"No, I remembered," I replied a little ruffled.

"But it's already four-thirty."

"What are you saying, Miss?"

"I am saying what is a simple fact," replied Miss Adele, taking out a small watch from her breast pocket.

"Unbelievable!" I feigned. "It seems that my watch has stopped."

The lovely lady probably figured this was a lie, but she added gently, "No harm done. Fortunately, we ran into each other, and if you have no other commitments, we can move on to our 'army headquarters.'"

"I am at your service. Not that I have a choice, since I am your prisoner, after all."

"Are you sorry about that?"

"Not at all."

We walked on from the Boulevard des Italiens to the Place de l'Opéra.

"Are we going far?" I asked.

"No, we're close, left of the Opéra, No. 3 Rue Scribe."

And so, we arrived several minutes later at the appointed address. We entered a building bearing the following inscription, "Salvation Army."

And only then did I realize what I had gotten myself into. I had often heard of the Salvation Army, even in Constantinople. But I thought that this army only existed in England.

We walked along a narrow corridor and finally arrived at a door. It was being guarded by an old woman.

"Is Major Charles in?" asked my companion.

"Yes, Miss."

The lady opened the door, and we walked in together.

It was a vast auditorium full of chairs. A burly, forty-something man was marching back and forth like a gendarme, one hand holding a small newspaper.

He approached us as soon as he looked up.

After the usual greetings, Miss Adele said, "Major Charles, please allow me to present you with our newest prisoner, Mr. Yervant Odian, a Christian Armenian..."

"Yes, the one who was captured in the fortress of Rue Trevise," interrupted the major smiling smugly.

"The very same... But how did you know? Had you already heard?"

"I just saw the report in our official newspaper..."

And Major Charles showed me the little newspaper in his hand.

"But how can that be? Did they already run the latest issue?!" exclaimed Adele. "That means I have to distribute it."

"They just brought it in five minutes ago," the man replied.

Of course, this exchange intrigued me. I wanted to know right away what they had written about me so, I said, "If I may, Sir. May I please see the piece about me?"

"Here you are," replied the Major, offering me the newspaper and pointing out the passage about me.

This small newspaper, *En Avant* – which I mentioned earlier – was the official organ of the Salvation Army. And although I cannot recall the article about me verbatim, it went something like this: "A Fresh Victory – Just as our paper was about to go to press, we received some great news from the Fortress of Trevise. After fighting for two months among the enemy's forces, a young man from the East by the name of Mr. Odian has surrendered to us and joined the Society of Temperance. This gentleman – a Christian with extensive knowledge of the Bible – has vowed to become a powerful new force in our army. Bless him and praise the Lord."

"May I keep this paper?" I asked the Major.

"Of course."

Miss Adele turned to me and said, "I have to distribute the paper. Please wait for me here. The military drills start in about fifteen minutes, at five, and last until seven. I'll be back by then, and we can go to the dining hall together. Don't even think of leaving without me. Otherwise, you will receive a reprimand!"

"Miss, I would never defy your command," I replied.

Turning to me, Major Charles explained, "Miss Adele is a bit strict with prisoners. But she is also very caring and accommodating, provided that you do not disobey."

Miss Adele rewarded me with a lovely smile and left.

"Does Miss Adele hold a specific rank in the Salvation Army?" I asked the Major when we were alone.

"She's still just a Non-Commissioned Officer," replied the senior military commander. "But she has a great future ahead of her, because she has courage and daring. You are lucky to be in the custody of such a brave officer."

"That is my sole consolation in captivity," I replied smiling. "But please do tell. How has she demonstrated her valor up to now?"

"She's demonstrating it this very instant!" exclaimed the Major.

"How so? Could you please explain?"

"Simply by distributing our newspaper in the streets of Paris, especially in working-class neighborhoods."

"Is that really so dangerous?"

Major Charles folded his arms across his chest, directed his eyes at me, and said, "Young man, what Miss Adele and our other female comrades are doing here in Paris is far more trying than what the missionaries were doing in deepest Africa or China or among the savages of South America… You, a man, endowed with physical strength and perhaps even audacity, can you carry the newspaper *En Avant* into those enemy circles of unbelievers and skeptics without apprehension, without hesitation, despite the scorn directed at you at every turn, despite the lewd taunts, lascivious propositions, shameless comments, and coarse gestures…? Could you withstand, oh young man, the cackles and jeers erupting around you and at you with every step you take? Could you withstand hearing the mockery aimed at your deepest convictions, at your most sincere beliefs, at the purity of what you hold most sacred…? Well, that is what Miss Adele and her friends are doing with unparalleled courage."

Unable to proffer a reply, I lowered my head in silence at the truth of the Major's comments.

In fairness, spreading such propaganda was much more difficult in the streets of Paris than in the deserts of Africa.

For instance, I did not have the pluck to do what Miss Adele was doing with such unfazed devotion. She did not expect a reward and simply acted on her single-minded pursuit to save the souls of those who had strayed.

After subjecting me to utter confusion, the Major said, "Goodbye," and left.

Alone, I withdrew into a corner and began to read the official newspaper of the Salvation Army.

From start to finish, it was drafted like a military pamphlet. And if one did not know any better, he could easily be fooled into believing that every corner of the world had sunk into vicious warfare.

The headlines alone were enough to terrify the reader: "A Horrible Battle in Switzerland," "A Glorious Victory in Southern India." "After fierce resistance in the United States of America, the enemy finally surrenders in the state of Texas." "Eighteen prisoners in one day on the

Cape of Good Hope." And so on and so forth. And then there was the section on official business, which announced that Sergeant Major John Marx had been promoted to the rank of Major as a reward for his most recent show of valor in Shanghai; that Major James Harold had been named Vice-Lieutenant to lead the battle in Belgium.

I had almost concluded this informative reading when I heard some music with deafening drums and blasting trumpets. The Salvation Army was approaching.

Sure enough, the door flung open, and the musicians entered, followed by a parade of male and female soldiers waving their flags and roaring a marching song that denounced Satan and his schemes.

Notwithstanding all the commotion, the Salvation Army consisted of a scant 60 – 70 people. Once they had marched into the hall, everyone took their seats, and the band assumed its position next to the podium at the front.

Major Charles stood at the podium and drowned the auditorium in his rumbling voice, "To arms, to arms…! The enemy's attacks are fiercer than ever. It has raised fortresses of evil and deviance to defeat us. It has laid snares of lechery to entrap us. We are facing an ambush of skepticism. A mob of drunks will soon be upon us. And we must scale the great wall of gambling obstructing our way. What are we to do, troops? Should we succumb to that united force commanded by Satan? Will we act like cowards, drop our weapons, and run? Will we let ourselves be trampled, destroyed…?"

The entire auditorium erupted with the resounding response, "Never! Never! War! War!"

A contented Major Charles looked around triumphantly and continued, "Furious by its losses, the enemy will persist. It will continue to attack from every direction, left and right, north and south, east and west; at all times of day, from dawn to dusk to the middle of the night; at every hour, minute, and second. Tireless and undaunted, it will strive at every turn to cast us into the abyss of defeat… Will it succeed…?"

"No! No!" repeated the assembly at the top of its voice.

"Yes, that is correct," continued the Major with growing rage. "We will not fall into the abyss of defeat! Forward march, troops! The unseen General of the Salvation Army is God Himself. And God cannot be defeated by Satan…

"Never! Never!"

"If Satan ever defeats God," continued Charles, "I would rather tear up my uniform than sprout a couple of horns and grow a dangling tail…"

This unexpected bit of humor lightened the crowd's mood.

The Major continued speaking for half an hour. And at the end of his sermon, he raised the battle cry, "Long live the holy war! Long live the good war!"

The band began a marching song, and the group piped up with, "Onwards, to War!"

That is when they began their gymnastics prayer.

I highly recommend the gymnastics prayer to anyone with a penchant for that sort of sport.

The Major is standing at the podium; the band is playing; and the group is belting out a marching tune denouncing the enemy.

Suddenly, during the song, the Major begins moving his arms and legs in what appears to be a Swedish gymnastics routine. And the Salvation Army's soldiers – both male and female – follow suit.

This gymnastics prayer lasts twenty minutes. Then everyone drops into their seats, panting.

What made this a very special sort of prayer was that it strengthened both body and soul.

Yet, there is nothing new under the sun, as wise Solomon, God rest his soul, used to say. Anyone who has ever attended a ritual at Pera's Dervish lodge near Tünel must admit that the aforementioned proceedings are just another version of those ceremonies – a European version, if you like. The synthesis of music, song, and physical movement always arouses a sense of spiritual intoxication in man. I have often witnessed this effect during the Salvation Army's "military drills."

When this salutary prayer was over, Major Charles – who was still standing at the podium – said, "I now invite our comrades up to the stage to make their public confessions."

A man wearing a long redingote and spectacles appeared. He came forward, his arms folded across his chest and his eyes riveted to the ground. He approached the stage slowly, climbed up the steps, and stood next to the senior officer at the podium.

As he raised his head, I could not help yelping in surprise.

It was Artaki!...

Artaki was a young Armenian man. He had been around the block a few times. After drifting about in Italy, Belgium, and England, he ended up in Paris, living hand to mouth every day by working whatever odd jobs he could find. He was an incredibly witty, impish, hilarious character. And he paid no mind whatsoever to what the future held in store. His company was a great laugh, provided, of course, that he did not prey on our gullibility.

I had not seen him for over a month. I figured he had left Paris for more welcoming shores. But here he was! I found him at the Salvation Army headquarters…

Artaki stood quietly by the podium. He seemed to be buried in deep thought. And then he suddenly proclaimed, "I was rescued from an excruciating trap. Thank the Lord… I wish to confess everything and ask that you help me gain my strength back with your prayers. I found myself in a struggle of terrible proportions. And I almost succumbed to its power… I must have fought harder against Satan's disciples than Jacob wrestling with the Angel of the Lord…"

This prelude sparked our curiosity.

"Confess, so that you may finally regain your strength and find release," rose the Major's mournful voice.

"It all happened last night," Artaki continued without a hint of irony. "I had just received my fifteen francs in benefits at our headquarters. I went back to my room for a few moments of prayer and rest. I usually take the side-streets. But, last night, I unfortunately went via the Boulevards. Satan must have sowed that impulse. At Café de Prince on the Boulevard Montmartre, I suddenly heard a whisper, 'psst-psst.' I turned around and saw a very young, beautiful woman beckoning to me. My reaction spurred her on. And soon she was taking my arm and telling me to buy her a drink…"

Artaki's confession provoked murmurs of outrage.

"I realized right then and there," continued Artaki, "that Satan had entrapped me… I tried to snatch my arm away from the enemy's claws, as the lewd creature taunted me with her excruciating vulgarities. Then she almost dragged me by force to the Rue du Faubourg-Montmartre…"

The auditorium gasped in terror and suspense. Many, especially the women, covered their faces in shock. Others cried out "Oh, oh, ooh!" in their horror.

Artaki continued unperturbed. "Of course, I could have resisted this temptation and walked away, although it may have taken a herculean effort. But, alas, I did not have it in me. That creature of damnation roused the beast within me, inciting my passions as she touched me, as her breath caressed my ear, as her hair faintly brushed against my brow… At that moment, I was blinded to the image of our Lord…"

The Major motioned for the band to play a hymn. And everyone sang "The Image of the Lord Is My Mirror."

When they concluded, Charles told the penitent, "Please continue."

"When the woman noticed my resistance slacking, she led me to a café on the same street. I stood there quiet and confused, tortured by my conscience. The servant of Satan beckoned the waiter and ordered two glasses of an alcoholic drink…"

"An alcoholic drink!" exclaimed several members of the group.

"That's right, my dear sirs," Artaki said calmly and in earnest. "Two glasses of an alcoholic drink, one for her and one for me…"

"And did you empty that glass…?" hollered the Major.

Artaki lowered his eyes and replied gravely, "Yes, Major Charles, we emptied our glasses together. And as soon as we did, that wicked creature called the waiter and ordered another round…"

"Oh, Lord, grant him your mercy," bellowed the Major.

"Oh Lord, grant me your mercy," repeated Artaki.

"Forgive him, Lord," pleaded the entire Salvation Army.

The sinner continued his confession.

"After the second glass, Satan had overpowered me… There was a third glass, and the woman finally said, 'That's enough. Let's pay up and go.' We settled the bill and left the cafe. I bid that evil creature, 'Goodnight.' And she replied as she tugged at my shirt, 'You are coming to my place tonight.' 'That's impossible,' I insisted. 'It's very possible,' she objected. 'Where do you live?' I asked. 'Near here. On the Rue Bréda,' she replied. As soon as I heard that scandalous street's name, my whole body shuddered. But, alas, we walked on together. When we arrived at the Place St. Georges, the woman said, 'Come on, let's have another drink on the way.' And before I could reply, she was pulling me into a tavern. We guzzled several more drinks and left. I mustered every drop of spiritual strength I had left in me to tell her, 'Goodbye. I am going home.' She burst out in a crude, vulgar cackle. And, alas, I kept walking beside her. Eventually, we arrived at a house. She rang the doorbell. And, in that moment, I awakened to the full horror of my situation. I could see below me the chasm of defeat, the abyss of sin. I shuddered and recalled the Salvation Army. I was one of its soldiers. And I had betrayed it to the enemy… I gathered all my strength, and just as the door opened, I fled as fast as my legs could carry me. The woman beckoned me to return. But I was now free from Satan's clasp…"

The auditorium filled with a hum of joy and relief. The Major beamed triumphantly.

"It's true. I did not look back. I just ran," continued Artaki. "I got home, shut myself in my room, dropped to my knees, and praised the Lord who had saved me in my hour of need… Blessed be the name of the Lord."

Artaki stepped down from the podium and was followed by a young woman.

She had also been drawn into temptation the previous day. She had been pursued by a young man as she was walking down the street. He had propositioned her. But the power of the Lord had risen within her, and she had found a policeman to get rid of the young man.

This confession provoked an objection.

"Why appeal to someone else when you have our army and its arsenal?" enquired Major Charles. "Is your own soul too weak to repel the enemy…?"

The Major turned to the woman and said, "What if you had not found a policeman? Does that mean you would have fallen into temptation…? Does your soul need a policeman for protection?"

"Oh, no," stuttered the young woman.

"What if there were no policemen around?" pressed the Major.

"I would have appealed to the Lord to give me strength," she replied.

I was satisfied with this answer. But the soldier was unconvinced and persisted, "So just because you found a policeman, you felt no need to appeal to the Lord. Rather the policeman than the Lord. You put more faith in the policeman than in the Lord…"

These harsh, hurtful reproaches bludgeoned the poor woman over the head.

"The Lord is the supreme Police Chief and the most senior General," concluded the Major.

Then an old man came up to the podium. His face was covered with hair, and he resembled a dervish. He had a long beard reaching down to his chest and wore green-tinted spectacles that gave him an oddly nefarious expression.

"I am dead," declared this strange man. "And I ask my friends to perform my funeral rites."

This announcement was followed by perfect silence.

"Is this man insane?" I asked one of the soldiers sitting next to me.

"What do you mean?" exclaimed the outraged man. "Don't you know him...?

"No, sir. I am setting foot in this place for the very first time," I explained.

"Then, I will have you know that this eminent elder is the Reverend Sir Perrier, the spiritual leader of the Salvation Army's regiment in Paris."

At that moment, the Major, who was standing by the podium, turned respectfully toward the elderly gentleman and said, "Reverend Sir Perrier. Could you please tell us whether you died of natural causes or whether you were murdered...?"

"I was murdered!" the old man's trembling voice resounded.

"Who murdered you?"

"Corporal Georges," replied the regiment's leader.

Searching looks went around the room at the sound of this name.

"Is Corporal Georges in this auditorium?" barked Charles.

"No, no," replied several people from their seats.

"We must record his absence in our army log," said the Major.

And then, turning to the old man, he continued, "Now, Reverend Sir Perrier, would you be so kind as to give us the details concerning your murder?"

"No!" replied the old man. "I have reported the facts in detail to our General, and there is no need to repeat them here. All I ask of you is to perform my funeral rites. It pains me that my murderer is absent and will not be able to take part in the ritual."

These words were followed by the funeral rites accompanied by music and another round of gymnastics prayers.

And yet, I was still in the dark about that living-dead man. So, when the military drills ended, I asked the soldier next to me, whom I had already engaged in conversation, "What is this murder business all about?"

Chapter 10

"This is not the first time that our eminent leader has been murdered in this fashion," he replied. "By one of our comrades. But it seems that this time, it was especially gruesome, since he felt the need to report the event directly to our General."

"But despite those murders, he is as alive and well as we are," I observed.

"Do you think so?" he said.

But nothing he said helped unlock this enigma.

"But what does the Reverend leader ultimately mean in reference to these strange murders?" I persisted.

"Our leader," explained the soldier, "feels that he is being murdered every time someone in our contingent commits a grave sin… So, for instance, it seems that Corporal Georges has succumbed to a terrible transgression. With a lesser sin, he might have simply told us without reporting it to the General."

"The Major asked him whether he had died of 'natural causes.' What does he mean?"

"That if the leader himself had committed the same sin, he would have confessed it to us rather than telling the General."

The auditorium was almost empty. I was standing around waiting for Miss Adele's arrival, when I saw our buffoon, Artaki, exiting with one of the soldiers.

"Artaki," I called.

He turned around, saw me, and ran up to me.

"What are you doing here?" I asked with a chuckle.

"Please, don't mess this up," he said quietly. "I'm in a very delicate position here… What about you? What are you doing here?"

"I'm a captive."

"You too…?"

"Unfortunately, yes. Didn't you see it in your official newspaper?"

"Well, then, wait here a minute so that we can catch up," said Artaki. He sent off his friend and returned to continue our conversation.

"I joined the Salvation Army two months ago," he told me. "I've finally made it. Food, drink, and merriment! Were you here for my confession?"

"Yes, I was. I heard it from start to finish. I think you made it all up."

"On the contrary," Artaki replied. "It was all true. I just changed the ending a little."

"You mean the part where you turned around and ran away…"

"What's a man to do, brother. You have to keep on living," was Artaki's melancholy reply.

"And what's your status here now, seeing as you're so desperate to hold onto it?"

"If I have several more similar confrontations with Satan and get the better of him, then I will get a promotion. But I must be careful that I don't get caught… Because, you should know that this place is full of spies."

"Is that right…?"

"You see all those innocent-looking young girls? The ones that were praying with downcast eyes? Every one of them is a shrewd spy. They submit daily reports of everything they see and hear."

"Are there any other Armenians in the Salvation Army apart from you?" I asked.

"There used to be two young Armenian men from the provinces," Artaki replied. "But they were sent to England two weeks ago."

"Why is that?"

"Because they didn't know the language and were of no use here."

"What are they going to do in England?"

"They are going to work on the farms owned by the Salvation Army, pure and simple… Because our army has extensive land holdings, which it entrusts to foreign laborers when they appeal for assistance. The men cultivate those lands without pay. In exchange, they get a bed and some basic sustenance."

"Why don't you just come out and call it what it is: exploitation of the poor."

"Or the stupid," replied Artaki. "If they had any sense, they would turn the situation on its head and exploit the Salvation Army instead."

"Like you, for example."

My fascinating conversation with Artaki would have continued if Miss Adele hadn't walked in just then.

"Mr. Odian," said the charming lady. "If you would be so kind, it is time for us to leave."

"I am at your service."

And taking my leave from our friend Artaki, I rushed to Miss Adele's side.

"What do you think of our military drills?" asked the young woman.

"They were very moving and uplifting," I replied. "The ritual confessions had an especially powerful effect on me. They reminded me of the early days of Christianity, which I've read about with rapt interest…"

"I can see that you have penetrated the Salvation Army's real aims," said Miss Adele, "namely, to return Christianity to its simpler origins without its complicated ritualistic aspects. Those were inherited as mere vestiges of pagan traditions."

Such profound observations from the lips of a seventeen-year-old girl seemed so extraordinary to me that I could not help remarking, "But, Miss, how could you be so deeply cognizant of such religious matters?"

"What would you have me do with my time?" asked the young lady as she turned to me in surprise. "Can you think of a better occupation…?"

"What?" I exclaimed. "You mean to say that this is the life you deem most suited to your needs…? I can only interpret this as a sort of self-sacrifice, a sort of penance, nothing more. And you are simply not old enough for such self-sacrifice and penance."

"What am I old enough for?" asked Miss Adele.

The answer was at the tip of my tongue, but I could not bring myself to spit it out. That young lady had an overpowering effect on me. I simply could not shake it off.

"I know what you're thinking. You don't want to come out with it," she continued, "but I'll do it for you… At my age, I should be enjoying myself. Is that right?"

"Yes," I mumbled. "That's exactly what I wanted to say."

"All right, then. You can rest assured that my actions are burdened neither by self-sacrifice nor penance, but consist rather of pure pleasure… Yes, indeed! Pleasure in the most physical sense."

"Excuse me?" I exclaimed. "You mean to tell me that distributing the Salvation Army's newspaper through the streets of Paris gives you that much pleasure, despite having to run the gauntlet of derision and mockery by a bunch of brutes every time… Forgive me, Miss, but even Major Charles would disagree with you on this point."

"How so?" enquired Miss Adele, her curiosity piqued.

"He told me during our meeting that what you have been doing is far more trying and challenging than what the missionaries are doing by martyring themselves among savages in the name of Christianity."

"Trying and challenging. Of course, I accept that. But can't such tribulation be a source of great pleasure...? Doesn't martyring oneself offer its pleasures? Didn't Jesus himself experience unsurpassed pleasure during his crucifixion...?"

And a peculiar brilliance illuminated my young interlocutor's eyes as she uttered these words.

We were crossing the Grands Boulevards on our way to the restaurant on the Rue St. Martin. I risked scandalizing the young lady and replied, "As far as I'm aware, the source of the greatest pleasure is love."

"No, it isn't," she said firmly. "Not love, lust!... See? I can go even further than you. For example, I love the Lord. I love my father and mother, sisters and brothers. But does that give me any pleasure? Not at all, never. On the contrary, love sometimes causes me great suffering."

"But, Miss, love only..."

"I know what you're about to say," interrupted Miss Adele. "You are going to speak of sensual love... A handsome young man who sweeps me off my feet and to whom I..."

"Yes, that's exactly what I wanted to say."

"I admit that there is some ephemeral pleasure or ecstasy in that, but so ephemeral and so physical that it does not merit any further thought. Whereas the ecstasy, which grants us spiritual pleasure, is both pure and eternal."

"Could you please explain to me the nature of such ecstasy?"

"Speaking only for myself, each time I save a wayward soul – or as we put it, take someone captive –, I experience a powerful and prolonged spiritual ecstasy that, I suspect, would make your version of romantic pleasure seem absolutely meaningless."

"Miss," I told her, "you are a genuine saint."

"Not at all. I am quite simply a hedonist..."

We eventually arrived at the restaurant, where the President, his family, and many other members of our organization had already gathered.

"And here is the prisoner accompanied by his captor," said Adele's father with a chuckle. "Is he being kept under such strict watch, because he might perhaps try to escape?"

"I dropped the gentleman off for the Salvation Army's military drills, and then I fetched him here," explained the young lady.

"Uh-oh!" exclaimed the old man. "One must be careful not to put him off with too much at once… We should ease him into it little by little. The Salvation Army is not in urgent need of soldiers at the moment."

"But Mr. Odian was very impressed with what he witnessed," replied the lady as she turned towards me.

"I am very grateful to Miss Adele, who was gracious enough to take me to army headquarters," I said promptly. "And please do believe me when I tell you that I will be going back for more."

The dinner went as merrily as it had on the previous night. To be honest, I was rather pleased with my new acquaintances, whose cheerful, honest conversation was extremely engaging.

It must be said that they never bombarded me with religious propaganda or intolerable sermons. And it was hard to believe that I was surrounded by such a pious circle. The elderly President, who was extremely erudite, always found an enjoyable topic of conversation. And he was so amiable that we were always reluctant to part with him.

"We need some dedicated soldiers," said the elderly President.

"What for?" asked several young men.

"For the Midnight Mission," replied an old man.

"It's a project that gives our Lord great pleasure," said our President. "And I am certain that we will be able to find willing participants among these young men."

And then, he turned to me and added, "Mr. Odian, here's a beautiful opportunity for you to get involved."

"But," I mumbled, "I still have no idea what I am supposed to do."

"I will explain presently," said the old man. "Unfortunately, Paris deserves the name 'New Babylon.' This unique capital city, which serves as the cradle of science, art, and literature, is simultaneously a center of depravity. Thousands of inexperienced young men come here with the best intentions of receiving an education and bettering themselves. But they fall headfirst into the abyss of depravity, inflicting terrible harm upon themselves and driving their parents to desperation. If this city has hosted the apex of perfection in science, art, and literature, it has also facilitated the unbridled proliferation of addiction and debauchery, immorality and indecency. A young man raised in Paris sees two paths stretching out before him: one leads towards responsibility, diligence, cultivation, and marriage; and the other, towards debauchery, extravagance, and addiction; one is challenging but directs him towards perfection, while the other is easy but steers him towards failure. That well-meaning but naïve young man, who remains blind to himself and weak in character, ultimately wanders onto the fateful path of disaster. He is then lost forevermore to his loved ones, his fatherland, and his God."

The old man's words reverberated in the profound silence. They were greeted with mumbling assent.

"What you say is true," confirmed the President.

"It is the intention of our Society," continued the elderly newcomer, "to caution those young men against the road to deviance and to compel them toward the straight and narrow path. It is our intention to stand at the junction of those two paths. And whenever we see a young man wavering between the two, to advise him gently, 'My friend, tread not the path to your left; stay the course on the right path.'"

"Bravo!" cried the President.

"We are seeking the kind of soldiers who will stand at that junction," continued the elderly newcomer.

I had more or less surmised what was being expected of me, but there was still much that remained in the dark. There were other young men who seemed to feel the same way. One of them said, "We do not deny the truth of your statements. I am sure that many of us here wish to devote ourselves to this sublime calling. But what will our participation entail? And what exactly does the Society mean with reference to the 'Midnight Mission?'"

"Your mission is made clear in that name," replied the old man. "Midnight is the preferred hour of crime and deviance. The devil seems to wake when the angels retire at midnight. Take a young man who has spent his day working assiduously. In the evening, he goes to a café for a tipple, supposedly to whet his appetite. Then, he goes out for dinner, orders a digestif, rum, cognac, Mar, or whatever. As if that weren't enough, he then heads to a cabaret where a bunch of half-naked women titillate his fantasies with their suggestive song and dance. Let us not forget that said cabaret does not charge for entry, but it requires its patrons to purchase an alcoholic drink to pay for their seats. The cabaret shuts its doors half an hour before midnight. Where does the young man go then...?"

"To bed," replied one of the listeners.

"No!" exclaimed the old man. "He goes to a brothel..."

"Not all of them," someone objected.

"Not all of them, but most of them."

The dining room filled with a moment of overwhelming silence. The old man looked around the room and continued, "And lo, it is at this psychologically charged moment, at midnight, that we must act, for deviance makes its appearance under the cloak of darkness. That is when we must confront it, combat it, fight it face to face, seek it out in its strongholds, and subdue it there... We must topple it within its own ramparts. Which young men here have the mettle to wage this battle?"

"There must be many, of course," our President replied.

"In that case, let them sign up on this registration form."

And the speaker pulled out a large, folded sheet of paper from his pocket. He unfolded it and said, "As you can see, there is a long list of signatures."

One could indeed see for oneself those numerous signatures at the bottom of the page.

The old man offered the form to his young companion and said, "Read it aloud. These gentlemen should hear what it says."

It was a long text repeating most of the old man's most poignant remarks in its preamble. This was followed by an announcement that a new society had been founded to battle deviance and debauchery. Interested parties would be obliged to perform the following tasks:

- a. At midnight, to take up their position at the entrance of a disreputable street
- b. To ask passersby whether they intend to visit a brothel
- c. In such cases, to try to dissuade passersby with indisputable proof of their intentions' negative moral, material, and physical consequences
- d. To strive to the best of one's ability to minimize potentially loud or unpleasant reactions to these sermons
- e. Should the individual become confrontational, to yield without hesitation
- f. Those who demonstrably succeed by steering individuals away from such streets will receive a reward of fifty francs
- g. Those who succeed thrice in one month will receive a set monthly salary

When the reading concluded, the old man turned to us and said, "Gentlemen, as you can see, we do not expect you to simply sacrifice yourselves. Whoever feels capable of performing this task is urged to come forward..."

Several young men went up and signed the form. I did not feel up to the task and remained seated.

But I noticed that the President and Miss Adele had fixed their eyes on me, and I felt chastened by their gaze.

"And you, Mr. Odian?" the President finally spoke up. "Won't you take part in this commendable society?"

"I wholeheartedly support its work," I replied.

"And yet, you show no sign of joining the effort."

"Because I do not feel that I am capable of carrying out that sort of mission."

"The Lord will give you strength. All you need is the will."

"Do you think so?"

"I have faith that He will."

"Your participation in this mission would please me greatly," added Miss Adele.

There was no way out then.

I walked steadily towards the table. The form lay open and waiting. And I signed up.

"We expect you to start this very night," said the President of the Institute of Midnight. I subsequently learned that he was this society's founder and President.

"So soon!" objected one of the young enlistees.

"It is never too soon to save a wayward soul," advised the man sternly.

"If we could at least get some guidance from people with some experience in this line of work. Then maybe we could start right away," replied the young man.

"Don't you worry about that. The enlistees can come with me. I will provide them with all the guidance they need." At those words, five of us took leave of our friends and left with the old man and his companion.

After a long walk, we went into an apartment building on the Rue due Faubourg-Poissonnière, which served as both the old man's residence and the new society's headquarters.

Three young men were already waiting in the reception hall. Must I add that they were all members of the "Midnight Mission?"

The old man, who was called Mr. Scott – and thus obviously hailed from England – made a great show of honoring us. After serving us some tea, he said, "Now, gentlemen, let us plan out the battlefronts. There are eight or nine of you here, so we can attack at least four different targets…"

Then he pulled a small notebook out of his pocket and said, "Here is a map of the enemy's exact positions."

What Mr. Scott called the map showing the enemy's exact positions was nothing more than a list of the most disreputable streets in Paris.

"Which of you live on the left bank and which on the right?" he asked.

The right and left banks refer to the areas on either side of the river Seine.

It just so happened that five of us lived on the left bank and four on the right. I was among the latter.

He perused his notebook and filled out four cards with different addresses. He handed them to the four young men, and told them, "You should pair up and go to the address on that card at around midnight to carry out your mission."

But this arrangement meant that the ninth young man was left out.

"So, one of us is extra," commented one of the men.

"He can be a reservist and monitor the others," decided Mr. Scott.

A member of the Temperance Society by the name of Mr. Henri also lived on the right bank. He approached me and asked, "Would you like to join me?"

"With pleasure."

It was not even eleven o'clock yet, and there was still plenty of time before we had to get to work.

Nevertheless, I and my partner took leave of the old man and went outside.

I was deeply distressed by the work that lay ahead of me. I had no idea how to do the weird, impossible job I'd been tasked with – all the more so, because I certainly did not possess the kind of inner strength and courage that fueled Miss Adele.

Mr. Henri also looked rather worried.

We walked quietly for a long time. My partner checked his watch and said, "We still have a whole hour."

"Yes," I replied automatically.

"Let's go sit somewhere," he suggested.

We went into a café and sat in the farthest back corner.

My companion was visibly anxious and kept throwing suspicious glances at me.

The server asked us, "What would you like to order?"

Henri looked at me and said, "What are you going to drink?"

And he cast another suspicious glance at me. That is when I cottoned on to what was bothering him.

"I'll have the same as you," I replied mischievously.

"No, please, you decide," he insisted.

"I will have half a carafe of white wine and some oysters," I said decisively.

Henri's eyes glowed with joy and relief.

I pretended not to notice the change in my companion's expression. And I told the server that we were ready to order.

"Bring me six oysters and half a carafe of white wine."

"And for the other gentleman?" asked the server.

"The gentleman still needs some time to decide."

The server walked away. Henri kept darting his eyes at me in astonishment. He looked both delighted and suspicious.

"I hope you're not going to turn me in," I said with a chuckle.

"Are you actually going to drink the wine?" he asked.

"Yes, why not…?"

"But you're a member of the Temperance Society, right?"

"We're pretty far from the Rue St. Martin at the moment," I replied.

The server brought the carafe of wine.

I filled my glass and took a sip. This gesture seemed to settle it for Henri.

"Garçon," he commanded, "bring me another half carafe of white wine and six oysters."

"But, Mr. Henri," I objected, "I thought you were a longstanding member of the Temperance Society?"

"But I'm just as far from the Rue St. Martin as you are," he replied.

We seemed to have an understanding.

We emptied our carafes and put away our oysters with great relish.

"Would you permit me to order another twelve oysters to have with a bottle of wine?" asked Henri.

"Whyever not?" I replied.

"Today is the first of the month, and I would like to invite you to be my guest," the young man added with a smile.

"Do you work for a company?" I asked.

"Yes, at a bank."

And after a moment's pause, he added, "Thanks to the President of the Temperance Society, Mr. Clemence…"

"You must be an old member."

"I signed up four years ago," replied Mr. Henri. "I am also a member of the Society of Christian Youth and the Bible Society."

"Are you Protestant?" I asked.

"No, I'm Jewish. But I converted to Catholicism, although I'm going to become a Protestant soon, when the Society keeps its promise."

"Which promise?"

"A raise on my monthly salary."

His confession was enough for me. It was my turn to explain the circumstances that led me to become a teetotaler.

But the clock was ticking, and it was close to midnight.

"What are we going to do now?" I asked. "Are we going to get on with the task at hand?"

"Let's go over to that address they gave us and take a little tour, since it's not too far from here."

We were now fast friends. We went out and made our way towards the Rue Bréda.

Henri was a witty, sensible, and energetic young man who couldn't stop talking and making jokes.

"I can see that you're not the type of man suited to the 'Midnight Mission,'" I told him. "Why were you first in line to enlist?"

"Because I could tell right away that it was an excellent opportunity for me to get ahead."

"But how? I mean, you have no intention of completing your mission."

"What do you mean I have no intention?" cried Henri. "On the contrary, I've decided to stop at nothing to save wayward souls from stumbling onto the road of debauchery. What about you? Being my partner, don't you intend to do the same?"

"I only signed up under moral duress," I confessed.

"To satisfy Miss Adele?"

"Perhaps…"

"I can assure you now that there are no prospects on that front… But that's not the real issue. Since you've already signed up, you might as well do something."

"All right, then. Let's go do something."

"Here we are at our workplace."

And indeed, we were already at the Rue Bréda. Henri said, "Let's give it a shot. If it goes well, great! If not, we'll get out of here."

We walked up and down the Rue Laferrière for a while, until we finally saw a teenage boy cautiously walking by, his eyes scanning the windows.

"And here we have the perfect prey," Henri said quietly. "Let's approach him and try to have a chat."

"I'll come along, but I'm not saying a word," I replied.

"I can see that you don't exactly have the makings of an apostle," he said with a laugh. "Alright, come along and say nothing."

And he strode assertively towards the boy.

"I'll bet you're looking for a house on this street, my dear sir," he suddenly told the boy, who looked up at us startled.

"And I'll bet that this is the first time you've been here on this street," continued Henri.

"Yes," the boy mumbled. "It's my first time here. But, sir, I don't understand what you want."

"I can see that," Henri continued. "It's just that my friend and I are also looking for an address that we can't seem to find."

The kid looked visibly disconcerted by this conversation and didn't reply to my partner.

The latter had made up his mind not to let the kid off the hook.

"I believe that you're also looking for an address," he said.

"Yes."

"Can I give you a piece of advice?"

"What kind of advice?"

"You should follow in our example."

"What do you mean?"

"What I mean is, we had the same idea as you when we first came here. But as soon as we walked down this street, we changed our minds and decided to go home and sleep."

The kid didn't respond.

Henri continued obstinately.

"It'll be for our own good. First, that money will stay in our pockets. Moreover, we won't be putting our health at risk. And…"

"Leave me alone!" exploded the kid's voice.

I gently tugged on my partner's arm to leave the kid alone. But Henri didn't budge.

"Just one last thing, young man," he persevered.

We were just passing an open door at that moment. The kid leapt in through the doorway and glowered at us.

"Now, we can go get some rest with a clear conscience that we have fulfilled our duties," said Henri.

"As for me, I can assure you that I will not be doing this again," I replied.

"What?!" he cried. "Are you going to resign from the 'Midnight Mission?'"

"Yes, tomorrow morning."

"I advise you not to do that, because it will elicit a terrible reaction."

"But what would you have me do?"

"Stay on as a member and do nothing."

"But why would I abuse the trust of Mr. Scott and Mr. Clemence?"

"I have a new plan. We'll be able to avoid an onslaught of sermons and still hold onto our benefits from the society. The key is to act shrewdly and prudently."

"What are you talking about?" I wondered.

"I'll explain presently, but let's go sit somewhere for a bit. It's still early, and tomorrow is a Sunday. I don't need to wake up early."

We went to another café next to my hotel.

"Now we can speak freely," said Henri. "First of all, tell me, do you have a friend who'd be willing to pretend that he is a sinner looking to repent?"

"How would he pretend to do that?"

"It's simple. For instance, imagine that one night, during one of our propaganda missions, we meet a young man. He is about to walk the path of deviance. We approach him, talk to him, convince him, and prevent him from taking that disastrous step. And then, we take matters further. We convince him to take refuge in our society. He is so moved by our sermons that he agrees, and that is how we escort him ceremoniously to our President…"

"But wouldn't that be fraud?"

"Oh, such a big unnecessary word. Don't we all need to scheme a little from time to time just to get by in life? The important thing is to find truly loyal friends."

"The truth is, I can't help you there," I replied. "I don't think we'll be able to find the kind of person you're looking for in my circle of friends. Besides, to be totally honest, I couldn't even bring myself to ask someone to do that sort of thing."

"I can see that you are not a man of action," replied Henri disappointed.

My refusal cooled our exchange, and for the next few moments, we sat in mutual silence.

Eventually, Henri said, "I hope that our conversations will remain between us."

"You can be absolutely certain of that," I replied.

"All right, then, let's go get some rest."

It was two hours past midnight when we parted ways.

Several days went by. I continued dining regularly at the hall on the Rue St. Martin. And I attended another one of the Salvation Army drills at Miss Adele's urging.

Occasionally, our President, Mr. Clemence, would enquire into how our work for the "Midnight Mission" was proceeding.

"We're working hard, but we haven't had any results yet," I would reply.

"Don't lose hope. You must persist, and I am certain that eventually, your work will bear fruit."

And then one day, I ran into the elderly Mr. Scott on the street. He stopped me and said, "If I am not mistaken, you are Mr. Odian."

"The very same, sir."

"One of the members of our society."

"Yes, although perhaps not the most productive."

"I believe you work with Mr. Henri."

"Yes, because we live practically on the same street."

"Why didn't you ever drop by at my place again?"

"I didn't want to inconvenience you. I wanted to make sure that we had something to show for our work. I thought it best to make my appearance once we had a victory to announce."

"On the contrary, now is when you should be coming round, when you're making your first strides and not getting anywhere. That way, you can take heart and not lose hope… Our weekly meeting is tonight. I will be waiting for you, after dinner, at nine o'clock. Be at that meeting… Come with Mr. Henri."

"Of course, Mr. Scott."

I searched the dining hall for Henri but had no success. It was unusual for him to be absent.

I kept my promise and attended the meeting on my own.

Eight to ten youths had already congregated around the old man.

"Where is Mr. Henri?" asked Mr. Scott when I entered the hallway.

"Mr. Henri wasn't at the restaurant tonight," I replied.

"I saw Mr. Henri an hour ago, and he told me that he was definitely coming," observed one of the other men there.

Indeed, half an hour later, there was a knock at the door, and Henri came in with a stranger.

"Mr. Scott," he declared triumphantly to the old man, "I have the honor of presenting you with Mr. Bigman, who, I hope, will meet with your approval."

"I approve of all my visitors," replied the old man, inviting the recent arrivals to take a seat.

"Mr. Bigman is a friend of mine. I was very fortunate to meet him last night," said Henri emphatically.

"All friends are welcome here, old or new," replied the old man.

"Our friendship will endure for a long time to come, due to the circumstances of our meeting," continued Henri. "At least, I hope so."

It was obvious that Henri was burning and aching to tell us about how he and Mr. Bigman had met.

The old man noticed and said, "Go on, then, tell us all about it, Mr. Henri. What were the auspicious circumstances that led to your friendship?"

At that prompt, the young man shot a victorious look around and said, "Last night, as I was carrying out my duties for the 'Mission' on one of those disreputable streets – at one of those addresses you gave me –, I saw this gentleman wandering in that direction looking terribly drunk."

I watched Mr. Bigman's face as this narrative unfolded. He was sitting motionless and quiet in his seat, head downcast, like a subdued offender.

"I gently approached this stray sheep," continued Henri solemnly, "greeted him, and engaged him in conversation."

"Wasn't Mr. Odian with you?" interrupted old Mr. Scott.

"Mr. Odian had just returned to his room at my urging," replied Henri, "because he looked unwell and could not accompany me – although despite his condition, he stubbornly insisted on performing his duties."

Henri was absolutely lying. It had been several days since I had taken any part in the Midnight Mission, and I only saw him in the evenings at the dining hall on the Rue St. Martin. Nevertheless, I did not dare contradict him and kept my peace.

After casting a conspiratorial glance at me, he continued, "As I was saying, our friend seemed to be very drunk. Initially, he replied curtly and even threatened me several times. But I remained unfazed and began my exhortations on the real matter at hand. As I spoke, I could sense a change coming over my listener. Finally, he turned to me and said in a quiet voice, 'Perhaps you're right. It would be best for me not to indulge my compulsions.' I naturally felt encouraged by his goodwill and began to advise him more fervently. At the same time, I was also trying to surreptitiously lead him away from our seedy surroundings. A quarter of an hour later, we had reached the Rue Lafayette. 'I thank you for your intervention,' said my new friend. 'Good night. I am going to bed.' He seemed to have sobered up. Still, I did not want to leave things at loose ends. 'Where do you live?' I asked. 'Nearby. On the Rue Mouffetard,' he replied. 'In that case, I'll escort you to your door.' And so, we arrived at his door, and I rang the bell. The door opened a moment later. 'On which floor do you live?' I asked. 'The sixth,' my friend replied. 'What's your name?' 'Maurice Bigman.' 'Would you permit me to pay you a visit tomorrow morning?' 'I would be most happy to receive your visit,' replied my new friend, and disappeared behind his closed door. I could have called it a day's work, gone home, and rested content. But I determined to stand by his door for another thirty minutes. Perhaps, I thought, Mr. Bigman might be prodded by the devil to change his mind and return to the same place whence I had worked so hard to save him. So, I thought it would be best for me to stay there. But it was eventually clear that his apartment door would not open, and that my friend had already gone to bed in his room. So, I too, went home to sleep with a perfectly serene conscience."

"Bravo, Mr. Henri!" cried the old man, who had been listening intently to this tale. "You could not have performed your duties any more conscientiously. I congratulate you on behalf of all our comrades."

Embarrassed, Henri lowered his eyes and said modestly, "Early this morning, I rushed to the Rue Mouffetard, to Mr. Bigman's home. Fortunately, he had just gotten out of bed when I got to his place. He greeted me with a smile and thanked me for my services the night before. I could tell that my new friend, Mr. Bigman, had fully regained his senses, and I wanted to take advantage of that opportunity by expanding upon my exhortations from the previous night."

"Bravo!" repeated old Mr. Scott. "It is rare for the Evil Demon to encounter an adversary of your caliber."

"I must credit Mr. Bigman for the fact that my exhortations were not for naught. An hour later, my new friend expressed his wish to join our organization as well as its affiliate, the Temperance Society..."

"Three cheers and hurray!" exclaimed the overjoyed old man. "Behold the Good Fight proclaimed by the Apostle Paul, in which victory belongs to both conqueror and conquered."

The novice, Mr. Bigman, who had been sitting there in perfect silence, finally spoke up and said, "I can corroborate Mr. Henri's report. Every word is true. I am a prodigal son returning to his native home, grieving over my past, and vowing to expiate my sins."

Henri's great feat was regarded with both awe and envy by everyone there. But he reacted with exaggerated modesty, as though he had simply been doing his job.

The rest of the evening was devoted to a discussion of more general matters.

And while Mr. Henri's star continued to rise, mine began to set. Hardly anyone paid me any attention, because they could see that I was good for nothing. I did not even deign to attend their meetings or the Salvation Army drills.

Miss Adele, who had harbored great hopes for me, was disappointed and gave me the cold shoulder.

This indifference towards me grew so intense that I even began to avoid dining at the hall on the Rue St. Martin. Instead, I passed my time with some friends in the Latin Quarter. We had settled on the Café François Premier as our meeting point, thanks to Souren Bartevian's profound reverence for the place where Paul Verlaine frequently indulged in absinthe.

Several days had gone by since my last meal at the hall on St. Martin, when one night, I received a card as soon as I entered my hotel.

"Please meet me at our office tomorrow morning at ten for an important notification. – Clemence"

I could tell that a deeply important matter was at hand. And I hastened to the office the following day. I found the President seated solemnly at his desk. He was joined by another member of the society.

"Welcome, Mr. Odian," said the old man in a painfully serious tone. "I am glad to see that you have accepted my invitation."

And then he continued, "Because for some time now, you seemed to be avoiding us. I suspected, therefore, that you would not respond to our invitation."

"It has never crossed my mind to avoid you…"

"And yet, it has been some days since you last dined in our hall."

"A friend of mine from Turkey was visiting. I was keeping him company for the past few days, because he's completely foreign to Paris, and he doesn't really know any French."

I went into some detail inventing an imaginary friend in the hopes that I could dodge the danger that lay ahead.

"Is your friend Christian?" he asked.

"Yes. He's a Christian Armenian…"

"And he does not consume alcohol?"

"No. He has absolutely no tolerance for what people consume in the West."

"In that case, it's a bit surprising that he refused to join you for dinner in our hall. We would have been delighted to meet him."

"My friend is on holiday in Paris, so he prefers to frequent well-known restaurants, especially since he's only staying for a few days."

"I understand," concluded the old man. "Our restaurant does not hold much interest for tourists, especially as it is rather tedious…"

Chapter 10

I did not reply.

"Tell me, what did you get up to with your friend yesterday? Did you take him around the more interesting parts of Paris?"

"Yes," I replied. "I took him to the Louvre and to the Luxembourg Gardens."

"What else…?"

"It was already evening by the time we were done…"

"And so, you went out for dinner, but first you had a brief rest in a café."

"Yes," I mumbled, dismayed by this interminable interrogation.

"Which café did you visit with your friend?"

"The Café de la Fée."

"Ah, so you were in this neighborhood."

"Yes, sir."

"Did you also dine in this neighborhood?"

"Yes, at a restaurant on the Boulevards. And then we went to the theatre… A variety theatre."

The elderly President did not reply. He looked despondent. He twirled a piece of paper in his hands for a few seconds and then he solemnly declared, "Mr. Odian, it pains me to say that you have not spoken a true word in more than half an hour…"

"What do you mean!" I cried.

"Last night, you were on the Left Bank, and that is where you had dinner… Before dinner, you were with three of your usual friends at the Café François Premier. And you joined them for dinner in a small restaurant on the Rue Cluny… Would you like me to tell you what you drank at the café and then over dinner? I should add that after dinner, you went to the Taverne Laurent with the same aforementioned friends, who were joined by a couple of 'Ladies.'"

He pronounced the word 'ladies' in such a tone that there was no question as to their ladylike credentials.

These details were so indisputably true that there was no point in denying them.

"Everything you say is true," I replied, absolutely defeated. "Now that everything is out in the open, I kindly request that you accept my resignation from the society."

"Mr. Odian, it was not my intention to go to such extremes. I had hoped that we could keep you on and forget this short-lived deviation."

"No," I replied firmly. "I feel that it is not possible for me to remain in your circle."

"Well, if it is not possible, there is nothing more to say," concluded the old man. "I accept your resignation and will make a note of it. May the Lord be your guide."

Our conversation was now over. I bid them farewell and prepared to leave.

"When my daughter, Adele, learns of your decision, she will be terribly upset," said the old man. "She believed that you had truly been saved."

I did not reply and took my leave.

I was genuinely upset myself.

That is how my membership in the Temperance Society came to an end after several months.

I met up with Mr. Henri a few times afterwards. He would tell me about his latest conquests. I learned that he was eventually promoted and had attained to a position of great distinction among Protestant circles.

A year later, when I went to London, I had an opportunity to meet several members of the Salvation Army there, as it was located near our place on Arabella Road in Notting Hill.

They gave me a similarly warm welcome but soon realized that I wouldn't amount to much. The Salvation Army in London is a much more powerful organization, boasting numerous branches. It also holds public gatherings in various parks.

Every Sunday, entire regiments consisting of several thousand people barge through the streets of London led by a marching band and waving their flags with great fanfare.

Maybe the reader has already lost track of the tangent that led us into this whole long-winded story. In any case, I think it gives a pretty good idea about the Salvation Army and other Protestant institutions, all of which are nothing more than systems of shameless exploitation at their core.

And now let us pick up the thread where we left off.

As I was saying, the last time I was in Cairo, I went to see Mr. Pique who was in town. Although I had already severed my relations with the Society of Christian Youth, I had nevertheless maintained my relationship with this institution's Secretary in Paris, who kept up his correspondence with me during my time in Egypt. His letters even provided detailed information about various members of the society, although none of it was of any interest to me. In return, he wanted me to help him get to know Egypt.

"Can we establish a branch of our society there?" he would sometimes query.

And I would always reply discouragingly. Had Mr. Henri been in my place, he would have turned it into an exquisite opportunity for his own profit.

We had a very congenial meeting at our hotel, where I went to meet him. Mr. Pique affirmed what I had conveyed to him in my letters.

"I can indeed see that it would not be feasible to initiate anything in Egypt," he said. "The Anglican and Protestant communities are simply too small."

"Yes," I replied. "Here we have cotton and rice fields, instead of the pastures of the Lord."

"Still, I will try to get something going," said the Director of the Christian Youth Society.

"You won't get very far."

"Don't try to discourage me, especially since I'm counting on your collaboration."

"But I've already made preparations to return to Constantinople. I'm only here to bid my farewells."

"What a disappointment!" exclaimed Mr. Pique.

And then, after a moment's pause, he added, "And if I ask you to stay?"

"That is simply not possible. I've already made my arrangements. I've even stopped printing my paper in Alexandria."

"I would like to offer you a new job."

"What sort of job?"

"The position of Director at the new Egyptian branch of the Society for Christian Youth."

My jaw gaped at this offer.

"I don't understand how that would be possible. I was practically expelled from your ranks."

"That's not important. Don't you know the fable of the prodigal son? You'll be received with redoubled joy."

"But I am no penitent."

"But I will still present you as one."

"Besides, how can you establish another branch when you don't even have any members?"

"The members will show up later, little by little."

"No, Mr. Pique. I'm not the man for that job."

"Being an editor and writer, you're probably quite well-known around here."

"Yes, I am indeed quite well-known to the entire Armenian refugee community. But the day I show up as the Director of Egypt's Society for Christian Youth, I'll become a laughingstock."

"Why is that?"

"Because I'm a renowned atheist."

My last statement stopped Mr. Pique in his tracks. He was rubbing his brow.

"Have you ever written and published anything anti-Christian?" he asked.

"Every chance I've had."

"How imprudent of you…!"

This was a revealing pronouncement, which more or less lay bare the fact that Mr. Pique was no more Christian than I was.

"What would the Director be paid?" I asked.

"For the moment, two-hundred francs per month."

"Isn't that a bit low?"

"But we're also going to rent an office space, so the Director will reside there, and rent won't be an expense. And then, when we start gaining members and setting up a dining hall, he also won't have any dining expenses. Besides, as our operations expand, his salary will also naturally go up. But what's the point of going into all this, since it's obvious that we can't work together… It would be absolutely absurd to put forward an atheist – not to mention a boozer – as the Director of the Christian Youth Society…"

"What do I know!" I sighed.

"So, my dear friend, let's discuss something else. Would you be so kind as to take me around the more interesting sites in Cairo?"

"With pleasure."

We spent the whole day together and dined at his hotel in the evening. I could not help but notice that after putting away a few glasses of whiskey, Mr. Pique also finished off an entire bottle of wine over dinner.

"I suppose you don't feel as strongly as you used to about drinking alcohol," I observed.

Mr. Pique gave me a penetrating look and replied, "For everything, there is a season, says the wise King Solomon. There is a time for consuming liquor and for not consuming liquor. Now, during my trip, I see nothing inappropriate in drinking, especially since our comrades aren't around and can't take offense at my behavior. Because that should be our true aim, 'not to offend our comrades.'"

Of course, this explanation was not nearly satisfactory. Nevertheless, I didn't want to put him in a tight spot. But I did realize that Mr. Pique was no better than Henri.

"And now that your hopes for me have been dashed," I said, "to help you set up a branch in Egypt, are you going to abandon the whole plan?"

"Not yet," he replied.

"So, what are you going to do?"

"I'm going to try to find someone else."

"I can assure you that you will not succeed."

"In that case, I am going to set up a branch without anyone's support."

"Do you think that's possible?"

"Of course!"

Mr. Pique was emptying one glass of wine after another like a man devouring forbidden fruit.

After dinner, he ordered cognac with his coffee. Then, after complaining that the food didn't sit well with his stomach, he drank a whiskey soda to help him digest.

That cocktail of various different drinks turned him tomato red and slurred his speech.

"Yes!" he exclaimed, returning to his idée fixe. "Despite all the difficulties, I will establish a branch of the Christian Youth Society in Egypt, because that is why I am here."

"Mr. Pique, do consider dropping that notion."

"Never!... And I hereby declare that our new branch has already been founded, and I will relay this news posthaste to our headquarters in Paris."

"Why don't you at least wait until tomorrow morning?"

"No, now immediately, I must write a letter."

And stubborn as only a drunk could be, Mr. Pique called the server over and asked for a sheet of paper and some ink.

I realized that it was pointless for me to be there, so I got up to leave.

"No!" insisted our Secretary. "You must stay here," and he immediately sat down at a desk.

I was obliged to stay if I didn't want to upset him. And as a reward for indulging him, Mr. Pique ordered two more glasses of whiskey.

The letter took half an hour to compose. After completing it, he turned to me and said, "Now, listen to this!"

The letter had turned out to be far more serious than I had expected. Mr. Pique recounted at length how, despite the opposition he encountered in Egypt, he had finally succeeded in founding a branch of the Society for Christian Youth in Cairo. The initial expenses had exceeded 1,200 francs. The Secretary expressed his hopes that this branch would in no time make huge progress and gain many members, but that for the time being, no expenses should be spared. He concluded by explaining that he would have to remain in Cairo for an extended period – at the very least, until the end of April – if this project was to succeed.

"What do you say to that?" he asked me when he finished reading.

"Actually, I have no idea what to say. There's a good chance you will dispatch this letter tomorrow morning."

"No, I'm going to drop it off at the post office right now."

"There's no point going at this hour, since the express doesn't leave until tomorrow morning."

"When I think of a great plan, I have to go through with it right away… Besides, I fear that I might change my mind by tomorrow morning and not send the letter."

And he inserted the letter into an envelope, sealed it, wrote out the address, and asked the server to stick on a stamp and drop it in the mailbox outside the hotel.

When the server went outside, Mr. Pique gave me a victorious look and said, "It's all done now. There's no way back."

"Believe me when I tell you that I have no idea what you're up to," I said. "How can you announce the creation of a new branch as a fait accompli when you haven't done anything towards that end?"

"What would you have me do?" he replied. "Headquarters has allocated 10,000 francs to establish a new branch. And they sent me here for the express purpose of doing just that. How can I go back emptyhanded?"

"But after this letter, won't you be going back emptyhanded anyway?"

"No, not at all! As far as headquarters is concerned, the branch has now been established. Therefore, my duties are now successfully completed."

"But what if they discover the truth?"

"Have no fear. I will be the one to handle the branch in Egypt. I'll be sending the correspondences, and headquarters will be getting all its reports about the branch's projects from me."

And so, Mr. Pique totally gave himself away. There was no reason for me to hold back now.

"Do you have any other imaginary branches like this one?" I asked.

"Of course," he replied. "And I'm not the only one setting them up. There are much more prominent members than me who've been doing the same thing all along."

"And their schemes have never come to light?"

"For the most part, no. But there were a few occasions when they did."

"And what happens in those circumstances?"

"In those circumstances, the society does everything in its power to stifle the whole affair."

"And what about the offender?"

"There has never been an offender. Do you have any idea how disastrous it would be for the society if one of its prominent members were to be exposed as a charlatan and then had to stand a public trial? As I said, in such cases, the society believes it would be best to immediately cover up the scandal and reveal nothing. Otherwise, how can you expect rich philanthropists and millionaire old ladies to bequeath us their fortunes, when they harbor suspicions of corruption in our midst…? We must make sure that our reputation remains immaculate."

And on that, Mr. Pique ordered another whiskey.

We parted late at night, having set another meeting for the following morning.

I was curious to know whether I would find Mr. Pique in the same mood the next day or whether his attitude would be completely different, perhaps regretful of having said too much.

But no. When I saw him again, he seemed far more cheerful and greeted me even more affectionately, taking my hand in his and telling me, "Dear Mr. Odian, now that we have founded our branch here and let our headquarters know, I believe that we deserve to treat ourselves. Given your Biblical expertise, you are of course familiar with its injunction, 'You shall not muzzle the ox while it is threshing.'"

"That is indeed what it says. And St. Paul even repeats it in one of his epistles."

"Well done! So, let's go for a little tour until it's time for dinner."

We spent almost the whole day together. But I eventually got sick of him and came up with an excuse that I had to leave for an important appointment. I had decided once and for all that I never wanted to see his face again.

The next day, I returned to Alexandria, where I intended to stay for another ten days before leaving for Constantinople.

The news from Constantinople gave us cause for hope. The Constitution was firmly in place. The Chamber of Deputies was holding regular meetings and preparing new legislation for Turkey's rebirth. His Holiness Izmirlian had occupied the throne of the Patriarchate. The Society of Armenian Women and the Society of Unity had both regrouped and were resuming their activities. The revolutionaries were sounding their trumpets at a deafeningly loud pitch. And activists were making their way through every street preaching their sermons to their enthusiastic supporters.

But despite all this, the initial enthusiasm felt by Egypt's Armenians faded after the Ottoman Constitution's reinstatement.

"Let's see how long it will last," was the speculation on everyone's lips.

No one trusted Abdulhamid to be true to his word. And many were bracing themselves for the disasters that were bound to ensue.

Those concerns were justified by some of the information relayed in the papers we were receiving from Constantinople.

It must be said that Egypt's Arab nationalist press completely opposed Turkey's new Constitutionalist regime. It had placed all its hopes on Abdulhamid and realized that this new regime signaled the collapse of his despotic rule.

As for Egypt's Greek community, they did not seem all that enthusiastic about a Constitutionalist Turkey either and regarded it with a sense of suspicion and caution.

The amazing thing was that many months before the Constitution's reinstatement, *Les Nouvelles* – a French-language newspaper published in Cairo –, predicted the event almost to the day with a lengthy article signed by Ali Haidar Midhat.

Return to Constantinople

We all smiled wryly to ourselves as we read the French paper's predictions. The author claimed that all these miracles would be performed by Abdulhamid himself of his own accord. At the time, there was no sign of rebellion in the Macedonian army. And nothing in the political climate gave us hope that the Ottoman Empire would undergo such a radical transformation.

I remember how my friend, Mikayel Giurjian, used his typical sense of humor to make a mockery of that article on the pages of *Arev*.

But then, over the next several months, every one of the predictions that Ali Haidar Bey had enumerated came true.

As I noted earlier, apart from *Les Nouvelles* – which never wavered in its vociferous support of the Young Turks – the entire Egyptian press was extremely wary of the Constitutional Revolution.

January 1909 may be deemed the calmest phase following the Constitution's reinstatement. The strikes, demonstrations, boycotts, and incidents involving the Keor Ali incidents had ended. After enjoying the lavish feast thrown by Yildiz Palace in its honor, the Chamber of Deputies was now busy with its various projects.

In the midst of all this, I left Alexandria on board the *Osmaniye*, one of the Khedive's steamers, and returned to Constantinople after a twelve-year hiatus.

The number of repatriates returning to Constantinople had shrunk appreciably. There were only three Armenian passengers on board: the modern and progressive Vosgan Effendi Mardigian, Minister of Posts and Telegraphs – who was returning home after a holiday in Egypt; Onnig Effendi Papazian; and I.

Before I left, Mihran Effendi Damadian handed me a large envelope containing the bylaws of the Constitutional Democratic Party. He requested that I deliver it to their erstwhile representative, Souren Bartevian, in Izmir. He was also founder and editor-in-chief of the daily, *Tashink*.

The day we left Alexandria was blessed with beautiful weather and smooth seas. Our acquaintances and friends had crowded onto the docks to bid us a final farewell.

I must confess that I was deeply saddened at leaving Egypt behind. That is where I had spent most of my life as an emigre. And I had come to regard it as my second homeland.

We enjoyed a comfortable trip to Piraeus, where the steamer had a four-hour layover.

Mr. Onnig Papazian and I took advantage of that intermission to visit Athens, which I had not seen in twelve years.

I found Athens greatly transformed in a remarkably brief span of time. They now had a fully operative electric tramline, whereas no such thing had existed before. Electric lights illuminated the entire urban landscape, and public telephone booths could be found everywhere. Here was an entirely Europeanized city, with exquisite new buildings popping up on every corner.

"Is this what's in store for us in Constantinople?" I asked my friend.

"Don't count on it," he replied.

"But twelve years is a long time."

"I'm sure we won't notice a jot of difference in Constantinople."

"Except for the regime change, which is what matters most."

We left Piraeus in the evening and arrived in Izmir the following day. Since the *Osmaniye* was scheduled to depart several hours later, it did not moor at the port. A dinghy transported us to the docks.

The boatman headed to the customs office.

"But we don't have any goods to declare," I told the boatman. "We're only staying for a few hours and then returning to the ship. Why are you taking us to customs?"

"What about the envelope in your hand?" said the boatman.

In fairness, I was carrying the Democratic party's bylaws, which I intended to deliver to Souren Bartevian.

"Do we have to go through customs for that?"

"Yes. Those are the regulations. Otherwise, we'll be held accountable."

"Is it difficult to bring in books?"

"I don't think so. You're free to bring in whatever you want."

We arrived at customs, where my friend, Mr. Papazian, and I disembarked.

An employee stopped me at the entrance.

"What's that envelope?" he asked.

"It's just a bunch of notebooks. I need to give them to someone who lives here. I can open the envelope and show them to you, if you like."

"What kinds of notebooks?"

"The Henchag party's new bylaws, *effendim*."

The employee replied with a great show of respect, "*Buyurunuz, gechiniz effendim.*"*

"I can now believe that there are some big changes in Turkey," I muttered to my friend.

I found Souren Bartevian in *Tashink*'s newsroom. We embraced warmly.

We hadn't seen each other for almost six or seven years.

The last time was in Paris. Then one day, he disappeared and resurfaced in London, where he went on to publish *Nor Gyank*. After that, he went to America first to edit *Tzayn Hayrenyatz*, and then *Azk*. He returned from America once the Constitution was declared. And, after a brief spell in Constantinople, he settled in Izmir.

Souren Bartevian and I had a history of minor spats, but they were so trivial that they didn't spoil our joyous reunion one bit. They started in Paris when he took aim at me – albeit very indirectly – in *Whip*, his awful diatribe against Arshag Chobanian.

Since I was a contributor to *Anahid* back then, Bartevian felt compelled to subject me to the same tirade.

But not long after *Whip* came out, we made up thanks to the interventions of Dr. Kololian and Levon Pashalian. We even decided to initiate a joint venture, *Azad Khosk*, and invited Pashalian and Arpiar to collaborate with us. Vahé Arzouyan joined the Henchag administration at around the same time. He took over from Arpiar and stripped him of his post as editor of *Nor Gyank*. And then he went to Paris to find someone else to replace Arpiar.

---

* Turkish, meaning, "Please, go ahead, sir."

Vahé offered me that position, but I declined. Then we learned that he had arranged something with Souren Bartevian and took him covertly to London. The fact is that up until then, Souren Bartevian was best known for his bitter anti-revolutionary barbs. And then suddenly, out of the blue, he was named editor of a revolutionary paper. Henchag party members were doubtless put off.

When we got wind that Bartevian had left for London with Vahé Arzouyan, we could not believe it, because his closest friends had been spreading word that he had left for Switzerland or Italy, or that he may have even returned to Constantinople.

But soon enough, we were receiving the latest issues of *Nor Gyank* from London. And there was nothing left to hide. From start to finish, the whole thing smacked of Souren Bartevian. Pashalian and I had started publishing *Azad Khosk* at about the same time. We made sure to add a few lines here and there to expose the identity of *Hentchag*'s new editor.

This exposure infuriated Bartevian, who sent me a nasty note from London in response. But only a month later, Bartevian's Henchagness was already out there for all to behold, like the secret of the Polichinelle.

After all these episodes, we were now reuniting in Izmir for the first time in a long while.

We decided to visit the widowed Mrs. M. Mamourian together.

"Every Armenian has a duty to make that visit," Bartevian told me. And I gladly complied.

It was on that occasion that I also met Mr. Hrant Mamourian, who was and still is publishing *Tashink*.

Then, Bartevian and I went to the Restaurant Crèmerie.

Bartevian tried to convince me to settle down in Izmir instead of returning to Constantinople. He proceeded to present the situation in Constantinople with typical hyperbole in the starkest possible terms.

"You'll settle down right here," he told me. "You can work for *Tashink* and start publishing a satirical weekly on the side… I can find you at least 500 subscribers in Izmir. That'll be plenty to cover your expenses."

"It is not going to happen. I have to go to Constantinople at least once."

"The climate in Constantinople is insufferable."

"Why…?"

"Because it's brimming with Tashags and Henchags… It's suffocating."

"But Shahnazar and I intend to publish *Hayrenik*."

"Shahnazar isn't going to publish anything…"

"Why do you say that?"

"Because he's part of an investigative committee that is slated to leave for Armenia."

"That hasn't been settled yet."

"On the contrary, everything is already in order. And the committee will be leaving any day now."

As further proof, Bartevian showed me the latest papers from Constantinople.

Indeed, everything seemed to be done and dusted.

"No problem," I replied. "The committee's mission is supposed to last a few months at most. We can start publishing *Hayrenik* once he's back."

Bartevian would not desist and eventually revealed his own plans.

What he wanted was to turn *Tashink* into a prominent newspaper, with the likes of Vahan Tekeyan and others on board; to make it an authoritative independent source free of any influence from Constantinople; one, which would become a mainstay of every Armenian home, regardless of class, in both Turkey and abroad; and, moreover, which would provide the Armenian intelligentsia with a beacon of light from its exalted heights.

"A little effort will go a long way," he said. "The chances of success are high, because there is a palpable need for an influential and thoughtfully produced newspaper. The only person who could pull that off in Constantinople might be Zohrab. He did have something like that in mind, but he's now given up the idea."

"You could get it done, but you need a substantial amount of capital to get started."

"We'll get the capital."

"How?"

"From the community in Izmir. If we put our minds to it and get started right now, I can assure you that it would be very easy to pool 2,000 liras."

"Have you had any discussions on that front?"

"Of course. I even got some pledges in writing."

"How much?"

"Eight hundred liras… You see, it's halfway there."

Bartevian was getting more animated.

"You cannot believe how generous the community in Izmir can be," he said. "They're incredibly patriotic and cultivated. They adore literature, and they have tremendous appreciation for anything that shows real merit…"

It goes without saying that I had absolutely no objections to my friend's lavish praise for the community in Izmir, nor did I harbor any doubts. Nevertheless, my decision to return to Constantinople remained firm.

"I promise," I said, "to return to Izmir and get on board *Tashink* if, as you suspect, we cannot find a way to publish *Hayrenik*."

Then Bartevian introduced me to several young men, who joined our table.

After dinner, we took a stroll through the city. And then I boarded the steamship, where Bartevian kept me company until our departure. Mr. Hrant Mamourian accompanied us, all the while doing his part to convince me to stay in Izmir and launch a satirical magazine.

What I am really trying to convey is how they were all swept up by the excitement of that time; and how they had been lulling themselves with fantasies.

The ship pulled out towards evening and at dawn the following day, we arrived at Chanakkale. The first thing I noticed were the snowcapped peaks – snow, which had become a distant memory over the past seven years. And with the snow came the bitter cold, which seemed to intensify as we approached Constantinople.

That same evening, a Sunday, we greeted the Saray Burnu. The *Osmaniye* made its slow approach into port, where a huge throng of people had pressed in to greet the steamship.

There was a high-ranking military pasha on board the *Osmaniye*. He was returning from Yemen after a long period of exile, and many had come to welcome his return.

As the steamship stopped near the shore, the air burst with deafening applause and exclamations of "Hurrah." Uproarious cheers erupted when the exiled pasha, dressed in full uniform, stepped out onto the bridge. The crowd below us was applauding furiously. I have no inkling of that official's identity, but there is no doubt that his feats did not merit this reception.

One could clearly see that he felt the same way, and that he was uncomfortable with this hyperbolic adulation. But there was no way around it. Every time he stepped off the bridge or moved aside, their cheers grew louder.

Eventually, he complied and stayed put, waving to the applauding crowd until we had finally moored.

As soon as the ladder was dropped, the crowd rushed up like one enormous demon.

I was standing next to my bags. A porter walked up to me, threw them over his shoulder, and commanded, "Follow me," at the top of his voice. "I'll push through so you can get down."

It goes without saying that were it not for his help, I would not have been able to disembark.

It took some effort to get down. But once we were on shore, I pulled out my passport and asked, "Where do I show this?"

The porter replied, "What is it…?"

"A passport."

"There's no need for that. Put it back in your pocket. Didn't you know that we have a *hurriyet*[*] now?"

"Yes, I know," I mumbled.

"Where are you headed?"

"Pera."

"By taxi?"

"Yes, by taxi."

"All right, follow me."

"But don't we have to go through customs?"

"Not anymore. We live in a *hurriyet* now," repeated the porter.

And he stowed my belongings into a taxi.

There was no perceptible change on the shores of Galata. It was all the same dingy, wooden, run-down cafes, the same rough cobblestones, the same muck… And suddenly, I recalled vividly the day that I escaped, the moment I sprinted across that beach terrified, charging madly to hurl myself onto the Messageries steamship. My heart sank instantly at the memory of those events. I took one last look at the *Osmaniye* – which had returned me to this place – and felt compelled to climb right back on

---

[*] Turkish, meaning "liberty." (Tr.)

board, shut myself inside, and wait until it had safely taken me once more to Alexandria.

The taxi took the side streets, following the tramline towards Pera through slushy, muddy roads.

I scanned my surroundings for any sign of novelty and progress but had no luck finding any. The same buildings, the same roads, maybe even the same people. It felt as though I had only been gone for a day.

I was simply devastated by my impressions.

They were made worse by the relentless downpour of sleet.

Epilogue

It took a week for me to readjust to life in Constantinople.

I had found my old friends and made some new acquaintances. I was already initiating various projects.

Shahnazar was going to resume publishing *Hayrenik*, but there were still some outstanding issues concerning the printing press. And, besides, there was still the matter of the investigative committee. But he would start publishing the paper even if he had to leave, and we would carry on in his absence. At least, that was the plan.

The Henchags had their own plans to launch a newspaper, and the Constitutional Democrats seemed to be in the same mood.

There were also individual initiatives to start up new dailies.

Everyone seemed eager to establish his very own special newspaper.

It appeared that the foundations of Constitutional Turkey were settling. And everyone was feeling hopeful.

Shortly after I arrived from Alexandria, Levon Shishmanian also came to Constantinople. He was there to stage a production of *The Shopkeeper Artin Agha* – previously called, *The Franco-Turkish War* –, a comedy co-written by Mikayel Giurjian and me. Levon Shishmanian had already performed the role of Artin Agha several times in Alexandria, and he thought that he would receive the same ovation in Constantinople.

One day, we were walking around Babiali when he said, "I have a Turkish friend not far from here. Would it be alright if we stopped by to see him?"

"Who is he?" I asked.

"The editor of *Volkan*."

"Sheikh Vahdeti…?"

"Yes, he is one my closest friends. And I'd like to pay him a visit while I'm still in Constantinople… I'm sure he'll also be very glad to see me."

"But how did you meet him?"

"In Cyprus… We published a revolutionary paper together, in Turkish. The problem is that I don't know his address."

"That's easy to find out. We'll pick up an issue of *Volkan*. I'm sure it will have their newsroom's address."

We picked up an issue and saw that their office was near the old *Zaptiyeh** neighborhood.

After some searching and asking around, we finally managed to find it.

Volkan's newsroom was a wooden house, which functioned simultaneously as the editor's residence.

Vahdeti welcomed us into his office. It was no more than a small cell with sparse furnishings, namely a desk and several chairs.

The two friends embraced.

Vahdeti was a rotund man with a puffy black beard and a cheerful, amiable face.

Levon Shishmanian began to discuss the political situation. "It seems that you have finally achieved all that you hoped for," he said. "The tyrannical regime has been overthrown, and we have entered a new era of freedom. I hope things have worked out as you wanted."

Vahdeti shook his head in a show of profound disappointment.

"On the contrary," he said. "I feel terribly let down. And I'm thinking of returning to Cyprus soon."

"Why is that?"

"Because the Constitution will not take. And I expect that what happens next will beggar belief."

"Why? Don't tell me Hamid has joined the *Jeunes Turques*†?"

"None of it is for real. It's all for show."

"But most people support the Constitution."

"That is simply untrue. The people do not want the Constitution. You'll see that for yourselves as the situation unfolds."

Shishmanian said that he was thinking of resigning from his post in Alexandria and relocating to Constantinople.

"You'd be making a really stupid mistake!" Vahdeti exclaimed. "You go right back where you came from. And while you're at it, see if you can arrange a job for me there as well. Things are terrible here, truly awful..."

Vahdeti went on to paint an extremely dark picture of the situation at hand. He was very candid, taking issue both with the Young Turks who,

---

* Turkish, "the Gendarmerie." (Tr.)
† French, meaning "Young Turks." (Tr.)

he claimed, would not be able to achieve anything and nor did they sincerely intend to revive their homeland; and with the reactionaries who, he averred, would soon annul the Constitution and reinstate the despotic regime.

"And when do you expect that to happen?" asked Levon Pashalian, who did not give much credence to his companion's opinions.

"At the very latest, in a month from now," replied Vahdeti. "And maybe even sooner."

"And what will you do in that case?"

"I will either flee or join the reactionaries."

"Is that even possible…? A former revolutionary like you?"

"We should all do our best to keep our bellies full," Vahdeti philosophized.

Shishmanian asked about his paper.

"Sales are extremely low," replied *Volkan*'s editor. "The income barely covers the printing costs and my daily meals… But soon, *inshallah*,* all of that will be a thing of the past."

We stayed for almost an hour. He seemed to be a droll, facetious man. And my impression was that he lacked character, conscience, and principles.

"He didn't used to be like this," Levon Shishmanian assured me. "He used to be a fervent revolutionary, liberal to the extreme. When he was in Cyprus, Hamid even tried to bribe him. But despite being hard up, he declined the offer."

I believe that this meeting took place in early March, just as the *Jemaat Muhammediye*† was getting to work.

Judging by Sheikh Vahdeti's comments, he was clearly already party to the treacherous plot. But we did not suspect a thing that day, since the events of March 31 were inconceivable to us.

I should add that the editor of *Volkan* had no resemblance whatsoever to a sheikh nor did he sport a turban. On the contrary, he had the appearance of a thoroughly Europeanized Turk.

---

* Turkish, meaning "God willing." (Tr.)
† The Mohammedan Union. (Tr.)

Several days later, Levon Shishmanian returned to Alexandria. His performances had left him disappointed, and he had been saddled with hefty financial losses.

We were approaching the end of March. The weather was beautiful, but the political climate was getting darker by the day. We could see the storm gathering on the horizon. And we could sense the gloom descending upon us, the shocking plots being put into play. People seemed to be getting angrier with each passing day.

At the time, Aram Andonian and I were publishing a daily called *Kharazan* – in addition to the weekly by the same name –, and our newsroom and printing press were located on Babiali Avenue. Not a day went by without demonstrations or disturbances.

And then, one morning, we heard that the editor-in-chief of *Serbest*, Hasan Fehmi, was shot dead as he and a friend were crossing a bridge the night before.

This news shook Constantinople to its core. And two days after that assassination, the Thursday of March 26, thousands of people – mostly university students and turbaned young men – gathered to stage a demonstration at the Sublime Porte, vociferously demanding that the murderer be punished. The demonstrators continued their protests outside the offices of various Turkish newspapers. Eventually, they arrived where we were at Ikdam *han*, which also housed *Ikdam*'s newsroom.

The entire length of Babiali Avenue was carpeted with countless human heads.

Suddenly, loud chanting burst through the air.

"We want Ali Kemal! Come out, Ali Kemal...!"

Ali Kemal, *Ikdam*'s editor-in-chief, came out to the entrance of the *han*, stepped up on a chair, and gave a speech. He was hurling blind accusations, swearing up and down that those who had armed the perpetrator would be made to pay.

The overwhelming consensus was that the attack was planned by Yildiz Palace.

Ali Kemal's speech received thunderous applause and cheers of "hurrah." Then the demonstrators moved on.

The rivalry among mutually hostile newspapers had come to a head. An endless stream of screamers flooded the bridge with an unimaginable din. The news vendors kept yelling suggestively about the warming weather to intimate the meaning of their papers' inflammatory headlines, things to the tune of, "*Otuzdokuz derece yaziyor…*" "*Kirkalti derece yaziyor…*" "*Elliiki derece yaziyor…*"*

The most worrisome development was that the old regime's spies and supporters – all of whom had scuttled into a hole once the Constitution was reinstated – suddenly came out of the woodwork in the midst of all this. They could be seen strolling through the streets and frequenting the cafes, as brazen and belligerent as ever.

The antagonism against the *Jeunes Turques* Committee intensified to such a pitch that even fervent constitutionalists and enemies of the Hamidian regime adopted a critical tone. The reactionaries had been extraordinarily shrewd. They had exploited every one of the Committee's mistakes expertly. And their hapless victims played unsuspectingly right into their hands, unaware all the while that their reproaches were nothing more than triggered reactions to a series of covert machinations.

The recently established political party, Ahrar, had marshalled a large militia and was gaining in strength every day.

The genuine progressives leaned collectively towards Ahrar, believing that only it could salvage the precarious situation.

We were already overwhelmed by all the ensuing turmoil, and on March 31,† a Tuesday morning, I was passing through Istiklal Avenue in Pera when a friend of mine asked, "Where are you going?"

"Galata and then Constantinople," I replied.

"Constantinople!" he exclaimed. "I would advise you to stay right where you are."

"Why? What's the matter…?"

"The army is in Aya Sofia Square demonstrating against the Chamber of Deputies."

"That has nothing to do with me. I'm not a deputy."

"All the shops in Constantinople are closed. People are terrified… Come on, let's go over to Tokatlian's. We may be able to find out more in there."

I went along with my friend's suggestion and changed my route.

---

* Turkish, meaning, "It says thirty-nine degrees; it says forty-six degrees; it says fifty-two degrees." (Tr.)

† The date is noted according to the Julian calendar.

Tokatlian's was overflowing with other people like us trying to find out whatever they could. But no one could provide any confirmed reports.

Occasionally, we could see armed military detachments marching towards Galata. Some of them seemed to be breakaway units, others were following their corporals' lead. But there was a strikingly conspicuous lack of officers. This provoked a great deal of anxiety.

"I don't see any officers out there," everyone observed.

"What exactly are these soldiers up to?"

"Armed with rifles, moreover."

People began to fill Tokatlian's restaurant, each with a fresh piece of news.

"Ten-thousand soldiers are occupying Aya Sofia Square. And they're calling for the Chamber of Deputies to be dissolved."

"The softas are behind all this."

"The soldiers are demanding that the Cabinet be dismantled."

In other words, all we were hearing was, "the soldiers are demanding this, the soldiers are demanding that."

Naturally, none of this news was doing much good for our peace of mind. On the other hand, it was not causing any panic either.

"Galata seems to be calm," everyone confirmed. "Everyone's busy at work."

"And Constantinople?"

"Things look like they've settled down there too. And some of the shops are open."

This piece of information reassured me, and I left Tokatlian's for Tünel.

I ran into Shahnazar in Galata. He seemed to be in very high spirits.

"Where are you off to?" I asked.

"I'm going to Constantinople…"

"But word has it that it's not safe in Constantinople. Where exactly are you going?"

"I'm going to Aya Sofia Square," Shahnazar replied. "Do you want to come along?"

"No, thanks… I'd rather take a walk along the beach. That way I can jump on board a steamer. The Khedive's leaves today…"

We parted, and I headed for the port. I got on board the Khedive's steamship and stayed there for a little while. All I wanted was to shut myself inside and leave Constantinople behind. The military protests – whose true aims remained a mystery to us – did not appeal to me at all.

A couple of hours later, I disembarked and returned to Pera. Tünel was overrun with congestion and traffic. Everyone was rushing to get where they needed to go. No women were to be seen anywhere in Galata. And the men's expressions were veiled with anguish and anxiety.

I met several friends and went to a café in Pera.

There were rumors of nefarious developments. We heard that soldiers had either murdered all the officers or locked them up in fortresses; that Hilmi Pasha's cabinet had been toppled; that several deputies were killed, and so on…

Each new patron brought more news of killings.

"Nazim Pasha, the Minister of Justice was killed."

"The representative of Beirut, Mehmed Aslan Effendi was mistaken for Javid Bey and killed."

"Kabuli Bey, the naval officer, was brutally murdered right outside Yildiz Palace."

And then someone mentioned a Mirabeau-esque comment by Bedros Effendi Halajian: "We cannot convene a meeting with bayonets hanging over our heads."

Several of the men were scanning their surroundings, picking out certain people of interest with their probing eyes. "Look, spy so-and-so is hanging around." "You see that spy…"

Their return after a six-month hiatus instilled dread in all of us.

"Could it be that the *ancien régime* is rearing its ugly head again…?"

"Surely, Hamid has a hand in all of this…"

***

The next day, a Wednesday, the streets appeared to be calm.

The shops had reopened, and everyone was busy with their work.

We knew that soldiers – whose numbers had grown significantly – were occupying the squares outside Aya Sofia and Sultanahmet Mosque. But they remained peaceful.

People seemed to agree, "The army isn't against the Constitution. They just don't want the Committee and are demanding the reinstatement of sharia law."

Some were claiming that an army corps from Salonica had joined the protesting troops. And that seemed to be proof enough that the Constitution was not under threat. Meanwhile, others claimed that most soldiers opposed the demonstrations and were prepared to disperse the protesters by use of force if need be.

I ran into Sarhad and Chris on Istiklal Avenue. They were going to meet their gun distributor in Constantinople. I joined them, and we crossed the bridge together. A continuous current of armed troops kept marching into Constantinople. And all the officers seemed to be purged from the capital city.

"Did they kill them all...?" we wondered, terrified at the thought.

The situation around Yeni Jami was quiet. But a mob of porters had lined up along the mosque's steps, their expressions menacing.

I left my friends and headed towards *Kharazan*'s newsroom on Babiali Avenue. Aram Andonian had taken ill and was being treated in the Bulgarian Hospital of Shishli. So, the weekly *Kharazan* had ceased publication. And the daily had not appeared since the previous Saturday. Regardless, the owner-publisher of the press, Mr. Zkon Papazian, had been busy printing extra editions for the past two days. And they were selling out in a matter of minutes.

The moment I walked into the newsroom he asked me to write something for the next supplement.

"Is there anything new to report?" I asked.

"No," he replied.

"So, what do you want me to write about?"

"Don't you have anything new to report?"

"Nothing that everybody doesn't already know."

"That's alright. We'll run whatever you can come up with. We must strike while the iron is hot."

"What sort of thing did you have in mind?"

"Did you see nothing on your way over here?"

"The large glass windows of Stein & Tiering were riddled with bullet-holes."

"Well, that's your bit of news right there. Take a seat. Write it up. I'm sure you'll have plenty more to say. Half a column should do it."

My insistent friend left me no choice but to acquiesce.

I was in the middle of describing the bullet-ridden windows when suddenly, shooting broke out. It was getting louder, and it was clearly coming from the direction of Aya Sofia Square.

"They're shooting at each other," said the news staff.

"Quick," Mr. Zkon instructed me, "add that to your report."

I sat down at a desk and started to write:

> Unfortunately, the internecine war that everyone had feared is now underway. It began at noon, pitting supporters and opponents of the Committee against one another. As these lines are being composed, their blood is being spilled in Aya Sofia square. There are hundreds of dead and wounded. All the shops are shuttered, and the streets are deserted. See our next supplement for further details.

The copy was immediately dispatched to the typesetter, as the shooting continued unabated.

"How do you intend to get further details?"

"I've sent someone over there. He should be getting back any minute now," he replied.

And sure enough, the reporter was back as soon as the shooting had stopped.

"What's the news? How many dead?" he asked.

"What do you mean, dead?"

"Haven't you just been to Aya Sofia Square?"

"Yes!"

"Aren't they killing each other over there?"

He laughed out loud.

"What about the shooting earlier?"

"The soldiers got a ration of mutton. They were shooting their rifles into the air to celebrate," replied the reporter. "No one's fighting. They're having a feast."

They had to undo the freshly typeset column and prepare a new one reporting the details of this mutton distribution.

By evening, the people of Pera were gripped with fear. The last couple of days had revealed the true purpose of this mobilization. Its main target was the Constitution. And the attack had been orchestrated or incited by Yildiz.

Sheikh Vahdeti's paper, *Volkan*, was pouring fire and brimstone on both the Committee and the new regime. And people could not get enough of it. It had become an overnight sensation, and people turned to it for their official source of news on current events.

The Ittihadist press was shut down. The Committee's club and *Tanin*'s print-house and newsroom were ransacked.

***

On Thursday, March 2 [*sic*.],* the situation remained unchanged. The troops were still occupying Aya Sofia Square, although all their demands had already been met. There were official declarations guaranteeing the full implementation of sharia law. In addition, a new Ministry was formed with Hakki Pasha at the helm; Edhem Pasha became Minister of War; and Noradoungian Effendi stayed in his role as Minister of Public Works.

Soldiers were strolling through the streets, emptying their rifles into the air whenever they felt so inclined. Those shots terrified the populace, but they eventually got used to it. Kids would follow the soldiers around to collect the empty bullet shells.

There was growing apprehension in Constantinople. People had dropped everything, locking up half the shops in the area as they waited for the crisis to pass.

Everyone was certain that the Constitution would be annulled, unless something unexpected happened.

Some could not resist the urge to see the damage on Sherif Street. I was one of them and went there with a friend.

Ittihad's club was practically in ruins. The windowpanes were completely shattered. Even the shutters and frames were dismantled. They had unhinged and removed the doors. And there was no furniture in sight. It was the same story in *Tanin*'s newsroom abutting the club. They had even looted the machines and huge reams of paper.

By evening, I was in *Jamanak*'s newsroom, when someone appeared with a small barrel of printing ink.

"It's for sale. Do you want it?" he asked.

"How much is it?" Kasim replied.

"Whatever you can pay."

---

* April 2, 1909 of the Julian calendar.

"That's no way to make a trade," replied Kasim. "You have to name your price."

"I'll give it to you for less than what you usually pay."

"First, name your price."

It was blatantly evident that the man had no idea how much his merchandise was worth.

"I'll give it to you real cheap," he repeated.

"I don't need any," Kasim replied.

"Here, take it and pay me whatever you want."

"I don't need it. Try somewhere else."

The man walked away disappointed.

"He probably looted it from *Tanin*'s press," said Kasim.

A little later, another man showed up carrying a small printing contraption.

"It's for sale. You need it?" he asked.

"How much?"

"A pound."

The contraption, which was in mint condition, was worth at least ten pounds.

"But this tool is worth a lot more than that," said Kasim.

"I know that," said the man.

"Then, why do you want to sell it for a pound?"

"That's none of your business."

"I don't need it. Try some place else."

That man left.

Then another one arrived to peddle some paper. He was also sent away.

Presently, the soldiers were filling in as censors, paying all the publishers a visit and instructing them to write one thing and excise another. They were also throwing their weight around in the bookstores. Within a couple of days, all the unflattering books about Abdulhamid had been removed from the display cases. All this gave us a good sense of what we were in for.

Yet, it seemed that Yildiz was not feeling quite powerful enough to drop the charade completely. The papers claimed that the Constitution did not pose any threat; that the sharia and the Constitution were two sides of the same coin; and that the Chamber of Deputies would soon resume its work, or that a new Chamber of Deputies would be elected, which would surpass its predecessor.

Nevertheless, whispers were circulating throughout Pera.

Those whispering voices were claiming, "The troops in Salonica have rebelled. They are marching towards Constantinople."

And the Ittihadists appeared to be more confident.

But it all amounted to nothing more than conjecture, expectation, and hope. No one could be sure of anything. No one had any confirmed reports from Salonica.

***

There was sporadic shooting on Friday. But the streets were filled with people again.

Many of the Greek shops in Constantinople were closed.

To explain it away, the remaining shopkeepers claimed, "Today is Balikli-Panayir. That's why they're closed."

Some sort of panic broke out towards midday. And all the shopkeepers quickly locked up their stores.

No one had any idea what had provoked it. But tensions had mounted so high that people were imagining worst case scenarios or losing their grip on reality. The most trifling incident, the tiniest tiff, or the slightest noise could have flared instantly into a full-blown incident.

That afternoon, I was in *Kharazan*'s newsroom again. We received word that the marines had raided *Sabah*'s newsroom, because it had published an article the previous day entitled, "Mutiny among the Armed Forces."

We had a good view of *Sabah*'s offices. We ran straight to the windows and saw hundreds of marines mobbing its door and surrounding its premises.

While we were watching, someone from Ikdam *han* ran into our office panting. He shouted, "Get out of here! They're coming! They're looking for you."

"Who's looking for us…?"

"The marines."

"What do they want from us?"

"I don't know. They're asking for *Kharazan*'s newsroom. Quick. You have to get out of here!"

Armenian participation in street demonstration during the Ottoman constitutional revolution, 1908.

Zkon Papazian was incredulous and asked him to elaborate, while I went down and began watching from our doorway.

The mob was, in fact, heading up from *Sabah*'s offices. The marines were marching straight towards us.

They paused briefly outside the Meserret Hotel to make some inquiries. In the meantime, our cohort had fortunately locked up the newsroom and fled.

The soldiers were definitely looking for the '*Kharazan matbuasi*,'[*] and their demeanor did not exactly inspire confidence.

They arrived at Ikdam *han* and were directed towards *Kharazan*'s office.

They climbed up, discovered that the door was locked, and came back down.

We later learned that their consternation was provoked by the previous day's publication of *Kharazan*'s Turkish supplement.

It seems that Zkon Papazian was unable to dig up a truly sensational bit of news and decided to run a supplement of prophetic proportions heralding the end of the world. The end would surely be nigh if his message was not relayed in time.

---

[*] Turkish, meaning "*Kharazan*'s newsroom." (Tr.)

But things did not end there. And, as the reader will discover in more detail, Zkon Papazian's supplements ultimately landed him in prison.

There were signs that despite inciting the army's protests, Abdulhamid now feared them. Moreover, rumor had it that the army was disunited; that infighting had broken out in the military barracks; that even the soldiers in Yildiz were losing their sense of solidarity; and that, in fact, they were turning their guns on each other and thus terrifying the old man in their charge.

Shooting could be heard in Tash-Kishla on Friday morning and in Pera that same evening. The news was on everyone's lips. People were talking of sinister developments and recounting the mutiny of soldiers who were at each other's throats. This four-day-long ordeal was becoming unbearable, and everyone just needed to know how this catastrophic situation would eventually pan out.

The truth is that until that point, we really had no serious cause for concern. But uncertainty about the future had put us all on edge.

Although all this shooting was aimed at the sky, it caused a great deal of accidental deaths. Some claimed that the number of those who were "accidentally" killed in the previous four days exceeded several hundred. As the bullets rained down from a height of 2,000 meters, they mortally wounded anyone who stood in their way. Obviously, we could not report all this as it happened. The soldiers were being far too intransigent in their new and highly disagreeable role as censors.

***

We woke up on Saturday morning to the sound of more shooting in Pera.

Army units were emptying their guns into the air as they marched through the streets.

They were arriving from Constantinople and heading towards Taksim.

We all thought, "They're returning to their barracks. It's all probably over now."

But events took a different turn on Saturday.

There were confirmed reports about the troops in Salonica. The army was marching towards Constantinople to rescue the endangered Constitution. Several battalions had even reached Hadimkeoy and Chatalja. The reports were reassuring for everyone who favored freedom and who could not countenance the return of Hamidian rule.

Meanwhile, the reactionaries had shed some of their cocky, brazen posturing. After crawling out of the woodwork, the former spies were now scurrying back into their burrows.

Sheikh Vahdeti's *Volkan* – the official newspaper of the moment and the military protests' staunchest supporter –, suddenly changed its tune. It started preaching the importance of mutual compromise, reconciliation, and brotherhood. And it vociferously maintained that the Constitution was not in danger.

That same day, a battalion from Chatalja arrived in Sirkeji. Armed with heavy artillery, it went straight via Babiali Avenue towards Aya Sofia Square to appear before the Chamber of Deputies. We watched the battalion march past from our newsroom in Ikdam *han*. At that hour, we had no idea why they had come to Constantinople. We learned later that the soldiers went to Yildiz, where Abdulhamid made a solemn vow to preserve the Constitution. Then he fed the troops a lavish feast and honored them with gifts.

The protesting troops retreated into their barracks. And there was no more shooting in the streets. Now, all anyone thought about were the units from Salonica. We were amazed at how quickly an entire army had reached the gates of Constantinople. Word had spread that 60-80,000 men had already arrived in Chatalja.

And, for the very first time, there was talk that Abdulhamid could soon be deposed.

The leaders and organizers of the military protests were starting to show signs of fear. They were trying to ingratiate the Constitutionalists in the hope that they would be spared if they ultimately failed.

A couple of days earlier, a faction was established with the assistance of the Tashnag party. It called itself "*Heyet-i Müttefika-i Osmaniye.*[*]" This organization was formed with the express purpose of protecting the Constitution and putting an end to the crisis. It was joined by the Ahrar party, which had begun to betray its true colors. It wanted to use the new faction as a platform to negotiate with the Salonica division, and, if possible, to have them withdraw from Chatalja. The Ahrar representatives in the Chamber of Deputies were working towards the same end. And, on

---

[*] Turkish, "Ottoman Committee of Alliance." (Tr.)

Saturday, they dispatched a special delegation to the army encampment to achieve that aim. But they could not persuade the Salonica division.

We were brimming with joy at news of this failure.

***

We were already in the throes of anxiety, when the following day – Sunday, March 5 [*sic*.]* – we received horrific reports. It left the entire Armenian community of Constantinople in shock. The Catholicos of Sis and His Holiness Terzian had sent detailed telegrams conveying heartbreaking news of massacres in Adana and Cilicia.

As it arrived on the heels of an ongoing crisis; this was a crushing blow. We had no idea about the extent of the catastrophe. And we were not inclined to believe that it could rival the magnitude of earlier outbreaks. But grief shrouded our hearts and souls. The Constitution's reinstatement had led us to believe that, at the very least, such massacres would become an unthinkable thing of the past – all the more so, because only a few months earlier, our Turkish compatriots were shedding remorseful tears upon the graves of our Armenian martyrs.

***

By Monday, the horrors of Adana had almost been forgotten. The troops from Salonica were all that the people of Constantinople could think about.

We were bombarded with a barrage of newsflashes.

"The troops from Salonica have occupied Kuchukchekmeje…"

"An army unit from Salonica has reached Aya Stefanos and Makrikoy…"

"The Salonica division has seized the powder mill and taken over the railway system…"

What was going to happen next…? Was it possible for the army to enter Constantinople unimpeded? Or could there be skirmishes in the capital? There was rampant disagreement about what we could expect, but no unusual signs of anxiety or agitation. We firmly believed that the Salonica division would prevail. The dejected reactionaries had already withdrawn from the public sphere. The softas and soldiers were no longer seen mingling in the streets. And intimidating young officers now patrolled the

---

* This should be Sunday, April 5, 1909 of the Julian calendar.

city, their swords dragging along the ground, ready to strike with vengeance.

***

On the morning of Tuesday, April 7, I was in *Jamanak*'s newsroom, when Kasim gave me a suggestion.

"Why don't you stop just hanging around here and go to Ayastefanos?" he said. "You'll get some fresh air; it'll be a nice change of scenery; you can keep an eye on the Salonica division; and you might even get a scoop for an article in *Jamanak*."

"Good idea," I replied. "I'll get going, seeing as it's such glorious weather…"

And so, for about a week, I became *Jamanak*'s war correspondent.

Sirkeji looked positively celebratory when I arrived. People were overflowing from the waiting area into the courtyard, the sidewalks, and the pier – an elated, laughing, cheering multitude. I had to force my way through to reach the guichets and buy a ticket for Ayastefanos.

The railway authorities had doubled, even tripled the number of train cars. Despite that, it was impossible to find a seat. So, the passengers squeezed in wherever they could find a spot, even if that meant standing in the gangways. But many could not even manage that and decided to wait for the next train.

People were ecstatic beyond words.

For the entire length of the route, all the fields, hills, plateaus, and fortresses on both sides of the tracks were crowded with countless men and women cheering 'hurrah' at the passing trains.

Those crowds were there for no other reason than to spend their entire day, from dawn to dusk, watching the passing trains.

Finally, we arrived in Ayastefanos.

The tops of people's heads were all there was to see all around the station.

I was beholding the liberating army from Salonica, including the gendarmes, for the very first time. They were light-footed, strapping, slim, and on the whole likeable young men. They sported their rifles and swords with an imperious air. And, as we later discovered, many of them were actually young officers dressed in the more modest uniforms of soldiers and policemen.

The reactionaries were refusing to disarm. And, just as they had done in Constantinople, they were trying once again to ingratiate the Salonica division. They had dispatched their turbaned representatives to Ayastefanos and Kuchukchekmeje with that agenda in mind. But, as soon as they stepped off the trains, the gendarmes arrested them and locked them up in the barracks.

There were eight to ten such turbaned men on our train. They tried to sneak off once they disembarked. But no sooner had they taken a few steps, they were surrounded by gendarmes and escorted away.

One of them tried to stay behind when he saw what happened to his friends. He took off his turban and tried to hide it under his coat.

But his little ploy failed, and they caught him as well.

"I'm not one of them. I came alone," said the man. "I'm not a softa. See, I'm not wearing a turban."

"Why aren't you wearing anything on your head?" asked one of the officers and smirked.

"My fez fell out of the carriage on the way here."

"You're lying."

"I swear I'm telling the truth."

"What about this robe of yours…?"

"That's what we wear in our city."

At that point, the officer pulled his robe open and exposed his turban.

"You just made your life a lot harder with this little cover-up," said the officer. "Off you go! Start walking."

"Where are we going?"

"To the barracks."

"But I haven't done anything wrong," shouted the bewildered man.

"Shut up, you no-good dimwit! We know what you're all up to. And this time we're not letting you slip through our fingers."

Two soldiers took the softa away as he continued to plead his innocence.

The couple of cafes around the station were full of curious visitors from Constantinople. I noticed several Tashnag activists: E. Ardzrouni, Zavarian, R. Zartarian, and then Adom Yarjanian, Mrs. Zabel Yessayan, Chifté-Saraf, Silvio Ricci, Henchags, Ramgavars – in short, members of every contingent, both revolutionary and independent. They were all there on the same mission: to speak with the officers.

And the officers were not being coy. They did speak with us. They were perfectly courteous in responding to all our questions. What I noticed immediately was how, above all else, they fervently opposed Abdulhamid. They seemed to harbor an almost personal vendetta against him. And the officers' sentiments seemed to be shared even by low-ranking infantrymen.

"We will only return once we have toppled Hamid," they declared unanimously. "Otherwise, the Constitution cannot take hold."

"When will you enter Constantinople?" That's what we all wanted to know. But we could not get a clear answer.

"The army hasn't arrived yet," they claimed.

"But isn't Kuchukchekmeje just a stone's throw away?"

"No."

"But the encampments on Chekmeje's hill are clearly visible from here…"

"That's just the advance guard."

We were disappointed by this revelation.

It meant that we would have to withstand several more days of uncertainty and even precarity.

"What if a massacre breaks out?" we asked.

"If that happens, we will not wait for the army to defend the people of Constantinople… But, at the moment, there is no cause for concern…"

I returned to *Jamanak*'s newsroom late at night to write the first of my 'military' pieces.

It was already dark when I crossed the bridge.

After what was otherwise a very uplifting day, there was a palpable pall of inexplicable sadness and uncertainty over the city. People seemed to be hurrying home, anxiety etched into their features. Although they were close, the liberating army had not yet entered Constantinople.

On Wednesday, April 9, I rushed back to Ayastefanos first thing in the morning. Sirkeji station was overflowing with the same chaotic crowds trying to get a glimpse of the liberating army in Ayastefanos.

But some of their enthusiasm was dampened by unconfirmed and deeply upsetting rumors.

"They won't let anyone into Ayastefanos, except the local villagers and members of the Ottoman Parliament."

Despite this rumor, it was impossible to find any standing room in the train cars.

People had resolved, "Let's go anyway. And we'll just come back if they don't let us through."

The number of female passengers had increased substantially from the previous day.

The rumors around Sirkeji were true.

As soon as the train pulled into Ayastefanos, the Salonica division's officers approached the carriages and told the passengers that they were not permitted entry into the village, unless they were local residents, deputies, or had a special dispensation.

"I'm a local," I yelled and jumped down from my carriage.

"Do you have a home here?" asked the officer.

"Yes, because I live here."

"Whereabouts?"

"Right here, near the station."

"Wait here, and I'll have an officer escort you home."

I had a plan up my sleeve. My uncle, Kevork Effendi Aslanian, lived in Ayastefanos. And I was going straight over there.

An officer did indeed escort me all the way to my uncle's house, where I stayed briefly before going out to roam freely around the village.

Meanwhile, the inquisitive visitors from Constantinople had to stay on board, go all the way to Kuchukchekmeje, and then return to Sirkeji.

It felt much calmer in the village thanks to these restrictions. The only people out on the streets were deputies, senators, military personnel, and the local villagers, in addition to several journalists and foreign correspondents.

I aimed for the Yachting Club on the beach, where the Chamber of Deputies was supposed to convene.

Suddenly, there were audible murmurs up and down the street.

"Ahmed Riza Bey is coming."

The President of the Chamber of Deputies had disappeared into thin air with the onset of the army's protests. For days on end, people had been speculating about his whereabouts. First, there were rumors that he was killed by the protesters; but then, there were confirmed reports that he was not in the assembly when the protests had erupted.

Some claimed, "He took refuge in an Embassy."

Others averred, "He's in a consular vedette."

Many insisted that he was hiding on a Turkish navy vessel. And there were even intimations that he had committed suicide.

The Ittihadists maintained that he was in Salonica. All these rumors had piqued our curiosity. So, when we got wind of his arrival, we all stood stock still in the middle of the road to watch him walk by.

And there indeed was Ahmed Riza surrounded by bodyguards. His tall, imposing figure eclipsed his entourage. He walked right past us with confident, imperious strides. And everyone on the street or huddling at their windows who had been watching this scene began to applaud.

They were yelling, "*Hosh geldiniz, sefa geldiniz.*"*

At the opposite end of the street, we could see Ebüzziya Tevfik Bey who walked quickly towards Ahmed Riza Bey. The men embraced and continued together towards the Yachting Club.

The assembly did not convene that same day, since many of the deputies were still absent. But there were unofficial deliberations, which were off limits to the press.

Unfortunately, only part of the Salonica division had arrived. According to our sources, it would take another three to four days for them to save us from our interminable living nightmare.

But the reactionaries had already lost all hope. And the same people who had turned on the Ittihadists several days earlier were now clinging onto them more zealously than ever.

The Turkish press had completely changed its position. It was now openly attacking Abdulhamid, denouncing him as the sole instigator of the latest incidents.

And every one of Hamid's cronies was trying to get away.

The papers reported those escapes freely and openly.

"Ali Galib Bey, the bodyguard, has fled; the bodyguard, Sami Bey has escaped," and so on.

All this gave the impression that the tyrannical rule of the past thirty years was finally about to fall.

And yet, there were mounting fears of an imminent massacre. There were suspicions that by orchestrating a general massacre in Constantinople,

---

* Turkish, meaning, "Welcome!" (Tr.)

he would try to precipitate European intervention and thus secure his hold on the throne.

As though to confirm those ominous suspicions, the mobs – especially those made up of Kurdish porters and guards – had assumed a menacing aspect over the previous couple of days. Large groups of them could be seen standing outside mosques, on street corners, in public squares, waiting, it seemed, for a code-word or a signal.

Thursday, April 9, became a historical day in the annals of Ottoman history.

That day, for the first time since the military protests had begun and with uproarious popular support, the Ottoman Parliament convened a session in the Yachting Club of Ayastefanos.

Most of the senators were in attendance.

We had all gathered on the club's beachside terrace before Parliament went into session. And we noticed a fleet of three Ottoman naval ships accompanied by an imperial yacht approaching Ayastefanos.

The sudden appearance of naval ships caused a momentary stir.

Although for the past several days, all the papers had been reporting that the navy was allied with the Salonica division, no one really knew for sure which way they were leaning. There were some who maintained that the converse was true; that the papers were merely reporting wishful thinking rather than confirmed facts.

I do not know what happened, but suddenly a mournful lament cascaded through the crowd.

And then apprehensive whispers: "The fleet is on its way here to disperse the assembly. And it's ready to open fire if it has to…"

Soon, the terrace was deserted.

The same dread gripped the crowds on the beach.

"They're removing the muzzle covers from the cannons…"

"The ships are moving into combat formation…"

"The seamen are armed…"

These murmurs sent tremors through the crowds.

Their earlier cheer and excitement were gone. And now everyone was dashing off the beach.

Even some of the deputies and senators made excuses to leave the Yachting Club. But others swore bravely that they would rather die upholding their office than to capitulate.

Meanwhile, the naval ships had closed in and were now facing the club head-on.

The *Mesoudiye* promptly lowered a dinghy. Several senior officers climbed in and were brought to shore.

Fears of imminent bombardment were thus quelled.

People were now convinced, "They're coming to negotiate."

The officers got to shore and walked in stony silence towards the Yachting Club, passing through a gauntlet of wary eyes.

Our hearts raced with anxiety as we awaited this visit's outcome.

Word got out that the naval officers were meeting with the Presidents of the Senate to make several demands on behalf of Abdulhamid.

And the next twenty minutes or so had us in knots.

Suddenly, there were excited cheers, and the club boomed with cries of 'hurrah.' Moments later, the naval officers appeared on the balcony alongside Said Pasha, Ahmed Riza Bey, and a company of other deputies. And they all embraced.

It seems that an onslaught of kisses can be a substitute for bombs.

The officers had come to swear their loyalty to the Parliament and the Constitutional government. And they had offered to place the navy in their service.

After the initially tense and frigid reception, there was now inconceivable excitement. And a chorus of 'hurrah' accompanied the officers on their way back to the ships.

Then, once everyone's worst nightmares had been put to rest, the Chamber of Deputies and the Senate convened a session with Said Pasha presiding.

It was a closed session. So, we journalists had to wait outside, burning with impatience.

We knew that the chief item on the agenda was the deposition of Abdulhamid.

The closed session lasted just under one-and-a-half hours. Almost all the notable deputies I approached afterwards for further comment gave the same answer: "We are sworn to confidentiality."

When I asked Dr. Daghavarian whether the Assembly would reconvene in Ayastefanos the next day, he gave the following impenetrable response: "I believe that we will all stay here tonight. I, for one, will definitely be here. As for another session, tomorrow is a Friday. That usually means Parliament will not be in session. But we might convene a General Assembly anyway, either in Eyub or at the Dolmabahche."

His concluding remark all but confirmed what the secret discussions of the closed session had been about.

I left Ayastefanos late at night. That day, the village was teeming with soldiers from the liberating army. They were more than several thousand strong.

At the station, I asked a lieutenant, "When will you be coming to Constantinople?"

"In a few days."

"Give me a specific date."

"I cannot. And in any case, I do not know. But there is a good chance that in less than a week, it'll all be over."

"There are rumors that today's General Assembly agreed on deposing the Sultan."

"I do not have any information on that matter," replied the smiling officer.

***

Early the next morning I rushed to Ayastefanos for the last time. The government leaders had decided to relocate there several days earlier.

It was a Friday, and Constantinople was bathed in an aura of peace. Yet, one could not help noticing the menacing faces around Yeni Jami, on Babiali Avenue, and along Sirkeji station. These were the hard, rough features mostly of Kurds, who were roaming through the streets in packs. They had materialized over the previous couple of days. But this day there seemed to be far more of them. And they looked much more threatening.

My train to Ayastefanos was virtually empty. The incredible bustle and energy of the previous day were long gone. The restrictions on entering Ayastefanos had been effective. And now, no one was in any mood to make a pointless trip all the way to Kuchukchekmeje.

The village felt tranquil. The Senate and Parliament were holding a General Assembly. But it was a closed session, and even the Yachting Club's garden was off limits.

The arrival of Shevket Pasha – the liberating army's Captain General – was the biggest event of the day. He was in Ayastefanos for a parliamentary hearing.

Shevket Pasha explained that the Salonica division's priority was not to depose Abdulhamid. However, should the need arise, they were prepared to take action towards that end.

The newspapers even printed an official memo penned by Shevket Pasha. It stated that the liberating army's sole mission was to secure the Constitution, not to depose the Sultan.

This statement came as a disappointment to many. These were mostly people who had not been following events closely.

It was late when I arrived at *Jamanak*'s newsroom. I drafted a report for the following day's morning edition detailing what I had gleaned about the latest developments.

I left the newsroom after dark. The streets were already empty. There was something stifling and uncanny in the air. And I was inexplicably ill at ease.

I quickened my steps through Babiali Avenue and walked past the posthouse, searching for a friendly face to accompany me to Pera.

There were packs of Kurdish guards and officers sitting expectantly outside the *hans* and closed shops. They seemed to be waiting for a prompt to carry out unspeakably heinous atrocities.

The scene outside Yeni Jami provoked sheer terror. Huge mobs had assembled along its sprawling staircase, armed with pipes, waiting patiently. Another cold-blooded mob was occupying Bahche Kapu Square, the sight of which provoked absolute terror.

That scene raised the specter of imminent massacres before my eyes. There were only a handful of us in the streets. And we all raced towards the bridge to catch our breath in Galata.

We were all noticeably on edge from the same palpable threat.

Unarmed soldiers had taken up positions all across the bridge. But their presence failed to inspire our confidence. I finally arrived at Tünel. A few minutes later, I was in Pera. And I could finally breathe free again.

It was the usual bustling scene on Istiklal Avenue. People were walking around without a care.

I joined several friends at Tokatlian's restaurant. We exchanged notes on our impressions of the day.

The same thing was on everyone's lips.

"There will be a massacre, either tonight or tomorrow."

We took turns divulging what we knew about this possibility. Some reported that the mobs had already started arming themselves around noon. They made no attempt to hide their guns and daggers or their general preparations for massacre.

"They're waiting for a signal to get started."

"What signal…?"

"An order from Yildiz, of course."

People were discussing this situation as though it was the most natural thing in the world. And everyone had a different point of view.

"Adbülhamid wouldn't dare give an order for massacres."

"On the contrary. It would work in his favor."

"How?"

"Because it would force the European powers to intervene."

"But that would threaten the government."

"What does he care? As long as he gets to keep the throne."

And then the conversation turned to self-defense. People were boasting about the guns hidden in their homes and goading the violent hordes to attack.

"We dare them to come and see for themselves… It won't be like last time."

But ultimately, they had placed their hopes on the Salonica division.

"Even if something happens, it won't last more than an hour," they said. "The army would surround them in no time."

And yet, we were living in overwhelming fear and rushed to get home early.

My apartment was on Mekteb Street in Pera. My neighbors were a mix of Greeks and Italians, and the doorman was an old Greek man. This made us feel relatively safe. Everyone who had a Kurdish doorman, on the other hand, was living in a constant state of terror.

It was only nine o'clock at night, and already, the foot traffic had stopped. Occasionally, we got a glimpse of an unintentionally tardy passerby trying to get home in hurried steps.

I was rudely awakened at dawn by a burst of shooting.

"Is the army protesting again?" I wondered.

I cocked my ear. This time I could also hear blasts of cannon fire.

Everyone was awake.

There was no doubt about it. The Salonica division was moving in.

But why were we hearing shooting and cannons?

Are the units in Constantinople resisting? But the newspapers had been reporting repeatedly that the army in Constantinople and the Salonica division had forged an alliance. They had gone so far as to claim that not even the Yildiz guards were wont to put up a fight.

The first thing we did was to survey the situation outside. The entire neighborhood was already awake. And people were shouting out of their windows to find out whatever they could.

The cannons roared and the shooting continued unabated all around us.

We saw a milkman round the streetcorner.

"What is all this? What's going on?" we shouted from the windows.

"It's awful," replied the man. "It's war out there."

"Where?"

"Everywhere… The barracks in Taksim and Tashkishla are surrounded, and they're being bombed. Do not leave your homes under any circumstances."

We went up to our roof and saw the army in the distance.

The shooting got louder then, but we could not see much.

Our neighbors were talking across their rooftops. One of the houses, about a hundred meters away, had a higher vantage point. Its residents were reporting back that the fighters, even the cannons, looked happy.

Someone said, "We should stock up on bread. We might be stuck at home for a few days."

There were agreements of, "Yes, yes, you're right. We should stockpile while things here are still calm."

There was a small bakery nearby, at the other end of the street. Everyone rushed over there. And in a matter of minutes, they had bought up all the bread.

The baker had to close his shop to dodge the latecomers who started hounding him.

At some point, several peddlers walked by, so we plied them for fresh information.

They looked dreadful and could not tell us much about the situation.

"They're attacking each other… The fighting is really bad."

That summed up about all they knew.

At around ten o'clock, the cannon blasts in Taksim stopped. Then, little by little the shooting also tapered off.

More and more people appeared on the streets. I did not want to be stuck at home any longer.

I went outside and walked cautiously towards Istiklal Avenue.

There was already a large crowd of people there. They were walking towards Taksim, and I went along with them.

The procession went all the way to Parmak Kapu. But when we arrived, a military cordon stopped us from going any further.

An officer told us, "You are not allowed to go through."

Several people objected, "But we have family up there. We need to know how they are."

"Rest assured, your family members are just fine."

"Just let us up there for a quick look. We'll come right back."

"That is not possible…"

"At least tell us what is going on."

"The Taksim barracks are surrounded. That's all I know."

"Haven't they surrendered yet?"

"No," said the officer and shook his head.

"But we don't hear any cannons."

"They're negotiating right now. And there's a temporary ceasefire. But things can change any second."

We had to content ourselves with this information and turn back.

Throngs of inquisitive patrons filled the cafes.

Despite the still audible din of shooting in the distance, everyone looked pleased and cheerful, since their fears of an imminent massacre had been allayed. They were now certain that the Salonica division would triumph.

Everyone, especially those who lived around Taksim, had a story to tell about that harrowing morning. They had been right in the crosshairs of all the shooting and seen everything.

No one had expected the troops in the barracks and garrisons to put up such stubborn resistance. And there had not been a single case of voluntary surrender.

I stayed around Galatasaray until evening. I could not walk back up to Taksim anyway. And there were reports that barricades had also been mounted in several other sections of Galata and Constantinople.

The usual Constantinople newspapers had not gone to press that day. Not until late afternoon were we able to find a copy of *Jamanak* in Pera. It was half its normal length, but we still eagerly snatched it out of each other's hands.

The city was placed under martial law, and the curfew began at dusk.

People were extremely frustrated by this directive, especially in Pera.

Towards evening, several friends and I walked all the way to Tünel Square.

The avenue that gaped before us looked gloomy. Many of the storefronts had been shuttered. And the Salonica division was patrolling the area. Students from the military academy were stationed as guards outside the Embassies. They had slung their rifles over their shoulders, and their faces beamed triumphantly.

That Saturday, the people of Constantinople finally enjoyed their first good night's sleep in many days.

By evening, there was no more shooting or cannon fire. And peace seemed to be restored.

Now that our wish had come true, we wondered whether our other hopes would also be realized. In other words, would the liberating army depose Abdulhamid, and, if so, when?

We knew that Yildiz did not surrender until nightfall and that it was still surrounded. We also knew that the liberating army was refusing to use force against it.

The next morning, a Sunday, Pera was still calm.

This day, however, the streets were full of curious crowds of men and women. Most of them were heading towards Taksim.

And the scene in Taksim did not disappoint. There were signs of the previous day's fighting everywhere.

Mausers had shot holes into iron storefront shutters. All the windows around Taksim Square were shattered. And Noradoungian Kapriyel Effendi's home had not been spared. Bullets had shattered the glass panes in his doors and left scars across the walls.

The barracks in Taksim were in worse shape. Cannons had reduced much of its façade into rubble.

But we saw all that from a distance, because they had blocked off the road leading out of the gymnasium.

"Why?" we asked a soldier standing guard.

"Because the shooting could flare up again at any moment."

"What? Hasn't everyone inside already surrendered?"

"Not everyone. We believe that over one hundred soldiers are sheltering inside. And they have no intention of laying down their arms."

"So, why don't you just keep shooting?"

"To avoid causing more damage to the barracks …"

"What if they don't give up…?"

"We will leave them to their own devices. Hunger will eventually force them out."

"And no one is allowed through until that happens?"

"If you are trying to get to Pangalti, you can go around the gymnasium."

Many – including me – followed the soldier's good suggestion and went around the gymnasium to get to Sourp Hagop.

Every window in every house facing the Armenian cemetery in Pangalti was shattered.

Their residents spoke to us about the previous day's events from their thresholds.

We asked, "Were any of you injured or killed by mistake?"

"Not at all. No one got so much as a nosebleed," they replied. "But we were plenty afraid."

"That seems strange. The apartments are absolutely riddled with bullets."

"The Salonica division gave us advance warning. We were told to shelter at the back of the houses and stay there until the fighting had stopped."

"So, did you see any fighting?"

"No, but we heard the gunshots and cannons."

Then we went to survey the situation in Tashkishla. It had seen much worse damage than the Taksim barracks, especially the side facing the Harbiye Academy.

The Salonica division had entered the military academy unimpeded. Its students had welcomed them with open arms. They had bombed Tashkishla mercilessly from there. And everyone who was inside had surrendered.

Rumor had it that several soldiers were still defiantly hiding in the barracks' cellar, refusing to come out.

There was no point trying to go any further from there. Nothing of note had happened around Shishli.

I returned to Pera and went into Tokatlian's, where I ran into our amiable deputy, Onnig Chayyan. I knew that he lived around Taksim and asked, "Do you have any news? Did you manage to survive everything unscathed?"

"Yes, but it was a terrifying day for all of us."

"Did you see any fighting?"

"I was right in the thick of it from start to finish," Onnig Chayyan replied smugly.

"You don't say."

"I certainly do. The army took up its position right outside our home."

"And did you grab a gun and join in the fighting?"

"No. But I tried to help in every other possible way. I took water to the parched soldiers. I stored their satchels in our house, offered them cigarettes, and so on. And I even offered one of our rooms to a wounded Salonican soldier."

"Is that right?"

"Yes, it is," continued Chayyan.

"Heavily wounded?"

"No, fortunately just lightly, according to the doctor."

"Where is the wounded man now?"

"Where do you think? He's still recovering at our place."

"May we see him?"

"Of course. If you don't mind walking all the way to my house."

"We'll be right over there," I exclaimed, hoping to scoop a good story for *Jamanak*.

When we arrived at his house, the wounded soldier was lying on a sofa in one of the ground-floor rooms.

He was a Turk hailing from Edirne, around twenty years old. He belonged to the second army corps.

We interviewed him at length but were unable to learn much. He was just a private and said little of note. All he knew was that his superiors in Constantinople had ordered him to discipline the insubordinate soldiers.

After this visit, I found myself around Pangalti again towards evening. Suddenly, fierce fighting broke out between the soldiers in the Taksim barracks and the academy. They started using Maxim guns, and, before we knew it, Taksim was a battlefield.

The crowd that had been surveying the damage around the city suddenly turned up just then in Taksim. All the men and women panicked and began to run for their lives.

An instant later, the streets were completely deserted.

The battle did not last long. Just thirty minutes later, the few remaining defiant soldiers finally turned themselves in.

The liberating army had now seized all of Constantinople – except for Yildiz, which was surrounded but still standing.

We were told that the palace's water and gas supplies had been cut off. And members of the royal court were starting to flee. They were forsaking the master they had so slavishly served for so many years, and the inexhaustible favors they had so lavishly enjoyed.

Rumor had it that many of the Yildiz palace guards had opted to join the liberating army rather than to put up a pointless fight.

It was increasingly clear that the final act of this 'drama' – the overthrow of Abdulhamid – was fast approaching. There was no doubt about it.

The newspapers openly accused him of orchestrating the latest incidents and repeatedly invoked his dethronement.

Monday, April 13 became a momentous day.

The surrender of Yildiz was on everyone's lips. The palace had surrendered to the Salonica division, and Abdulhamid was placed in solitary confinement. Officially, however, he was still the sovereign ruler.

In the evening, we witnessed an unforgettable scene outside Galatasaray.

The entire Yildiz palace retinue – comprising perhaps one-thousand individuals from the lowliest agas to the seniormost pashas — was led in a procession to Galatasaray. First in line was Abdulhamid's Brigadier

General, Tahir Pasha. He looked gloomy and menacing. Behind him was a motley crew of chamberlains, servants, eunuchs, doorkeepers, and so on. Some of them were wearing long vests, others were sporting shalwars or uniforms. It was an altogether pathetic, albeit comical, sight.

Humiliated, stupefied, and bewildered, they moved along with downcast eyes, oblivious to their surroundings.

The crowds reveled in abusing them with their taunts and insults. Far deadlier abuse may have followed were it not for the soldiers in their guard.

People yelled out the names of the palace officials they recognized and launched into an onslaught of obscene jeers.

Before us marched the parade of filth and abomination which had ruled from Yildiz for thirty years.

And to think that it was these same pathetic men who went unpunished for decades as they extorted an entire Empire with their heads held high.

Hundreds of curious spectators kept loitering outside even after the palace officials were locked up in Galatasaray. Some of them were even trying to push their way in. At a certain point, the police intervened to disperse the crowd.

In addition to the palace staff, more than 600 reactionaries were also arrested and taken to the Ministry of War on Monday.

Wherever we turned, we saw the police taking people away. Sometimes, they were arrested right in the middle of the street. The reactionaries were terrified. They were nothing like the cocky show-offs of the previous week.

The spies who had crawled out of the woodwork after March 31 went back into hiding. But, this time, many of them were also collared and thrown in jail at the Ministry of War.

There were rumors that Abdulhamid had managed to escape from Yildiz and was taking refuge in the German Embassy. Others claimed that he was smuggled on board an Ottoman navy vessel. They were waiting with bated breath for the cannons to fire the 101 blasts announcing the good news.

***

Everyone was already out and about at dawn on Tuesday.

We knew that Abdulhamid was about to be dethroned and replaced by his successor.

The streets were filled with Salonican soldiers and a corps of volunteers. Constantinople was brimming with excitement. Men and women had occupied the entire route from the Bahche Kapu to Aya Sofia and Sultan Beyazit Square.

The regiments had to cut through the excited crowds on their way to the imperial procession route.

Our hearts were aflutter. We believed that Abdulhamid would surely be deposed. Nonetheless, we waited anxiously for the roaring cannons to give us some added assurance.

It was after noon, around two o'clock. I was near Sirkeji Station when I heard the first blast.

Hundreds of lips shouted, "One," in unison.

But there was an abiding sense of uncertainty. It could have been a fire alarm.

But there were more blasts, and the people counted anxiously up to seven.

When the eighth cannon boomed, thunderous applause filled the air. An explosion of excitement followed quiet apprehension. And cries of 'hurrah' burst through the resounding applause.

The blasts continued. We must have reached twenty or twenty-five when we eventually lost count.

Someone suddenly yelled, "Long live Sultan Reshad," and we realized that the new Sultan had reached the port of Sirkeji.

Then the imperial carriage appeared. The new Sultan's warm, kind expression captured the people's hearts instantly. The air thundered once more with deafening cries of "long live." And, without a moment's hesitation, he waved in response to that great multitude.

I believe that never in the history of Constantinople had its citizens showed such elation at the first sight of their new Sultan.

***

On April 28, another Tuesday, the sword-girding ceremony took place before even more ecstatic crowds.

This time, there was a much bigger turnout in Constantinople. Human faces appeared everywhere – in Sirkeji, Aya Sofia, Babiali Avenue, Sultan Beyazit Square, in the streets and window-frames, on the rooftops and in the trees.

Turkish women occupied most of the highest outposts. They sat for hours waiting to catch sight of their new padishah.

More violence: The Adana Massacres, 1909.

Sultan Reshad emerged from the Topkapu Palace, reclining in an elegant carriage drawn by four horses. The vast multitudes slowed the carriage's advance. And the spectators thus had an excellent opportunity to see their sovereign up close.

He was the same amiable man we had seen the day he acceded to the throne. However, this time he looked much older, because he had grown a beard.

He was welcomed by resounding cheers and applause all along the procession route.

I saw him for a third time in the Ottoman Parliament. On May 8, a Friday, he gave his solemn oath to protect the Constitution, calling on the deputies to do the same.

The liberating army had now achieved its mission. Blood had been spilled for the Constitution, which seemed to be permanently restored. A future of fruitful collaborations now lay before us.

It is true that the Adana Massacres had been a crushing blow – to us Armenians, at least. They felled our spirits and smothered our hopes. But we tried to conceal our pain and, whenever possible, to simply put the whole thing behind us as we yielded to what lay ahead.

***

After all these solemn ceremonies had been performed, it was high time for a complete purge.

The state of siege intensified. The number of restrictions continued to grow. There were ongoing arrests. But there were no expressions of discontent, except, of course, from those who were being pursued. The fact is that the authorities were acting fairly. And their stringent measures were a matter of necessity.

One May morning, as I was walking along the pier, I noticed a large crowd of people scrambling to see an arriving steamer.

"What is going on?" I asked a curious spectator.

"Sheikh Vahdeti is on board. They're about to bring him out," he replied.

Sheikh Vahdeti had fled when the Salonica division had entered Constantinople. And he was finally apprehended in Izmir or Bursa, I forget which.

I remembered how Levon Shishmanian and I had gone to meet that charlatan at his newsroom. And I wanted to have another look at him.

A military cortege soon escorted him out of the steamer.

He was practically unrecognizable. I would have mistaken him for an unkempt peasant in his shalwar, mules, and tassel-free fez. His eyes were downcast as he walked past us, and the mob besieged him with relentless taunts.

I saw Vahdeti for the last time one early morning on Sultan Beyazit Square. He and four of his friends were hanging from the gallows...

Over the course of the next several days, those gallows became our living nightmare.

Then, it was all over. And our lives resumed in the shadow of our restored Constitution...

About the Translator

Nanor Kebranian is a researcher, writer, and translator working at the intersection of history, literature, and law. She received her doctorate from Oxford University with fellowships from the Jack Kent Cooke Foundation and Oxford's Clarendon Fund. In addition to her appointment as Assistant Professor in the Department of Middle Eastern, South Asian, and African Studies at Columbia University, she has also held research positions at Queen Mary University of London and Nanyang Technological University (Singapore). This translation was completed in part during her appointment as Visiting Fellow in the Faculty Centre for Transdisciplinary Historical and Cultural Studies at the University of Vienna (2023 - 2024). She has commissioned and edited several published translations of Armenian literature and scholarship, as well as producing her own translations of poetry by Krikor Beledian and Taniel Varouzhan. This translation is her second collaboration with the Gomidas Institute, following the 2023 publication of *Zabel Yessayan on the Threshold: Key Texts on Armenians and Turks as Ottoman Subjects*, which she also compiled.

Also by Nanor Kebranian

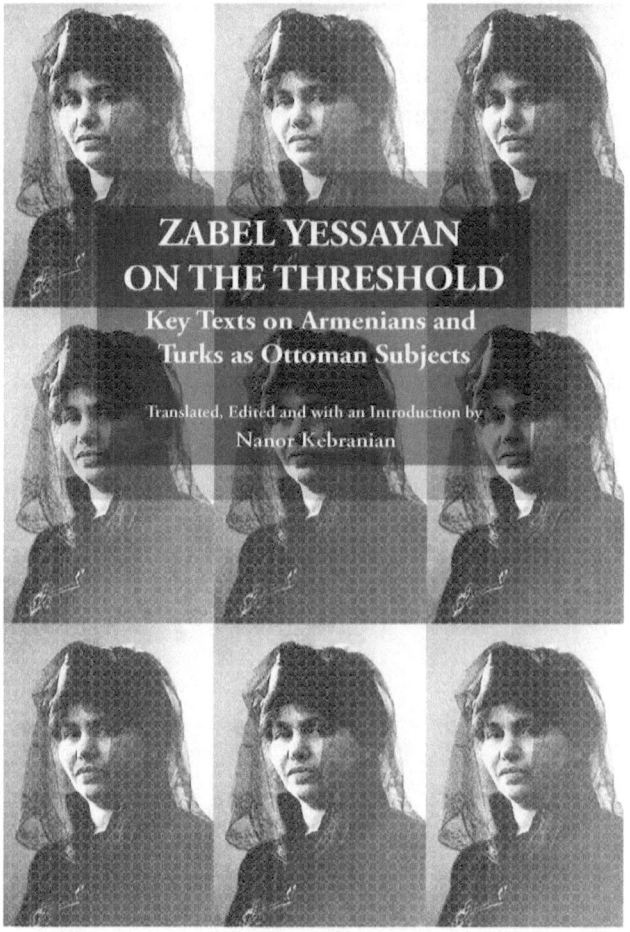

Nanor Kebranian, *Zabel Yessayan on the Threshold: Key Texts on Armenians and Turks as Ottoman Subjects*, (London : Gomidas Institute, 2023), 144 pp., illust, ISBN 978-1-909382-75-6. For more information contact *info@gomidas.org*.

www.ingramcontent.com/pod-product-compliance
Lightning Source LLC
Chambersburg PA
CBHW021835220426
43663CB00005B/252